S0-EYW-306

DISCARDED

INVERSION IN MODERN ENGLISH

STUDIES IN DISCOURSE AND GRAMMAR

EDITORS

SANDRA A. THOMPSON
University of California at Santa Barbara
Department of Linguistics
Santa Barbara, CA 93106
USA

PAUL J. HOPPER
Carnegie Mellon University
Department of English
Pittsburgh, PA 15213
USA

Studies in Discourse and Grammar is a monograph series providing a forum for research on grammar as it emerges from and is accounted for by discourse contexts. The assumption underlying the series is that corpora reflecting language as it is actually used are necessary, not only for the verification of grammatical analyses, but also for understanding how the regularities we think of as grammar emerge from communicative needs.

Research in discourse and grammar draws upon both spoken and written corpora, and it is typically, though not necessarily, quantitative. Monographs in the series propose explanations for grammatical regularities in terms of recurrent discourse patterns, which reflect communicative needs, both informational and socio-cultural.

Volume 6

Heidrun Dorgeloh

Inversion in Modern English
Form and function

INVERSION IN MODERN ENGLISH

FORM AND FUNCTION

HEIDRUN DORGELOH
University of Düsseldorf

JOHN BENJAMINS PUBLISHING COMPANY
AMSTERDAM/PHILADELPHIA

∞™ The paper used in this publication meets the minimum requirements of American National Standard for Information Sciences — Permanence of Paper for Printed Library Materials, ANSI Z39.48-1984.

Library of Congress Cataloging-in-Publication Data

Dorgeloh, Heidrun.
   Inversion in modern English : form and function / Heidrun Dorgeloh.
     p.   cm. -- (Studies in discourse and grammar, ISSN 0928-8929 ; v. 6)
   Includes bibliographical references and index.
     1. English language--Word order. 2. English language--Discourse analysis. I. Title. II. Series.
PE1390.D67   1997
420'.41--dc21   96-6511
ISBN 90 272 2616 4 (Eur.) / 1-55619-372-6 (US) (alk. paper)   CIP

© Copyright 1997 - John Benjamins B.V.
No part of this book may be reproduced in any form, by print, photoprint, microfilm, or any other means, without written permission from the publisher.

John Benjamins Publishing Co. • P.O.Box 75577 • 1070 AN Amsterdam • The Netherlands
John Benjamins North America • P.O.Box 27519 • Philadelphia PA 19118-0519 • USA

Table of Contents

Abbreviations	viii

Chapter 1
Introduction   1

Chapter 2
Word order in English: Some theoretical preliminaries   7
2.1 Basic concepts   7
    2.1.1 Topic   8
    2.1.2 Focus   10
    2.1.3 The clause as representation, exchange and message   11
2.2 English within word order-based language typologies   13
2.3 Basic and natural word order   16

Chapter 3
Inversion in English: The state of the art   19
3.1 A preliminary typology   20
    3.1.1 Types of inversion excluded   21
    3.1.2 The FI and SAI types   23
       3.1.2.1 Full inversion (FI)   23
       3.1.2.2 Subject-auxiliary-inversion (SAI)   26
3.2 Diachronic aspects   29
    3.2.1 Inversion in earlier stages of English   30
    3.2.2 Inversion and grammaticalisation   32
3.3 Two formal hypotheses   34
    3.3.1 Inversion as a root transformation   35
    3.3.2 "Mixed" subject status in full inversion   36
3.4 The functional claims   40
    3.4.1 Focus-marking and the presentative function   41
    3.4.2 The information-packaging claim   47

3.5 Related phenomena	50
3.5.1 *There*-insertion	51
3.5.2 Preposing and initial adverbial placement	53
3.5.3 Left-dislocation	59

Chapter 4
The semantics of inversion   63

4.1 The semantics of choice: inverted vs. canonical word order	65
4.1.1 On the nature of the semiotic process	65
4.1.2 Full inversion vs. canonical word order	67
4.1.2.1 A deictic presentative prototype	67
4.1.2.2 The lexical presentative type of FI	74
4.1.2.3 The lexical predicative type of FI	79
4.1.2.4 The anaphoric/cataphoric type	89
4.1.3 Subject-auxiliary-inversion vs. canonical word order	91
4.2 Viewpoint and subjectivity in inversion	96
4.2.1 Inversion in embedded constructions	97
4.2.2 Viewpoint analysis of main clause full inversion	102
4.2.3 Focus management through point of view	105
4.2.4 Markedness, unexpectedness and emotive meaning	116
4.3 Summary: a functional classification of English inversion	119

Chapter 5
Inversion in discourse   125

5.1 Inversion and other textual relations	126
5.1.1 Spoken vs. written mode	127
5.1.2 Colloquial vs. literary style	131
5.1.3 British vs. American English	135
5.2 Inversion and categories of discourse	139
5.2.1 Discourse types and discourse typologies	139
5.2.1.1 Function and structure — basic discourse types	141
5.2.1.2 Convention — the status of genre	144
5.2.2 Inversion in a corpus of written non-fictional discourse	147
5.2.2.1 Syntactic variation and a corpus-based approach	147
5.2.2.2 Inversion in five text categories of the LOB and the Brown corpus	148
5.2.2.3 Typical uses and characteristics of text categories	151

5.3 Inversion and discourse under conditions of displacement 164
    5.3.1 Basic affinities in non-fictional discourse 165
    5.3.2 Displaced immediacy, organisation of discourse
           and comment in political news reporting 174
5.4 Summary: inversion as a discourse marker 188

Chapter 6
Summary and conclusion 193

Appendix 201

Notes 204

References 214

Index 225

Abbreviations

add-inversion	SAI after additive adverb
AdjP-inversion	FI after adjective phrase
AdvP-inversion	FI after adverb or adverbial phrase
corr-inversion	SAI in correlative construction
neg-inversion	SAI after negative constituent
NP-inversion	FI after nominal phrase
PP-inversion	FI after prepositional phrase
pro-inversion	FI or SAI after pronominal element
VP-inversion	FI after verb phrase
FI	full inversion
SAI	subject-auxiliary-inversion
CWO	canonical word order
V-1	verb-first
V-2 (XVS)	verb-second
V-3 ((X)SVX)	verb-third
VS	verb-subject-order
AuxSV	subject-auxiliary-inversion
BRW	The Brown University Corpus
DailExpr	*The Daily Express*
DailTel	*The Daily Telegraph*
Econ	*The Economist*
Guard	*The Guardian*
Guardw	*The Guardian Weekly*
IHT	*International Herald Tribune*
LOB	The Lancaster-Oslo/Bergen Corpus
NW	*Newsweek*
Time	*Time*

Times	*The Times*
WashP	*The Washington Post*
bbe.	'belles-lettres, biography, essays'.
ed.	'press: editorial'
rep.	'press: reportage'
rev.	'press: review'
sc.writ.	'scientific writing'
CD	communicative dynamism
CG	Cognitive Grammar
FSP	Functional Sentence Perspective
HPSG	Head-Driven-Phrase-Structure Grammar
LFG	Lexical Functional Grammar

Chapter 1
Introduction

The study of syntax has long had its focus on "the formal relation of signs to one another" (Morris 1938:6). It has thereby been c onsidered, within linguistics as a semiotic discipline, as one of the three major branches of inquiry into language: the relation of signs to objects or propositions falls within the domain of semantics, while pragmatics is concerned with the relation of signs to their users. In this sense syntax has been less investigated in terms of meanings or contexts of use, but rather as for the rules which determine *grammaticality*. Nonetheless, it has not really been claimed that the principles underlying the *adequate use* of syntactic patterns are less decisive or do not form part of the ultimate interpretation induced by them. Over the last few years this question has been increasingly tackled within discourse, pragmatic, or functional approaches to syntax, and it is in this framework that the present study is situated.

The discourse conditions upon which the actual use of a syntactic form depends are particularly relevant for those syntactic patterns which have the same propositional meaning — i.e. truth-conditions — as what could be considered a more basic sentence form. As far as word order is concerned, SVO constitutes the basic form of Modern English, while there are a few semantically equivalent alternatives. Among them, the reversal of the subject and the verb is called an *inversion*. Against the background of grammaticalised word order in English, which interprets the position of the NP before the verb as subject-marking, an inversion represents a deviation from the norm and as such lends itself particularly well to a functional account: syntactic form is in this case not exclusively in service of expressing propositional content, but can only be accounted for by the conditions of use which have to justify the norm-breaking. It is in this sense that the present study of Modern English inversion has two main goals: on the one hand, it is concerned with the ultimate, including a non-propositional, meaning that a speaker licenses a hearer to infer when using inverted verb-subject order as syntactic variation within a rigid word order system. On the other hand, this is a corpus study which analyses the patterns of use of inverted forms over various kinds of natural text.

There have been previous accounts of inverted constructions in English, among them other functional ones. Some of these deal with individual types of inversion only, some with certain subsets, and only very few, to my knowledge, with the whole range of possibilities of subject-verb-order variation in declarative sentences. The principal criterion by which most studies define their focus of interest runs along the division between *full inversion* (henceforth FI) and *subject-auxiliary-* (sometimes *semi-*)*inversion* (henceforth SAI), i.e., they define the constructions under investigation as to whether either the finite part only or the entire verb phrase precedes the subject. This difference is exemplified by (1) and (2) below:

(1) Under the chair lies a cat. (= FI)

(2) Never before had a cat been in this house. (= SAI)

The present study does not treat FI or SAI to the exclusion of one or the other, but in principle defines inversion as comprising fully as well as semi-inverted forms. As explicated later, certain individual types of inversion had to be excluded for methodological reasons. The reason for this comprehensive approach is that, against the structural prerequisites of Modern English, both types of inversion arise out of reordering choices and are thus concerned with linearisation, not to forget that they are also historically related. It is therefore a particular concern of this study to explicitly integrate the types of inversion of Modern English into an overall functional and usage-based account; different though the various types may be in many structural and other respects.

To briefly illustrate why much remains to be said about inversion that requires corpus-based evidence, (3) and (4) provide some natural occurrences from fictional texts, which I have otherwise excluded from the corpus. Examples like them have given rise to two kinds of observations which have stimulated the approach chosen for this study:

(3) He looked round, and <u>not far off, behind a clump of bushes, rose a thin column of smoke</u>. He put the diamond in the pocket, and walked towards the smoke. Soon he saw a queer little hut, and <u>at the</u>

door, upon the ground, sat a man without any legs. [...] ; he did not need any trousers, for he had no legs to put them on, as I have told you. In front of him was a fire, and over the fire was a spit, and on the spit was a young kid roasting. (Rouse, *The Crocodile and the Monkey*, p.17)

(4) Francesca stepped off the porch and walked unhurriedly through the grass toward the gate. And out of the pickup came Robert Kincaid, looking like some vision from a never-written book [...]. (Waller, *The Bridges of Madison County*, p. 27f.)

The passage given in (3) is from a children's tale and offers no less than five inversions within a single paragraph. This is not unusual for the genre, as just a few brief glances at some tales have confirmed.[1] The same applies to criminal stories, novels, or guidebooks: sometimes, in these kinds of discourse, or in specific subparts of them, inversions occur in virtual clusters, while in others, for long stretches of or the entirety of a text, one finds no occurrence at all. On the other hand, frequency is not the whole story: (4) is one of a couple of inversions spread into the love story about *Francesca* and *Robert Kincaid* in *The Bridges of Madison County*. Interestingly, the few instances of inversion predominantly occur in that part of the story when the two characters meet and which is told from *Francesca*'s perspective, as the naming of her by first name, against his introduction by full name, indicates. (4) therefore exemplifies an inversion which is striking, not because of the frequency of the construction, but for the kind of character it introduces: *Robert Kincaid* is, definitely from *Francesca*'s subjective point of view, the main character of the book. Parallel to this example, in many novels the occurrence of an inversion correlates with a particularly prominent point of the story or character.

These are the kind of observations which I considered worthwhile to be substantiated and to be accounted for by empirical, corpus-based work. In particular, there was need for quantified data based on a collection of texts, rather than on a collection of occurrences, since non-occurrence of inversion deserves at least as much interpretation as clusters of instances found. The results were to be related to the respective types of discourse and genres, not only as a quantitative picture, but also evaluating the placement and contexts of occurrence. It is in this sense that the present study is corpus-based in part, but also extensively discusses in a text-based manner individual tokens in their individual contexts.

The main part of the analysis is thus based on instances drawn from naturally-occurring discourse; restricted, for reasons which will be made clear later, to written, printed, non-fictional texts. These have been taken from the LOB and the Brown corpus, out of which several categories of discourse have been selected and sub-corpora been accordingly defined; for want of more recent samples of Modern English, and in order to subject them to my own categorisation, I have also used extracts from some issues of various, mostly British, newspapers and magazines.[2] Where instances of inversion are contrasted with their constructed canonical or related word order counterparts (especially in 3.5 and 4.1), the different versions of equal propositional content are judged on the basis of information from the context, of judgments taken from other studies, as well as by my own or native-speaker intuitions. Examples which are in this sense constructed can be recognised by lack of an attribution.

The analysis of corpus texts had to be performed manually and does not follow the "total accountability principle" (Svartvik/Quirk 1980:9) of corpus study. It is therefore not claimed that it covers the matter of inverted word order as syntactic choice as such, i.e., the number of inversions is not related to the total number of clauses. Instead, the corpora have provided a substantial database of 534 tokens of inversion, structured and interpreted according to their distribution over the various categories of text and according to the shares of the individual inversion types identified. Therefore, the quantitative results have the form of *mean* frequencies over categories of discourse and of *relative* frequencies of the individual types with respect to each other, but are not subject to any further statistical analysis.

The structure of the book is as follows: Chapter 2 contains some theoretical preliminaries. It first tries to clarify some basic terminology, in particular topic, focus, and different layers of sentence meaning, and then provides the theoretical background to word order and word order variation by dealing with criteria for basic and natural word order in general, as well as with the structural preconditions of English. Chapter 3 introduces in more detail the phenomenon of inversion as delimited here, it excludes some types of inversion, and presents a formal taxonomy of the remaining types of it. Major claims from previous studies of inversion — diachronic, formal, and functional ones — are summarised here, and some related word order phenomena are discussed.

The core of the analysis is developed in chapters 4 and 5. The overall aim is to show that, beyond other discourse functions and propositional meanings identified, all of the inverted constructions considered here bear a component of subjectivity, and that this is due to what is perceived by the hearer as a speaker-based choice concerning the relative ordering of sentence elements. For reasons which can ultimately be understood from a diachronic perspective only, the various types of inversion have developed different degrees of grammaticalisation and therefore differ in a range of structural properties. They are thus differently related to their canonical word order counterparts and lend themselves more or less easily to various contexts of use and to the production of subjective meanings. The borderline between FI and SAI types is most notable in that respect.

In the first step of the analysis, which deals with the overall semantics of inversion (chapter 4), it will be shown that FI is basically a device for expressing point of view in discourse, whereby the speaker adopts the subjective position of a discourse entity from the universe of discourse and directs the hearer's focus of attention accordingly. SAI, by contrast, is more directly concerned with speaker-based prominence attached to individual constituents, expressing direct emotivity or involvement attached to the contents expressed. In some cases, however, SAI constructions have become mere grammaticalised devices of anaphoric or cataphoric reference and thereby of sentence-linkage. Since the different structural properties of the various inversion types are in this way linked to different kinds and degrees of subjective meaning, it is one objective of this study, summarised in the closing of chapter 4, to complement the formal typology of inversion by a more comprehensive functional classification.

Various criteria for classifying discourse could be potentially relevant for predicting occurrence or non-occurrence of inversion, which is the focus of the corpus analysis about inversion in discourse, and inversion as related to conditions of displacement, presented in chapter 5. Previous studies as well as my earliest corpus work had suggested an overall affinity for inversion in the written language, which is the starting-point for a more differentiated analysis of its usage in different kinds of written discourse. The classification rests on a distinction between basic types of discourse in terms of structural or functional characteristics, and rather conventional patterns of usage, i.e. genres. Furthermore, the treatment of displaced discourse worlds in a text is shown to play a substantial role. The results are summarised into two main claims, namely, that inversion is a marker of subjectivity on the one hand, and a discourse marker serving the organisation of a discourse on the other. A summary and an evaluation of those findings are provided in the concluding chapter 6.

Chapter 2
Word order in English
Some theoretical preliminaries

Word order and word order variation are linearisation phenomena, which, for a language such as English, have to be seen against the background of its basic constituent order and the word order type to which English belongs. However, linearisation is a universal property of language — speakers/writers can only produce one word at a time, one sentence after the other, etc. — and thus also obeys natural principles, namely, that a starting-point always influences the interpretation of everything that follows. This principle not only concerns sentences in isolation, but also can be approached from a discourse perspective. One thus needs a functional terminology for talking about word order, for covering the discourse dimension as well as sentence structure: since reordering processes such as inversion formally differ from an English basic sentence by the mere order itself, this difference is not captured by traditional grammatical functions or roles. This chapter therefore introduces some basic functional terminology, such as topic, focus, and various levels of sentence structure (2.1), before discussing the status of English within word order-based language typologies (2.2), and the relationship between basic and natural word order (2.3).

2.1 Basic concepts

Functional approaches to syntax make extended use of the notions *topic* (*theme*)[1] and *focus*, as well as of many of their derivations. Also — and not always with compatible outcomes — these terms are used in discourse analysis when taking an " above-sentence", discourse perspective. There is thus a large amount of different, though related, uses of topic and focus, which this section tries to clarify (2.1.1 and 2.1.2). It will conclude by determining the level of sentence analysis that is most plausibly said to be affected by word order variation (2.1.3).

2.1.1 *Topic*

In approaches to word order, topic is used in at least as many as the following senses:

(a) To refer to a construction under investigation itself: using a formal definition of topic as "first position in the clause" (Geluykens 1992:14), all movement operations that involve front-shifting to sentence-initial position are sometimes termed *topicalisations*. This term encompasses what is distinguished later as preposing and inversion. It has also been used both in a narrower sense, namely, to denote NP-preposing only (cf. Prince 1981a), and in a broader sense for all rules that move constituents to the left (cf. Creider 1979).

(b) To emphasise a functional status, as opposed to a syntactic constituent or a grammatical role, of one element of a construction under investigation: its topic is "what the sentence is about" (cf. Brown/Yule 1983:70). However, this definition obscures the role of the subject (cf. Chafe 1994:84), and there has been ample discussion in the literature that this notion of topic is, at least for English, hard to operationalise (cf. Chafe 1976, 1994; Geluykens 1992).

(c) To indicate a status of discourse items which refers to their relation to previous as well as to subsequent discourse: some or all of the elements involved in a reordering process are sometimes considered and compared in terms of their *topicality* (*thematicity*). The topicality of an item covers properties such as "recoverability" from previous and "recurrence" in subsequent discourse (Geluykens 1992:8), two aspects which have also been described as *lookback* and *persistence* in terms of topic continuity (cf. Givón (ed.) 1983). From a cognitive viewpoint, topicality is to be understood as *activation cost* or mental effort necessary to convert an item or an idea into an active mental state (cf. Chafe 1994:71ff.); in that sense, it can also be equated with *accessibility* (Ariel 1988, 1990). More fine-grained taxonomies have been developed to distinguish different degrees of topicality, or *givenness* (e.g., Prince 1981b, 1992; Gundel et al. 1993), which have been applied to inversion in an *information-packaging* analysis of it (Birner 1992, 1994; cf. 3.4.2 below).

(d) To refer to "what is being talked about" (Brown/Yule 1983:73) in units of discourse beyond the sentence level: if the topicality of items constitutes the global and local coherence of a discourse, *discourse topics* emerge as aggregates "of coherently related events, states, and referents that are held together in some form" (Chafe 1994:121). Word order can plausibly be said to contribute to the identification of a discourse topic, namely, it often reflects greater or lesser *topichood* of the items involved. The status of discourse topic, however, often belongs to "a larger amount of information" (Chafe 1994:120) and cannot necessarily be attributed to a single noun phrase (cf. Brown/Yule 1983:71ff.). Furthermore, there is no necessary correlation between a global or local discourse topic and discourse *topic entities*, understood as more specific characters, objects, and ideas (cf. Brown/Yule 1983:137).

In view of this terminological complexity, limiting one's usage of topic and related terms is strongly advisable. First, this study defines the phenomenon of inversion, its subtypes, and the related phenomena, on the basis of formal syntactic criteria alone; it will thus not have to refer to *topicalisation* or *sentence topics*. By contrast, *topicality* of sentence elements is what previous functional accounts of inversion have mainly been concerned with; in particular, as will be summarised below, by stressing the relevance of the relative *discourse*-familiarity of elements affected by reordering as opposed to their relative *hearer*-familiarity. In this sense, word order depends on conditions of Prince's (1981b) "Givenness$_s$" (*saliency*), rather than her "Givenness$_k$" (shared knowledge), but not only in that it *reflects* relative topicality. The *local* or *contextual* salience "has to do with the degree to which a referent 'stands out' from other referents" (Chafe 1994:100) at a particular point of discourse, and this plausibly depends on how recently it was mentioned (the topicality criterion) and on the manner in which the item is presented (cf. Kemmer 1995:59). Word order thus also *determines* what is salient in subsequent discourse, i.e., what becomes a *discourse topic*, an analysis that will be developed in later chapters (cf. 4.2.3).

2.1.2 *Focus*

Salience is closely related to focus because what is salient for the speaker and hearer constitutes or becomes their *focus* of consciousness or interest. The term itself, however, calls for an even more careful definition. Contradictory senses of it have engendered analyses of inversion both as a *focussing* and as a *defocussing* device, so that at least three uses of focus should be noted:

(a) On the sentence-level, focus has traditionally been applied to set off the sentence element that carries the newest "most important or salient information" (Dik et al. 1983:42) from what has been considered the "presupposition" or "the information in the sentence that is assumed by the speaker to be shared by him and the hearer" (Jackendoff 1972:16). Originally, focus identification in this sense was mainly concerned with phonological prominence (Chomsky 1971); since then, this concept has also been widely applied to syntactic phenomena (Prince 1981a; Dik et al. 1983; Rochemont/Culicover 1990). It is referred to more precisely as *sentence* or *information focus* and is in the *unmarked* case identified with sentence-final position: "when the information focus [...] coincides with final position, focus placement is clear even without further marking" (Enkvist 1980:152). On the other hand, by *marked focus* is meant "that special prominence which is given to elements [in the sentence]" (Enkvist 1980:134), usually by prosodic signals in spoken language, while written language has to make use of "those operations [...] that affect the linear order, and therefore the thematic information structure, of a sentence" (Enkvist 1980:148).

(b) Still on the sentence-level, a contrary notion of being *in-focus* is sometimes applied to nominative case or subject position, to "what the speaker's attention is centred on" (Penhallurick 1984:46); a related use is found in Erdmann (1990), who identifies focus with grammatical prominence. Since this is prominence usually granted to the subject, these authors refer to the removal of it from its normal position, as in inversion, as *defocussing*.

(c) The two definitions of focus on the sentence-level share one aspect of focal meaning. More recently, focus has come to be associated with the update potential of a sentence, composed of a *focus* and a *ground* (cf.

Vallduví 1992), with the latter nonfocus part of the sentence being thought of more as *activated* rather than presupposed (cf. Dryer 1994). This leads to a definition of a *discourse notion of focus* as the listener's/reader's current focus of attention with its "management" performed by various devices (among which word order). A focus of attention thus represents a particularly prominent activation status, achieved through some kind of instruction which triggers the activation of formerly non-activated (or semi-deactivated) referents. In this sense, the sentence focus constitutes the current focus of attention, while the in-focus interpretation of subjects refers to an as yet high level of activation, normally due to a previous focus of attention.

It is the discourse notion of focus which is most relevant for the analysis to follow. Linguistic devices, especially the forms of referring expressions, have long been understood as signals — or instructions — for focussing discourse entities (cf. Gundel et al. 1993; Kemmer 1995); however, the point has perhaps been made less clearly about word order.

2.1.3 *The clause as representation, exchange and message*

Finally, one needs to distinguish various layers of sentence structure — levels of sentence meaning — in order to describe the kind of change induced by word order variation. One useful approach is Halliday's (1970, 1985; Halliday/Hasan 1976) system of the meta-functions of language, consisting of an ideational, an interpersonal, and a textual function. On their basis, three kinds of sentence meaning are distinguished:

> *Ideational meaning* is the representation of experience: our experience of the world that lies about us, and also inside us, the world of our imagination. It is meaning in the sense of 'content'. The ideational function of the clause is that of representing what in the broadest sense we can call 'processes': actions, events, processes of consciousness, and relations [...].
>
> *Interpersonal meaning* is meaning as form of action; the speaker or writer doing something to the listener or reader by means of language. The interpersonal function of the clause is that of exchanging roles in rhetorical interaction: statements, questions, offers and commands, [...].
>
> *Textual meaning* is relevance to the context: both the preceding [and following] text, and the context of situation. The textual function of the clause is that of constructing a message [...]. (Halliday 1985:53; my emphasis)

These three functions of a clause — representation, exchange, and message — all have a structure of their own: On the level of *representation*, the structure is made up of semantic categories that derive from the real world. It "consists potentially of three components: (i) the process itself; (ii) participants in the process; (iii) circumstances associated with the process" (Halliday 1985:101). The *actor*, the one that — in the widest possible sense — does the deed (cf. Halliday 1985:102), is what has traditionally been called *logical* subject, emphasising that it has to do with "relations between things", as opposed to grammatical relations that are "relations between symbols" (Halliday 1985:34). For this reason, the structure of the clause as a representation of experience is affected neither by the distribution of grammatical roles nor by word order.

Then, as concerns the interpersonal function of *exchange*, one crucial kind is exchange of information, leaving aside here offers and commands (Halliday's (1985) "exchange of goods-&-services" (p.71)). When language is used for the exchange of information, the clause takes on the form of a proposition, in Hallidayan terms made up of subject, finite and residue. The *subject* supplies "something by reference to which the proposition can be affirmed or denied" (Halliday 1985:76), i.e., something of which something is predicated. It is also the *grammatical* subject, determined in English on the basis of various grammatical features such as nominative case or concord of person and number with the verb. Changing the position with the verb does thus not change the status of subject according to these criteria, but it is nonetheless questionable whether the proposition as a whole remains the same. The question will be taken up in chapter 4, and later in the analysis it will be claimed that inversion in fact changes the interpersonal meaning of a clause.

Finally, the clause as a *message* has what Halliday calls a *thematic* structure, and this structure is expressed by word order itself, by what is chosen as the *theme* and the *rheme*. The theme, in English, is realised by the first position in the clause, while its function is that of *starting-point* for the message (cf. Halliday 1985:39). Despite some obvious problems with Halliday's notion of *marked* theme (cf. the discussion in Ward 1988), or in general with the formal identification of theme in English (cf. Chafe 1976), the functional status of starting-point is important. In that an inversion affects the starting-point of the clause, it changes the meaning of the clause as a message and thus serves the textual function of language.

On the basis of these three levels of sentence analysis, it is important to note that "the typical UNMARKED form, in an English declarative [...] clause is the one in which Theme, Subject and Actor are conflated into a single element" (Halliday 1985:36; his emphasis), an observation which has been repeated and accounted for in many other studies (Tomlin 1983; van Oosten 1986). A typical, unmarked form is also the one "we tend to use if there is no context leading up to it, and no positive reason for choosing anything else" (Halliday 1985:36). This is an argument for a *motivated choice*, which will be developed in detail in chapter 4 and which is treated there as the principal source of the semantics and discourse function of inversion.

2.2 English within word order-based language typologies

There is abundant literature on the topic of word order, going far beyond the scope of the present study, including comparative and language-typological studies (Greenberg 1966; Hawkins 1983; Hammond (ed.) 1988; Siewierska 1988; Downing/Noonan (eds.) 1995) as well as studies of word order in individual languages (cf. Yokoyama 1986; Payne 1990). Though these are useful for clarifying the structural prerequisites of English inversion, they need not be reviewed in their own right here. Instead, this section tries to clarify on which basis, from a typological point of view, the status of word order in English can be defined, and what the language type to which it belongs implies for those structures that represent deviations from the norm. The discussion of the interaction between a language-specific basic order and principles that have been brought forward as "natural" or "iconic" will be left for section 2.3 at the end of this chapter.

W*ord* order most often really refers to the order of sentence *constituents*, in fact, more precisely, to the order of sentence elements or grammatical relations. This is a well-established custom in the literature (cf. Payne 1990:23), but it is interesting to ask why at this very level of syntactic analysis linguists and grammarians have been so concerned with linearisation. In natural language, "signs cannot but follow each other in the chain, whether or not they bear a direct grammatical relation" (Lehmann 1992:398), but ordering has nonetheless different functions at different levels of complexity: below the level of sentence constituents, the sequence of words alone does not determine grammatical relatedness, it is rather a result of their "relational potential" (Lehmann 1992:398) to combine into certain phrases. This relational potential is defined for each grammatical or lexical category and includes ordering rules. Here, as well as for sentence constituents, i.e. below the sentence-level, "the typical relationship is a constructional one, of parts into a whole" (Halliday 1985:xxi), while, above the sentence-level, the position is reversed: "the non-constructional forms of organisation take over and become the norm. [...]. Changing the order of sentences in a text is about as meaningless an operation as putting the end before the beginning" (Halliday 1985:xxi). It is therefore exactly at the level of sentence constituents that constructional and non-constructional matters meet, in other words, that structural prerequisites and functional possibilities interact. The interaction is determined both by the language system and by pragmatic principles, and it also depends on the matter of whether a language uses word order *grammatically*, i.e., in service of expressing constructional (grammatical) relations, or *pragmatically*. This is one sense in which word order has been used as a typological parameter for classifying languages, at least since the pioneering work of Greenberg (1966).

Classifying languages according to word order rests on the assumption that all languages have a *basic*, syntactically defined, constituent order. The universality of this claim has lately been put into question (cf. Mithun 1987; Payne 1990), but there can be no doubt that Modern English, with SVO, possesses such a basic order. Nonetheless, the basis of this statement has still to be specified. Mithun (1987) names as "the usual criteria for establishing the basic word order of a language [...] statistical frequency, descriptive simplicity, and pragmatic neutrality" (p.311). Of these, for a usage-based account of basic and non-basic patterns, the criteria of *statistical frequency* and *pragmatic neutrality* are particularly relevant; they closely correspond to what is elsewhere, especially in Givón's (e.g., 1993) work, referred to as the *markedness* condition of "discourse distribution" (p.178). While, on the basis of the distributional criterion, in Modern English deviation from SVO in declarative clauses is *generally* marked (cf. Denison 1993:27), it has to be born in mind that the specific markedness value of a construction in use cannot be determined in isolation from text type (cf. Siewierska 1988:12), nor from matters of position and context (cf. Mithun 1987:313). For instance, it is argued in many discourse studies (cf. Fox1987; Pu/Prideaux 1994) that discourse-initial sentences belong to highly marked situations and therefore give rise to so-called *markedness reversal*, i.e. to a local affinity with marked constructions. Even if one might not want to treat syntax in terms of a static or systematic markedness (cf. García 1994), such observations nonetheless imply that non-basic patterns are not necessarily less frequent — less expected from the addressee's point of view — than their unmarked counterparts, at least not in any kind of discourse and not without positional constraints.

More consensus about classifying languages on the basis of word order exists for the distinction between

> (a) languages in which order is primarily used for syntactic functions such as signalling grammatical relations, (b) languages in which order is primarily used to signal the discourse-pragmatic status of information [...], and (c) languages in which order displays a good mixture of syntactic and discourse-pragmatic functions. (Payne 1990: 25)

Due to the mixed nature of (c), these alternatives in fact form a continuum; one might therefore just distinguish between *pragmatic* or *flexible* word order languages and *grammatical* or *rigid* word order languages (cf. Thompson 1978; Givón 1988).

In this context, the status of English as an SVO (Greenberg 1966), grammatical (Thompson 1978), or rigid word order (Givón 1988) language has an important implication for the function and pragmatic meaning of deviant word order. Despite a fair degree of rigidity, English possesses devices of pragmatic reordering, one of which is inversion. Only, "in syntactically based languages, pragmatic reordering is highly marked" (Mithun 1987:325). A plausible consequence is that,

> while the underlying pragmatic principles [...] controlling word-order remain the same [....,] milder degrees of those same conditions would not precipitate word-order variation in a rigid-order language, but would in a flexible-order language. (Givón 1988:276)

There is one more effect which word order flexibility as a structural prerequisite of English has on the syntactic devices available to express pragmatic meanings and which touches upon the issue of ordering within or beyond the clause-level raised above: as Lehmann (1992:411) notes, in a rigid word order language, where syntactic means are grammaticalised, "in order to get greater order freedom, one has to step up to a higher grammatical level". In that respect, inversion (together with preposing) belongs to those highly marked and strongly restricted devices for expressing pragmatic meaning *within* the clause; in addition to them, forms of *complex* sentences, such as dislocations or clefting, fulfil similar tasks.

To sum up, the so-described typological status of English provides two crucial prerequisites for an analysis of inversion: first, word order is largely determined by syntactic functions, and second, reordering options, though possibly following pragmatic principles, at the same time bear an additional meaning of deviation or markedness. The pragmatic principles underlying word order, however, call for some further discussion, if, for instance, Givón (1988:276) is right in that they are universal and would thus have to have an iconic or natural motivation.

2.3 Basic and natural word order

An inversion always involves that some sentence constituent other than the verb is shifted to the front of the clause and is followed by subsequent VS (FI) or AuxSV (SAI) order. This happens obligatorily or optionally; there may thus be a second word order choice involved, namely, mere front-movement as opposed to inversion. If there are natural word order principles governing inversion, these will therefore have to relate to the sentence-initial position in the first place, but must also touch upon the final position, to which the subject is shifted. Only in SAI constructions does ordering within the rest of the clause, apart from the front-shifted item triggering *do*-periphrasis, remain the same.

Natural ordering follows natural or cognitive principles in language, which have usually been thought of as non-linguistic in origin:

> The cognitive structures underlying comprehension [...] and production [...] develop in prelinguistic, perception-based experience, these already available structures quite naturally being 'taken over' by the linguistic system. (Osgood/Bock 1977:93)

These authors furthermore claim that the sentence-initial position has inherent cognitive salience, as does Givón, who, in various works dealing with non-arbitrary coding in syntax (Givón 1985) and topic continuity as related to word order (Givón (ed.) 1983), repeatedly formulates his well-known principle "attend first to the most urgent task" (Givón 1985:199).

In apparent contrast to such a claim stands the much discussed principle of increasing communicative dynamism (CD), developed by the Prague

School linguists (cf., e.g., Firbas 1979), and adopted since then by many other, especially functionally oriented, linguists: the degree of CD carried by a sentence element is understood as "the extent to which the sentence element contributes to the further development of the communication" (Firbas 1979:31). Elements with the lowest degree of CD have been called *thematic*, those with higher degrees *rhematic*. For English, but even more for more flexible word order languages such as Czech and Russian, a *theme-first* pattern, i.e. a preference for "Old Things First" (cf. Downing 1995:13), has repeatedly been stated, operating to the extent that language-specific word order flexibility allows for variation.

Both principles are well attested by empirical studies of various languages (cf. Mithun 1987; Downing/Noonan (eds.) 1995), and have a common core of cognitive plausibility: "the theme->rheme pattern or the rheme->theme pattern [...] both reserve a particular position for the crucial high CD (rhematic) material" (Downing 1995:15). The theme-first, or *given-new*[2], pattern provides an anchor, establishes an orientation and a perspective (Mithun 1987:307), which is needed early in the sentence. The most highly rhematic material ends up in clause-final position, whereby it constitutes the unmarked sentence focus. The rheme-first or *newsworthy-first* principle, by contrast, is mostly found in flexible word order languages, where all ordering reflects pragmatic considerations: the work the initial position does in these languages indicates high cognitive or natural salience, as does, not to forget, the natural prosodic prominence of that position (cf. Mithun 1995).

The way in which flexible word order languages exploit the sentence-initial position in fact reflects how this apparent contradiction comes about; as Mithun (1987) concludes from her study of three pragmatic word order languages:

> In the pragmatically based languages examined here, [...] constituents appear in descending order of newsworthiness. This does not result in a simple rheme-theme order, however. New themes, newsworthy in their own right, appear early, as do other orienting elements like time and location. Continuing themes, however, as well as continuing times and locations, usually do not appear as separate constituents at all. (p. 335)

While the latter option is due to the polysynthetic nature of these languages, i.e. to structural prerequisites entirely different from those in English, *subject-prominent* languages such as English (cf. Li/Thompson 1976) have to realise even highly predictable topics as separate constituents; what Givón (1985:198) considers an iconic way of coding highly continuous topics, namely "zero-topic" constructions, are not available. This also implies that the category subject is in principle independent of topic qualities; hence, in English, it may be indefinite (cf. Li/Thompson 1976:461), rhematic (cf. Thompson 1978:26), and in spoken language it may even come to carry the sentence accent (cf. Lambrecht 1994:24).

To sum up, natural or cognitive principles of word order and the structural prerequisites of English must be assumed to interact as follows:

(a) Since the sentence-initial position is cognitively salient, it is in principle available for urgent or important tasks. One important task at the beginning of a sentence is to give an orientation or anchoring for what is to follow. Pragmatic word order languages choose this option only in case of a new theme, while a grammatical word order and subject-prominent language like English shows a more consistent preference for theme-rheme, or given-new, order.

(b) From a discourse perspective, shifting a constituent other than the subject to the sentence-initial position in a grammatical word order language signals wider discourse relevance (Thompson 1985; Ramsey 1987; Ford 1993). This involves links to the preceding context as well as relevance for what is to follow. In the same vein, Givón (1987) characterises front-shifting as a "combination of anaphoric and cataphoric *grounding*" or a "re-orientation" (p.182; his emphasis) device for the structure of the text.

(c) Combining (a) and (b) suggests that inversion in English is probably not just a result of pragmatic (theme-rheme) reordering, but that it attributes a particular discourse function both to the front-shifted constituent as well as to the subject postponed. Given the rigidity of the English word order system, inversions also represent a strong deviation from a more basic sentence pattern and must therefore be taken to bear an additional newsworthiness of their own.

Chapter 3

Inversion in English
The state of the art

For a language to have an inversion construction presupposes that there is a basic pattern from which the order of subject and verb can invert. If this basic word order is SVO, or VX in more general terms, word order rigidity has been claimed to be a natural consequence (cf. Vennemann 1974). Inversion in Modern English thus implies the background of the typological status of English as an SVO and a rigid word order language (cf. König 1988:55).

For a functional account, the range of inversion constructions that are meaningfully treated together is limited. A preliminary exclusion of interrogative sentences, which English also encodes through word order, is expedient, in line with the position explicated above that only those word order changes are of interest here that signal changes in textual, and perhaps interpersonal, rather than ideational, meaning. This focus of the present study has further necessitated the exclusion of some individual inversion types, for which the relevant criteria will be set up in 3.1.1, and the types and labels will be introduced in 3.1.2.

The formal definition of inversion applied here will cover a heterogeneous group of constructions. This is symptomatic of the synchronic perspective adopted in the analysis. Historical studies, by contrast, have noted an "unevenness of applicability of V-2 [= verb-second, henceforth *V-2*]" (Stockwell 1984:578) and assume that the reasons why inversion phenomena range from grammatical coding mechanisms, apparently obligatory consequences of front-shifting, to textual choices in their own right "may have to be sought in a historical description rather than a synchronic one" (Green 1980:598). This chapter, which reviews the claims made by previous studies of inversion and of other word order phenomena, therefore also touches upon some diachronic aspects (3.2). As concerns the synchronic approaches, emphasis has been laid on the functional claims (3.4), while only two hypotheses that come from formal syntactic frameworks provide some relevant input for the later analysis (3.3). Finally, what has been said about the discourse functions of *there*-insertion, preposing and sentence-initial adverbial placement, as well as left-dislocation is also of interest here, since these are related phenomena, to be discussed in 3.5.

3.1 A preliminary typology

The phenomenon of inversion is understood very broadly here. The definition follows Green (1982), who defines inversions as "those declarative constructions where the subject follows part or all of its verb phrase" (p.120). One might object that this definition can "include not only SAI, but also existential and presentational *there*-insertion, right-dislocation, and extraposition" (Birner 1992:28), but this very much depends on the kind of syntactic analysis applied; in right-dislocation and extraposition at least, most studies identify the cataphoric pronoun occurring in them as the grammatical subject (cf. Erdmann 1990). *There*-sentences seem to be even more of an inversion, especially since existential *there* is probably "an extension of locative *there*" (Bolinger 1977:91). However, not every dummy *there* has a locative meaning, and, in questions and other cases of subject-auxiliary-inversion, it behaves very much like a grammatical subject (cf. Birner 1992:38). An adequate syntactic analysis of constructions other than inversion is outside the scope of this study; so suffice it to note that the *there*-construction does not fall under the definition of inversion applied here. It is nonetheless a construction superficially similar to an inversion and as such it will be discussed as a related phenomenon below.

Green's definition of inversion covers FI and SAI constructions, which, in many respects, appear to "have almost nothing in common beyond the relative order of subject and first V [= verb]" (Green 1985:122). Reasons for such a claim are given, e.g., in Birner (1992:27ff.), but her main argument is that SAI formally encompasses inversion in interrogative sentences. Since interrogatives are a grammaticalised function, "which has never been (and is not likely to be) attributed to [full] inversion [...] or any subtype thereof" (Birner 1992:29), it is indeed plausible to keep them apart from inversion in declarative clauses. FI and SAI in declarative clauses, by contrast, are intentionally treated together here; even though, from a synchronic perspective, they are in many respects functionally different. It is an interest in their overall discourse function as word order *choice* as such that justifies a joint treatment: on the one hand, both FI and SAI constructions in Modern English have remained non-basic or *marked* alternatives to the basic (henceforth canonical =*CWO*) word order and/or preposing variants. In other words, both FI and SAI are not entirely automatised. On the other hand, all inversion types introduced below involve the sentence-initial placement of some sentence element. With a few exceptions, this element would canonically stand elsewhere in the sentence, and it triggers or is optionally followed by inversion. In the terms laid down in section 2.3, the sentence-initial position potentially has wider discourse relevance and is thus a particularly promising candidate for the function of a *positional* choice in discourse.

3.1.1 Types of inversion excluded

The inversions excluded here follow from the criteria presented above; what is in addition taken into account is the likelihood of occurrence in the corpus texts used, i.e. in written monologue discourse. In the following, the most substantial types excluded are listed and examples from other studies are given. Inversion phenomena have been classified under several systems, of which Green's (1982) coverage of inversion types is probably closest to mine. I therefore refer to her terminology, if not stated otherwise.

(a) The focus of this study is sentence-initial placement and subsequent V-2; hence, no cases of inversion displaying remnants of former verb-first (*V-1*) position are included.[1] In particular, this concerns the inverted conditional (as in (1)) and formulaic inversions (as in (2)); more marginally, this also excludes the more colloquial inversion types after a negated verb (as in (3)), with an implied temporal phrase (as in (4)), in appended clauses (as in (5); cf. Schmidt 1980:14), as well as exclamatory inversions (as in (6)):

(1) Should I leave this job to go to the bathroom I risk being fired. [= (35a)]

(2) Be it resolved that ... . [= (14b)]

(3) Didn't nobody teach me this. [= (15a)]

(4) Came a terrific flash of lightning and clap of thunder. [= (50a)]
(Green 1982)

(5) He lied a lot, did that man. [= Schmidt 1980:(81)]

(6) God, have I seen attitudes change! [= Green 1982:(25b)]

(b) Limitation to declarative sentences has already been noted; furthermore, some constructions which Erdmann (1990:30ff.) calls "sentence-type inversions", namely, dependent interrogative clauses (as in (7)), other (non-V-1) exclamatory sentences (as in (8)), as well as concessive clauses (as in (9)), are also excluded:

(7) Truman had been trapped once before by that device, when a reporter asked him did he not consider the Hiss case a red herring. [p.31]

(8) What a feast of the imagination too are the interminable meals he eats [...]. [p.33]

(9) In fact the demonstrations of the past few days — substantial though is the public reaction and repugnance for them — [...] have not resulted in disorder. [p.36]
(Erdmann 1990)

(c) Quotation inversion (as in (10)) is excluded for more pragmatic reasons, as are the related types of inversion with onomatopoeic words (as in (11)) and so-called "journalistic style inversion" (as in (12)) (Schmidt 1980:10f.):

(10) 'Sugar is recommended in this cereal,' [...] said Robin. [= Green 1982:(7)]

(11) "Bang" went the gun. [= (56)]

(12) Says lovely actress Mary Malone, "I always have a wonderful time in Columbus." [= (57)]
(Schmidt 1980)

Despite some affinities with other types of FI, other studies have provided sufficient evidence that quotation inversion, "being syntactically, semantically and intonationally distinguishable from other inversions, is also functionally distinct" (Birner 1992:29ff.; cf. the discussion there).

3.1.2 *The FI and SAI types*

This section presents a typology of the inversions investigated in the following and introduces the categories used. Since this is a formal typology, the joint treatment of FI and SAI implies that no single criterion can be applied consistently. For instance, fronted adverbs, such as in (13) and (15), or fronted prepositional phrases, such as in (14) and (16), are followed both by an FI or by an SAI type of inversion, while different syntactic categories, such as in (13) and (14), or (15) and (16), in principle trigger the same mechanism.

(13) Then came the peace dividend. (Econ, 3 Apr.93, p.15)

(14) Over Europe's thinkers and leaders hangs a pall of gloom reminiscent of the deep "Euro-pessimism" of the early 1980s. (NW, 12 Apr.93, p.10)

(15) Never before have fans been promised such a feast of speed. (LOB, rep.)

(16) In no other period since the war have we doubted our Government's ability to take the right decisions, except perhaps during Suez. (Guardw, 20 Dec.92, p.8)

It therefore makes sense to use two different systems of classification. For FI, there is the practice established by Birner (1992), who classifies inversions by the syntactic category of the preposed constituent. Her system of notation is used with some minor modifications. SAI, by contrast, is classified into broader categories on the basis of a combination of semantic and syntactic criteria.

3.1.2.1 *Full inversion (FI)*
Full inversion denotes all those constructions in which the subject[2] follows *all of its verb phrase*, i.e. a full (= lexical) verb or copular *be*. In cases where the

distinction is necessary the former type is referred to as *lexical-verb-inversion* and the latter as <u>be</u>-*inversion*. On the basis of the syntactic category of the preposed constituents followed by FI, five major types are distinguished. The examples that follow illustrate how these types are formally identified, notwithstanding the semantic and functional diversities within the categories, which will be dealt with in chapter 4.

(a) <u>AdvP-inversion</u>: FI following an adverb (as in (17) and (18)) or an adverbial phrase (as in (19)) is referred to as *AdvP-inversion*. Inversions with adverbs followed by a prepositional phrase, as in (20), however, belong to the *PP-inversion* type, discussed under (b).

(17) <u>Now is the time</u> for the first of these omissions to be rectified. (Times, 15 Dec.92, p.23)

(18) <u>Out came the journal</u> and in it went Ann's own description of the scene. (BRW, bbe.)

(19) <u>Now and then could be seen southward through the scrub the vista of the great plain</u> parallel to which the tracks were running on and on before Bony: [...]. [= Birner 1992:(45b), p.49]

(20) <u>Off to the United Nation forces in the Congo goes a load of 1,000lb bombs</u> sent with the compliments of the British taxpayer. (LOB, ed.)

Anaphoric adverbs such as *thus* and *so* are excluded from *AdvP-inversion*. This is justified by the introduction of a *pro-inversion* category among the SAI types, even if sometimes these adverbs are followed by FI.[3]

(b) <u>PP-inversion</u>: FI following an initial prepositional phrase is labelled *PP-inversion*; examples are given in (21) and (22):[4]

(21) <u>Among the loudest advocates of regulation are members of the airline unions</u>, who hope that this will preserve their high paid jobs. (NW, 12 Apr.92, p.44)

(22) <u>With greater individual freedom should come greater individual responsibility</u>. (Times, 15 Dec.92, p.29)

This is the type of inversion often referred to as "locative inversion" (cf. Coopmans 1989; Bresnan 1994) in the literature. Note, however, that "the correlation of locativity [...] and preposed constituent type is imperfect" (Birner 1992:51ff.).

(c) *VP-inversion*: If the initial sentence constituent either consists of or is introduced by a present or past participle form of a verb, one can speak of a *VP-inversion*. Both cases are exemplified here, by (23) and (24) respectively:

(23) <u>Gone are the days</u> when Europe's monopoly carriers would fix prices and pool revenue on high traffic routes. (NW, 12 Apr.93, p.44)

(24) <u>Applauding on the river banks at Leningrad were thousands</u> now told that in 20 years they will have free food, housing, light, heat, transport and medical treatment all for a working week of 34 to 36 hours. (LOB, rep.)

There is a close similarity between *PP-inversion* and *VP-inversion*, especially when, as in (24), both constituent types follow each other. As exemplified by (25), however, co-occurrence with a PP is not a necessary condition for *VP-inversion*, and the affinity is rather a functional one:

(25) <u>Flanking the gates were low walls</u> topped with railings. [= Birner 1992:(49), p.52f.]

(d) *AdjP-inversion*: FI following a preposed adjective phrase is called *AdjP-inversion*. This category has a notable dominance of comparative and superlative forms (as in (26)), but simple forms, in that case frequently followed by a prepositional phrase (as in (27)), also occur:

(26) <u>Most disturbing is conservationists' willingness</u> to spend money to appease local government honchos. (NW, 12 Apr.93, p.47)

(27) <u>Conspicuous among the losers was Britain</u>, which went in with a list of 71 items to be removed from Brussels' control in the name of subsidiarity [...]. (Guardw, 20 Dec.92, p.7)

(e) *NP-inversion*: Finally, an *NP-inversion* type is established, despite the fact that the sequence NP-*be*-NP is difficult to identify as a CWO or an inversion on purely syntactic grounds. Basically, one can speak of an *NP-inversion* in case of a fronted "characterisation", as opposed to an "identification", predicate (cf. Quirk et al. 1985:742). Syntactic evidence for an

NP-inversion is the use of the indefinite article or no article in the sentence-initial NP, such as in (28) and (29):

(28) An exception to this rule are the wealthy merchants, Ministers, and senior Government officials who have invested in cattle. (Guardw, 3 Jan.93, p.23)

(29) [...] and bridesmaids were Miss Pat Dawson of Austin, [...]. (BRW, rep.)

One could also argue that, "given VP inversion, AdjP inversion, and PP inversion, one might expect to find NP inversion as well" (Birner 1992:69), but there are also arguments for a shared function. Nonetheless, an *NP-inversion* type remains difficult to analyse into subject and complement, which is why it has been excluded from the corpus analysis.

3.1.2.2 *Subject-auxiliary-inversion (SAI)*

The subject of an SAI — or of a "subject-operator-inversion"[5] (e.g., Quirk et al. 1985; König 1988) — follows *the first auxiliary of the verb phrase*. Four groups of SAI constructions are distinguished here, on what is a mixture of semantic and syntactic grounds:[6]

(a) *Pro-inversion*: is defined by the fact that, following a pro-form that stands for an entire predicate or at least a substantial part of it, SAI — sometimes a *be-* or even a lexical-verb-inversion — introduces a subject that ends up in sentence-final position. This goes for sentences introduced by *so*, *such*, *thus*, and *as*, as well as for *nor* and *neither* when they do not function as negative additive adverbs. Examples are given in (30) – (32). (33) is not *pro-inversion*, but exemplifies the use of *nor* as additive adverb, as classified under (c):

(30) That was written in a cold noisy, flapping press tent [...], as was the following forecast. (Guardw, 27 Dec.92, p.24)

(31) Thus was born the Barbados Coup, a variation of the Grosvenor Gambit, in which you can ruff a loser [...]. (Guardw, 3 Jan.93, p.23)

(32) Food and sweets, fuel and light are not taxed; nor are books, magazines, children's clothes, some kitchen equipment, sheets and towels. (LOB, ed.)

(33) These were not ideal heralds. Nor is his undoubted success entirely accountable in terms of his personal charm [...]. (LOB, ed.)

In this category, the sentence-focus is still on the subject, which is due to the fact that the pro-element is a grammaticalised device which stands for the preceding predicate or some substantial part of it. In cases like (34), by contrast, the — equally anaphoric — sentence-initial constituent introduces a new predication; it is not just a back-referring constituent, but contributes new information itself. For this reason, an instance like (34) is classified under (d) below:

(34) [...] in this small way do the leaders of a city, or of a nation, inure the masses to watching, [...]. (BRW, ed.)

Pro-inversion is related to the linkage between clauses. The same goes for:

(b) *Corr-inversion*, which covers all SAI types in correlative constructions (cf. Quirk et al. 1985:999ff.). To these belong clauses linked by *so/such...that, more/-er/less...than, no sooner...than, the...the, not only...but also, if/as...so*. Examples of this type of construction are given in (35) – (40):

(35) So great is the apathy that the Government could probably go in or stay out without vitally offending either its own followers or the country. (LOB, ed.)

(36) So wholly disparate do they seem, indeed, that it comes as something of a shock [...]. (LOB, bbe.)

(37) No sooner had the ailing monarch departed for Italy, it was learnt, than would-be modernizers had begun to loosen [...]. (LOB, bbe.)

(38) [...] the faster one goes the greater is the need for concentration. (LOB, ed.)

(39) [...] for not only has Mercer proved himself to be one of the few great lyricists over the years, but also one who can function remarkably under pressure. (BRW, bbe.)

(40) The Japanese over the last three years have spent more money [...] than has the United States. (NW, 20 Jan.92, p.25)

The reason why this group of constructions is included here is that there remains an optional element as far as the inversion is concerned.[7] Similar to *pro-inversion*, correlative constructions can in fact take on the form of copular *be*-inversions; in that case, they have the subject in sentence-final position (cf. (35), (38) and (40)). Sometimes, the subject even follows a complex verb phrase, as in (41):

> (41) So successful has been this program, worked out by white and Negro civic leaders, that [...]. (BRW, ed.)

(c) *Add-inversion*: Some of the above-named pro-forms, in particular *nor* and *neither*, also occur as additive adverbs, exemplified by (42) and (43):

> (42) Thus can the fate of nations be decided. (Guardw, 20 Dec.92, p.31)

> (43) [...] they do not come to its meetings, nor are they informed of its decisions. (LOB, ed.)

(d) *Neg-inversion*: The final class of sentence-initial elements followed by SAI can best be grouped under a semantic heading. In particular, there is obligatory SAI after negative and restrictive adverbs such as *only*, *scarcely*, *hardly*, *never*, *little*, *less* (cf. (44)) and the like, as well as after negative direct object preposing (as in (45)):

> (44) Never before have fans been promised such a feast of speed. (LOB, rep.)

> (45) Not a soul did we see. [= Schmidt 1980: (62)]

Since this is the only SAI category that does not rest on a linkage between clauses, *neg-inversion* is extended to apply to non-negative adverbs that optionally trigger SAI, i.e., to "positive frequency, degree, and manner adverbs" (Green 1982: 125). Instances are *often*, *well*, or *truly*, as in (46):

> (46) Truly are the tax gatherers an unbeloved people. (LOB, ed.)

Some of the adverbs followed by *neg-inversion* also have an additive meaning component, for instance *particularly* (cf. (47)). Still others contain an anaphoric element, as shown in (34) above, repeated here as (48):

> (47) [...] it merely wished to minimize subjective views of officials who wielded public authority.

Particularly was this true as laissez-faire capitalism became the dominant credo of Western society. (BRW, sc.writ.)

(48) [...] in this small way do the leaders of a city, or of a nation, inure the masses to watching, [...]. (BRW, ed.)

The relevant criterion for setting up this group by itself is that the elements in sentence-initial position are not predominantly placed there to connect clauses or to create a complex construction; instead, the *neg-inversion* triggers usually have a canonical position within the clause, they are themselves part of what is predicated. As will be discussed later (cf. 4.1.2 and 4.2.4), that is why their front-shifting produces a particularly strong effect.

3.2 Diachronic aspects

Constructions in which the verb follows a sentence-initial constituent other than the subject (henceforth *XVS* order) have existed in all stages of English. However, the Modern English situation differs from earlier stages, in particular from the Old English one, in three respects: first;

> Old English was a mixed V-2/V-F [= verb-second/verb-final] language [...], with V-2 predominant in main clause declaratives and V-F predominant in subordinate clauses. Modern English, on the other hand, is consistently V-3 [= verb-third= SVX] or SVO.[8] (Denison 1993:29f.)

Secondly, "[s]ince in VX languages order is a major grammatical marker, the order becomes increasingly rigid" (Vennemann 1974:359). Only within such a context of an increasingly rigidified word order system have inversions become deviations from a norm, i.e. marked constructions. Finally, the emergence of *do*-periphrasis in the course of the history of the English language (cf. Stein 1990) provided a structural prerequisite for the distinction of fully inverted as opposed to semi-inverted constructions. These are the diachronic factors that have largely contributed to the form and function of inversion in Modern English. They will be sketched out in a bit more detail here below.

The discussion of inversion in earlier stages of English (3.2.1) mainly rests upon the findings of Schmidt (1980) and Stockwell (1984). The historical process is basically one of the grammaticalisation of V-3, whereby "the position of NP before V was interpreted as subject-marking" (Stockwell

1984:584). In several inversion types, V-2 has today become "limited to narrow domains, fully grammaticized there" (Stockwell 1984:584) and is no longer a matter of syntactic choice. Grammaticalisation is therefore an equally important issue for an understanding of the different inversion types of Modern English (3.2.2).

3.2.1 *Inversion in earlier stages of English*

Schmidt (1980) is a detailed study of the history of English inversion, ranging from Old English to Early Modern English,[10] while Stockwell (1984) traces the history of the Old English verb-second "rule" in search of its remaining manifestations, as opposed to true innovations, in Modern English. Both studies thus depart from the situation in Old English, and they attribute to V-2 the status of at least a word order *norm*. Stockwell (1984:577f.) characterises it as an "optional rule, [...] not fully grammaticized [...], but apparently moving in that direction", while Schmidt's (1980:85) findings add to this that after some adverbs, namely "after *tha* and *ne* (and to a lesser extent *nu*)" V-2 was almost *obligatory* (p.85). Apart from sentences started out by these adverbs, V-2 manifested itself as a choice between either an SVO or an XVS sentence pattern.

This choice, however, was probably not accidental. Hopper (1979) argues for a relation of word order in Old English with the foregrounded and backgrounded parts of narrative texts: SV order is associated with backgrounded material, for which "the *casual* presentation of new personages is characteristic" (Hopper 1979:223; my emphasis). VS syntax, by contrast, "coincides with the start of the actual events" (p.222), i.e., with the foregrounded body of the text. It is concerned with the introduction of new characters again, but in foregrounded narrative these usually have "a *role of some kind* in the narrative" (p.223; my emphasis). XVS order is therefore mainly found sequence-initially, i.e., starting a new event structure, and initiates "thematic shifts" or "a sort of breathpause" (p.221).

Hopper's analysis is in line with Schmidt's (1980) claim that inversion in Old English was part of a *subject-shift* system. VS order occurred with first-mention subjects, but also with given, i.e. recoverable, subjects if these were introduced as subsequent topics (cf. Schmidt 1980:151). According to both authors, inversion in Old English had thus relatively local textual significance, while more complex functions, i.e. major shifts within discourse, were not yet apt to be signalled by word order alone. Stein (1995:146) attributes this to the structural prerequisite of word order grammaticalisation, which was still to come: "[p]rior to the central structural process, the grammaticalisation of SVO, inversion (or not) did have non-propositional meaning, which is best described as 'textual' or discourse meaning, but no affective meaning".

In the course of the transition to Middle English, the subject-shift condition gradually got lost, as did the OE regularities of V-2 after the above-mentioned adverbs in general. Replacing this regularity of V-2 order, there evolved the functional potential to highlight *individual* constituents by the use of an inversion: the subject, the verb, or the preposed constituent. This tendency anticipates "a functional distinction between semi- and full-inversion" (cf. Schmidt 1980:215), which thus arose temporally prior to its structural prerequisite, namely, the availability of periphrastic *do* where no other auxiliary was available for SAI. The result at the stage of early Middle English was a strong, though far from generalised, tendency to use SV order for given, especially pronominal, subjects, and full inversion for topic introduction, and to use semi-inversion with thematic and pronominal subjects for highlighting the preposed constituent (cf. Schmidt 1980:217).

From then on the process of the gradual grammaticalisation of SVO order sets in, accompanied by an emerging availability of *do*-support (S*do*V) for the verb.[11] Only two types of inversion finally survive: XVS order becomes the main device of topic introduction or topic shift, which, after a seeming decrease in the Middle English period, re-emerged and brought with it an innovated type of inversion: Stockwell (1984), in his preliminary evaluation of a limited range of Middle English data, suggests that Modern English has "(i) surface V-2 constructions that are true reflexes of OE V-2 ; [and] (ii) surface V-2 constructions that have been innovated and merged with true reflexes" (p.589). To the latter belong *VP-inversion*, *AdjP-inversion* and some types of *PP-inversion*, which Stockwell subsumes under "*predicative* fronting with V-2" (Stockwell 1984:579f.; my emphasis). This characterisation of the innovated inversions is relevant for the later subsumption of those various formal types under a joint functional heading. According to Stockwell's data, they were "found rarely if at all in OE, and very rarely in EME [= early Middle English], increasing in frequency toward the end of the ME [= Middle English] period" (p.585). But, of course, what "re-emerged" as XVS at that time became comparatively restricted to a narrow range of verbs, notably intransitive verbs.

SAI constructions, by contrast, in the Early Modern English period underwent a different development, in fact a drastic rise and change in use, alongside with *do* as a dummy auxiliary becoming freely insertable. Until the late Middle English stage, semi-inversions with *do* seem to have occurred when "the verb rather than the PC [= preposed constituent]" (Schmidt 1980:259) was to receive some additional emphasis. This function of *do* in SAI gradually changed, at a time when a general increase in the use of *do* inversions can be noted (cf., e.g., Schmidt 1980:262), away from the verb and towards the sentence-initial position. By the Early Modern English period, S*do*V had become the device for giving additional weight to the verb phrase, while X*do*VS occurred in contexts "related to intensity" (Stein 1990:279). These contexts were also created by non-negative adverbs "akin to negation in focusing on the truth of the proposition", but, in addition, there was an epistemic meaning tied to them, a subjective dimension in that they contained "a judgment relative to the speaker's beliefs" (Stein 1990:279).

That most of these expressions are today obligatorily followed by SAI is a reflection of word order grammaticalisation within that process, interpreted by Stockwell (1984:584f.) as the "limiting" of V-2 to narrow domains.

In principle, a rigid word order system can highlight a sentence element by merely shifting it to the beginning of a clause. Constituent types, however, which are commonly found in that position gain only moderate prominence in that way, for them SAI is a further option and produces a further and stronger effect (cf. 4.1.2).[12] The reason why certain constituents came to be obligatorily followed by SAI has been sought in their being particularly heavy and "inbuilt emotional" (cf. Stein 1995:141).

3.2.2 *Inversion and grammaticalisation*

This brief sketch of the history of inversion has shown that the English word order system has undergone a development whereby the former optional norm that non-subject-shifted subjects were placed in front of the verb got lost. Instead, the position itself became identified with subject-marking. This may be considered a case of "reanalysis" (Stockwell 1984:584), and as such one of grammaticalisation, though in a broader sense of the term. Grammaticalisation is usually applied to lexical items or phrases which "come [...] to be reanalysed as having syntactic and morphological functions" (cf. Traugott 1995:32). Following, e.g., Hopper/Traugott (1993), "a broader definition of grammaticalisation as the organisation of grammatical, especially morphosyntactic material" (p.82), however, can also include word order changes.[13]

Within the process of grammaticalisation, the relative order of subject and verb in English became a device of grammatical expression, at work alongside other devices such as prosody, morphological modification, or function words (cf. Lehmann 1992). Note that it is not by word order alone, but rather in accordance with selection restrictions of the verb, that functions such as subject and object are assigned. In this respect, FI in Modern English, restricted to intransitive verbs, exploits a word order choice in exactly those contexts where the grammatical meaning of subject is already guaranteed. SAI, by contrast, is not limited to a certain class of verbs, nor does it affect the relative ordering of subject and object in relation to the main verb.

If, in the course of the grammaticalisation process, the subject-first instances of V-2 were reanalysed as marking subjecthood, the remainders of the XVS part of the optional norm are reflected in the different inversion types of present-day English. Stockwell (1984:585) distinguishes three types of consequences of the grammaticalisation process:

(a) Those constituents that trigger V-2 obligatorily are instances of limiting of the formerly optional norm; in these cases, V-2 has become *fully grammaticalised*. The two major domains[14] to which V-2 is limited are "initial negatives" and "affectives" (p. 585), i.e. *neg-inversion* as established above. Within the three other SAI groups, it is also via negative meaning (*nor/neither* as pro-forms and additive adverbs, correlative constructions introduced by *no sooner..., not only...*) or affective meaning (*so/ such...(that)*) that an obligatory, thus grammaticalised, SAI construction comes about.

(b) A second class of constituents is one in which inversion has been "common in OE and ME, but optional at all dates, as it is today" (Stockwell 1984:585); in these cases, inversion has thus not become fully grammaticalised, but has maintained the status of an *optional norm*. This status is valid for most cases of *AdvP-inversion*[15] and *PP-inversion*. There is a certain common semantic denominator within that group, related to the notion of locativity, and covering spatial and temporal location as well as direction (cf. Stockwell 1984:581). A case of optional SAI are manner adverbs, but for different reasons: already commonly placed in sentence-initial position, they can receive additional prominence by virtue of being followed by inversion.

(c) Those inversions that, according to Stockwell's data, did not exist prior to the end of the Middle English period are not necessarily reflexes of the former V-2 optional norm. This goes for *VP-inversion* and *AdjP-inversion*, as well as for a subclass of *PP-inversion*, called "predicative" by Stockwell and "abstract" by Green (1982). These types seem to constitute real *innovations*, while the fact that inversion is obligatory after these constituents is attributable to the equational nature of the construction. The empirical side of this hypothesis cannot be tested within the limits of my synchronic study, but it is important to note that the obligatory nature of inversion is in these cases not the result of a grammaticalisation process.

3.3 Two formal hypotheses

Formal approaches to syntax usually treat word order using a body of rules, such as movement rules in Government and Binding theory (cf. Travis 1984; Haegeman 1991) or separate immediate dominance and linear precedence rules within phrase structure grammars (e.g., Gazdar et al. 1985). An alternative position to these *derivative* conceptions of word order has recently been adopted within an HPSG framework: Reape (forthc.), for instance, no longer considers word order as an epiphenomenon of hierarchical sentence structure. Instead, it becomes an *autonomous* counterpart to phrase structure and dominance relations, with linearisation phenomena such as inversion licensed by only a limited class of verbs (cf. Kathol/Levine 1992:217f.). The formalism is not my concern here, but I am sympathetic to this view of word order, less as derived, but produced by discourse conditions of its own and carrying a discourse meaning proper. Support for the plausibility of this view is provided by the fact that the choice of verbs which can occur with full inversion is far from random; it is in fact strongly restricted and semantically motivated.

Apart from raising this aspect of word order, there are two hypotheses originating from formal syntactic models which I want to briefly present here because I refer to them later in the analysis: one is the ongoing discussion of the status of inversion as a *root transformation* (Emonds 1976; Hooper/

Thompson 1973), or a "main clause phenomenon [= MCP]" (Green 1976), with special attention paid to its putative inability to occur in embedded clauses (3.3.1). The observations which have been brought forward for and against this claim are particularly important for the semantics of inversion in terms of viewpoint and subjectivity (cf. 4.2). The other more formal issue about inversion is its syntactic analysis, notably that of FI, which remains a controversial issue as to whether the postverbal NP or the fronted constituent involved should be considered its subject. Arguments which speak for a "mixed" subject status of the sentence-initial constituent will therefore be summarised in 3.3.2. They support the claim which I make later that the different types of FI in Modern English are in fact *all* derived from a basic presentative mechanism (cf. 4.1.1).

3.3.1 *Inversion as a root transformation*

The formal version of this claim is that inversions move phrasal constituents to a position immediately dominated by the sentence node and are thereby root transformations. Since such a transformation is not structure-preserving, it cannot occur in an embedded clause (cf. Emonds 1976). There are obviously counterexamples to the structure-preserving hypothesis, as Emonds himself concedes, but he assumes "that the use of these rules in embedded sentences is ungrammatical in the strict sense, and that the structure-preserving constraint is broken for purposes of emphasis, clear communication, etc." (Emonds 1976:35).

Over the past two decades, extensive discussion about the validity of this constraint for inversion has taken place in the literature, and there is no need to repeat the arguments here. As a result of this discussion, it has in fact been sufficiently shown that "the embeddability of so-called MCP [= main clause phenomena] is influenced not only by syntactic forms and semantic functions, but also by pragmatic functions, by what the speaker is trying to do" (Green 1976:397). In the same vein, Birner (1992:80ff.) concludes that "the various approaches to inversion that have taken as a starting-point its putative status as a root transformation have proven flawed" (p.92), considering that there are enough cases of embedded inversions that are "uncontroversially acceptable" (p.84). However, the lack of a watertight argument in favor of the root transformation status must not blur two facts: by far the majority of inversions in natural language in fact occur in main clauses (98.7% of my corpus,[16] 93%

in Birner (1992)) and, vice versa, many of the so-considered counter-examples to the structure-preserving hypothesis would probably never show up in natural data. An analysis of the meaning and discourse function of FI should in my view be able to account for this.

3.3.2 *"Mixed" subject status in full inversion*

The discussion centring upon an adequate syntactic analysis of FI has so far mainly treated inversion following *locative* constituents, which, in a broader sense of the term, subsumes "spatial locations, paths, and directions, and their extensions to some temporal and abstract locative domains" (Bresnan 1994:75). It therefore takes place as concerning "locative inversion" (Coopmans 1989; Bresnan/Kanerva 1992; Bresnan 1994) or "focus inversion" (Levine 1989) and neglects FI after nonlocative phrases, which are restricted to the verb *be*.[17] This is symptomatic of the fact that, especially in the syntactic literature, certain types of FI are treated to the exclusion of others, a proceeding which it is also my concern to challenge.

The starting-point of any syntactic analysis of FI is that it is a construction "where the position of the locative and subject arguments are inverted without changing the *semantic role* structure of the verb" (Bresnan 1994:75; my emphasis). Schachter (1992) and Bresnan/Kanerva (1992) refer to this as the *thematic* clause structure, which remains unaffected by word order; both terms ultimately denote the clause as *representation* level as introduced above. If word order, however, derives from syntactic structure, word order variation should plausibly give rise to some kind of structural variation as well. The only question is at which level of syntactic analysis both the preverbal constituent and the postverbal NP in FI differ from the canonical alternative. Solutions have been suggested within various frameworks of basically two kinds: either a *configurational* formalism is used, taking FI as a syntactic dislocation process which results in a topicalised PP and an adjoined NP (Safir 1985; Coopmans 1989; Rochemont/Culicover 1990), or the analysis follows a *lexical* approach, which touches upon the syntactic valence (Levine 1989) and the grammatical function assignment (Bresnan/Kanerva 1992; Bresnan 1994) of the verb. It is the latter kind of approaches which have brought up the claim that the preposed constituent in an FI is in fact the subject of the clause. They use various kinds of syntactic evidence, such as Heavy-NP-Shift, subject raising, tag formation, or constraints on subject extraction (cf. Bresnan/

Kanerva 1992:121), as well as the discourse status of the putatively topicalised PP to support the subject claim, but, of course, there is one strong structural counter-argument: "English has subject-verb agreement (and no object-verb agreement), and the verb in a Locative inversion construction must agree with the Theme [= postverbal NP]" (Schachter 1992:107).

One attempt to reconcile the "mixed" evidence for the subject status of both the front-shifted locative PP and the postverbal NP in inversion is Bresnan (1994), who, within the framework of Lexical Functional Grammar (LFG), raises some interesting issues. Like other lexical approaches, Bresnan argues for a switch in grammatical function assignment that takes place in locative inversion. However, the LFG framework is more refined in that respect because, in addition to the level of representation (*semantic roles*) and the level of exchange (*grammatical functions*), it provides for a further level of *categorial structure*. While the former two are considered universal, languages may differ in their inventories and configurations of syntactic categories. As a result, a construction such as locative inversion may, on an abstract level of representation, display a mismatch of role ("a-structure"), syntactic function ("f-structure") and syntactic categories ("c-structure"). It thereby exploits an underspecification of the argument roles of the verb that allow the syntactic functions to alternate in order to meet the requirements of discourse functions. The alternation is usually triggered by "marked requirements of presentational focus" (Bresnan 1994:90), which makes a natural selection of the argument structure closest to its needs:

> In presentational focus, a scene is set and a referent is introduced on the scene to become the new focus of attention. In the core cases, a scene is naturally expressed as a location, and the referent as something of which location is predicated - hence, a theme. This imposes a natural selection of the <*th loc*> argument structure. (p. 90)[18]

In the default case, the <*th loc*> role structure would make the theme the subject of the clause. However, this is in conflict with the discourse conditions. Since a theme is in principle able to be subject or object, the locative becomes the subject of the inverted clause. But English locatives are non-nominal categories; thus, "the inverted locative is [...] the subject at a level of representation that abstracts away from their categorial expression" (Bresnan 1994:103). This explains the "mixed" subject properties of the constituents, reflected in their formal syntactic behaviour (cf. Bresnan 1994:105ff.): for instance, fronted locatives undergo subject raising and show the same constraints on subject extraction as do NP subjects, while they do not agree with the verb and do not undergo subject-auxiliary-inversion. Further support for NP-like properties of PPs in English are sentences like (52), which have a real prepositional subject:

(52) Under the chair is a nice place for the cat to sleep. [= Bresnan 1994:(103a)]

In (52), the prepositional phrase behaves syntactically like a nominal phrase and could in fact be regarded as a place NP (cf. Bresnan 1994:110). PPs thus possess a certain flexibility of getting re-interpreted as referential expressions; possibly, these are "instances of ellipsis" (p.110). In the terms of another framework, namely that of Cognitive Grammar (CG), this process depends on the "reference-point" of the PP, on the basis of which a "search domain" is defined (Langacker 1993:15). This domain becomes "conceptually reified" (p.15), thereby designates a place rather than a relationship, which is a process made possible precisely by the subject function of the PP. Alternatively, (52) could still be read as an inversion, in which the PP would be a characterisation rather than a predicate of identification.

Interestingly, it is copular *be*-sentences that are most flexible as far as a re-interpretation of PPs as NPs, or predicative constituents as referential ones, is concerned. Sentences other than predicative copular constructions are less flexible in that respect, for instance (53):

(53) ??Under the chair makes me happy. [= Bresnan 1994:(109a)]

Other types of FI "swivelling" rather freely around the verb *be* (cf. Enkvist 1987:20), however, in fact undergo a re-interpretation similar to the one giving rise to prepositional subjects. Notably, this goes for the nonlocative inversions restricted to *be*, which were originally not taken into account in this discussion. They have been said above (cf. 3.2) to differ from the locative types in at least two respects: presumably, they are diachronically younger, and they are obligatory after fronting, but not because they are grammaticalised. Now a further difference between inversions containing a lexical verb and copular *be*-constructions becomes apparent: with a lexical verb as in (54a), the PP, despite being fronted, remains unambiguously predicative, i.e., it states something about the referent expressed by the postverbal NP. By contrast, all constituents followed by copular *be* can in fact undergo a re-interpretation from a *predicative* to a *referential* constituent. This is the case for all *be*-inversions, including locative inversions with *be*, such as in (55a) – (57a):

(54a)   In the garden stands a fountain.

(55a)   In the garden is a fountain.

(56a)   Also present is a beautiful statue.

(57a)   Even more beautiful is the small pavilion in the back of the garden.

The potential referential status of the first constituent in *be*-inversions becomes apparent in their similarity with *wh*-clefts, such as (54b) – (57b), which make the re-interpretation explicit on the categorial level:

(54b)   What stands in the garden is a fountain.

(55b)   What is in the garden is a fountain.

(56b)   What is also present is a beautiful statue.

(57b)   What is even more beautiful is the small pavilion in the back of the garden.

Although (55a) – (57a) do not induce the same contrastive semantics as *wh*-clefted sentences (cf. Prince 1978; Declerck 1984), they show the same tendency to be read, not as *predicational*, but as *specificational*, statements. (54a) as opposed to (54b), by contrast, are two different statements, a predicational one and a specificational one, respectively. *Wh*-clefts, which are potentially ambiguous in that respect (cf. Declerck 1984; Partee 1986), are *not* reversible under the predicational reading, i.e., when the latter part of the cleft "does not identify the referent of the subject NP but says something more about it" (Declerck 1984:253); vice versa, specificational statements invert quite easily.

It is this specificational nature of nonlocative *be*-inversion that must in my view have encouraged the innovation of these types, which thus need not be leftovers of the former V-2 norm in English. Since the predicates of *be*-constructions are particularly easy to re-interpret as referents, the model may have been locative *PP-inversion* around *be*, subsequently giving rise to other, equally static, types of inversion. In that sense, Bresnan's (1994) assumption of a possible mismatch between grammatical roles and categorial expression ultimately uncovers a relatedness of all types of FI, despite their historical and categorial discrepancies.

3.4 The functional claims

Despite a focus on syntactic analysis, formal theories of syntax, when studying inversion, are of course aware of the fact that the motivation for word order variation has to be sought less in syntactic or structural terms, but in discourse and contextual conditions. For this reason, FI is treated in these frameworks as a *focus construction* (Rochemont/Culicover 1990) or a *stylistic* inversion (Safir 1985). On the other hand, inversion constructions have also been subject to functional analyses proper, which can be roughly divided into two groups: one group of approaches treats inversion as a *focussing* (Rochemont 1986) or a *defocussing* device (Penhallurick 1984; Erdmann 1990), depending on the notion of focus applied (cf. 2.1.2 above). Since one kind of a marked focus (cf. Enkvist 1980) is presentational focus, these accounts are in fact closely related to a *presentative* function of inversion, as claimed by Drubig (1988) or, from a Cognitive Grammar angle, in Langacker (1993). The essentials of these claims are summarised in 3.4.1. The other type of functional studies on inversion follow an *information-packaging* approach; of these, Birner (1992, 1994) constitutes the most recent and comprehensive work on FI. It basically centres on the relative hearer- and discourse-familiarity of the preposed constituents and the post-verbal NPs of FIs. Hartvigson/Jakobsen (1974) talk of *weight* inversion, and Penhallurick (1984) of only one condition, namely, that the subject must represent *new* information, but there is a common core in all of these arguments, which will be summarised in 3.4.2.

Some work on inversion is of a more descriptive or taxonomic kind (Hartvigson/Jakobsen 1974; Green 1982; Erdmann 1979, 1990) and therefore treats FI and SAI constructions together. However, these studies stress the differences, rather than any shared functions, of the individual inversion types.[19] SAI is overall studied less comprehensively in the functional literature; due to its mostly obligatory status, it is treated as an *attraction* inversion, i.e. an automatised construction (Hartvigson/Jakobsen 1974), or it is emphasised that the word order pattern of the rest of the sentence remains unaffected, that SAI is only inversion of *clause elements* (Erdmann 1990). These, especially the negative, items "triggering" SAI are the focus of some other individual works on inversion (Kjellmer 1979; Erdmann 1988; König 1988), reference to which, however, will only be made where necessary in the course of the analysis in later chapters.

3.4.1 *Focus-marking and the presentative function*

As stated above (2.1.2), the unmarked information focus of a clause is usually identified with sentence-final position, while a marked focus plausibly requires special prosodic or syntactic effort. In that an FI shifts to the final sentence-position those constituents that thereby come to carry the informational focus, it is a *focus-marking* device; in that it does so by the syntactic effort of word order variation, it is a construction which creates a *marked focus*.

This claim that inversion is a focus construction has been made by various linguists. According to the more recent ones (e.g. Rochemont (1986); Rochemont/Culicover (1990)), focus is still a syntactic notion with "both a phonetic and a semantic interpretation" (Rochemont 1986:17). The semantic interpretation is defined in terms of "c-construability", whereby a constituent is c-construable if it is "under discussion" (or indexical; cf. Rochemont 1986:174). Two types of focus are distinguished on the basis of this criterion: those constituents that are not c-construable constitute a *presentational* focus, while there is a *contrastive* focus in a sentence, if, after the extraction of that constituent, the rest of the sentence is c-construable.[20] Contrastive focus is therefore a sub-case of presentational focus: it rests not only on a condition for the focussed constituent (non-c-construability), but also on one for the rest of the sentence (c-construability).[21] Following this distinction, FI has been analysed as a focus construction, in which the post-verbal NP is identified as the presentational focus. This means that it has not been "under discussion" before. By contrast, it presumably does not constitute contrastive focus.

Birner (1994:237f.), however, discusses some examples in which the post-verbal NP has been explicitly evoked before and would therefore be c-construable. (58) is one of her examples:

(58) Nusseibeh's unusual predicament causes concern all around. His friends fear that Arab hardliners will turn on Nusseibeh, thinking he is an Israeli ally.
   The Israelis, who certainly want to squelch the 17-month-old uprising in the West Bank and Gaza Strip, are under intense pressure from the United States not to jail moderates who may figure in

their election proposal for the territories occupied since the 1967 war.

<u>Most immediately affected is Nusseibeh himself</u>. [= Birner 1994:(9a)]

This looks like a genuine counter-example against the claim that FI marks a presentational focus. Note, however, that the inversion presents a discourse entity which, though evoked by prior discourse, is only re-mentioned after the intervention of a considerable amount of text, in that case a full paragraph. The occurrence therefore supports a position adopted in Bresnan (1994), namely, that "presentational focus may be used to reintroduce previously evoked referents into the scene or some parts of the scene" (p.86, footnote 21). In other words, absence of c-construability, or not being "under discussion", is a local and also a gradient phenomenon. The use of *himself* in (58) is symptomatic of this: as put forward in Kemmer (1995:58), one typical use of the reflexive pronoun is a "return-to-topic" use.

Further evidence for a presentational focus analysis of FI is provided by Bresnan (1994): using the examples given in (59) – (62), she argues that, in the inversion, only the post-verbal NP can become the focus of contrast. Since contrastive focus is only a sub-case of presentational focus, the NP must therefore constitute the presentational focus relative to the preposed constituent. In CWO sentences, by contrast, both constituents can become a contrastive focus:

(59) On the wall hung canvasses, but no paintings. [= (46a)]

(60) ??On the wall hung canvasses, but not on the easels. [= (46b)]

(61) Canvasses hung on the wall, but no paintings. [= (45a)]

(62) Canvasses hung on the wall, but not on the easels. [= (45b)]

(Bresnan 1994)

Apart from such contrasts explicitly evoked by an appended phrase, inversions do not seem to mark contrastive focus. Birner (1992) also addresses this question, but finds no evidence for the strict condition that the rest of the sentence constitutes "salient shared knowledge" (p.206). There are basically two reasons for that: on the one hand, FI often follows preposed constituents which themselves contain rather complex information; from her corpus data, Birner (1992) concludes that it was seldom the case in the corpus that the entire preposed constituent represented relatively familiar information; rather, some element within the preposed constituent represented relatively familiar information in the discourse. (p.214).

A representative example would be (63):

(63) On the foreign-policy front, Nixon continued to protect the national security by not telling anybody, not even his secret (sic?) wife, Pat, what his secret plan to end the Vietnam War was. At the same time, he undertook a major clandestine foreign-policy initiative by sending chocolates and long-stemmed roses to legendary Communist Chinese revolutionary leader Mao ("Mo the Dong") Ze-dong. <u>Helping him with this initiative was the brilliant, avocado-shaped genius Henry Kissinger</u>, who became the nation's top foreign-policy strategist despite being born with the handicaps of a laughable accent and no neck. [= Birner 1992:(29), p.213]

In this instance, only *him* and *this initiative* represent shared knowledge at the time of the inversion, whereas the whole of the VP has not yet been "under discussion". Consequently, the post-verbal NP cannot become a focus of contrast, though certainly it is the presentational focus. On the other hand, in many inversions, the preposed constituent is only "plausibly inferrable in the context" (Birner 1992:214), but is not yet shared knowledge at the time of the inversion. (64) is again taken from Birner (1992):

(64) Of the VCR's tested, the RCA VKP950 and the Hitachi VT89A were the easiest to program. They have on-screen programming, a series of prompts that appears on the TV screen to help you enter the appropriate programming information. <u>Highly vexing were models that have a "one-way" timer</u>. [= Birner 1992: (30), p.215]

Thus, while FI is justifiably claimed to be focus-marking, the narrower conditions for contrastive focus are in fact rarely met. But the focus-marking analysis is probably not a sufficient one, given the complexity of many of the preposed constituents. Birner argues that most inversions involve "more than one nuclear accent — minimally [...] one in each of the preposed and postposed constituents" (1992:212); in the same vein, Drubig (1988:85) claims that FIs are bi-focal rather than merely focus-marking.[22] It is in this sense that the entire construction has been said to fulfil a *presentative function*.

This claim was again originally restricted to the locative types of inversion and goes back to at least Bolinger (1977). He characterises as *presentative* a "bring into" function and applies it to *there*-constructions and inversions, i.e., to all cases "where a locative, or *there*, or both, precedes the verb" (p.93). As the main motivation for *there* or its absence, he assumes that "[the FI] presents something on our immediate stage (brings something literally or figuratively BEFORE OUR PRESENCE) whereas [... the *there*-construction] presents something to our minds (brings a piece of knowledge into consciousness)" (Bolinger 1977:93f.; his emphasis). Furthermore, "the more vividly on the stage an action is, the less appropriate *there* becomes" (p.95). That is why, according to Bolinger, (65) and (66) are equally acceptable, but not (68) as opposed to (67):

(65) Out of nowhere appeared a mysterious figure. [= (29)]

(66) Out of nowhere there appeared a mysterious figure. [= (30)]

(67) Out flew a funny bird. [= (33)]

(68) *Out there flew a funny bird. [= (34)]

(Bolinger 1977)

Drubig's (1988:89) point that inversion creates a "visual-impact reading" is related to Bolinger's claims. Such a reading requires that a "scene" is before us (in sight or in mind). For the same reason, we can say *here is...*, but not *here there is...* (cf. Bolinger 1977:95), because *there*-insertion abstracts away from the immediate scene. There is therefore a close connection between FIs following deictic adverbs and those that follow more complex lexical phrases; they could in fact be considered "complementary in distribution and discourse function" (Drubig 1988:91). The common core is the presentative function, a central *deictic* act, which consists of "directing the addressee's conscious attention to an object in his environment by making him focus on a region in his perceptual field" (Drubig 1988:91). By contrast, a presentative function is fulfilled by *lexical* means "in non-optimal situations characterised by the relative distance or displacement of one speech act participant [...] from the region of optimal perceptual access" (p.91). In this way, Drubig's account plausibly relates various FI types to each other, such as *AdvP-inversion*, *PP-inversion*, and even *VP-inversion*, as in (69) – (72):

(69) Here comes the waiter right now. [= (31a)]

(70) I opened the bedroom door, and out/in walked the cat. [= (27a/b)]

(71) On our left was the Mediterranean. [= (1)]

(72) Exhumed were at least a dozen of corpses. [= (23a)]

(Drubig 1988)

However, nonlocative FI types such as *AdjP-inversion* or *NP-inversion* are explicitly excluded from both Bolinger's and Drubig's presentative claims and they are not sufficiently accounted for by a notion of a — literal or figurative — "physical stage"; furthermore, as the range of constructions in (69) – (72) suggests, the starting-points of this presentative mechanism are very divergent. Thus, while, in principle, the analysis undertaken below rests on a presentative function of FI, the aim is both a more comprehensive and at the same time a more fine-grained analysis of the different presentative processes involved.

One way to extend the presentative analysis to the nonlocative FI types is to interpret presentative statements as "reference-point constructions" (cf. Langacker 1993). In a Cognitive Grammar framework, a reference-point function is attributed to front-shifted constituents "that serve to introduce an element onto the scene" (Langacker 1993:26), and, similar to the LFG-approach, these need not be noun phrases. For Langacker (1993), in presentative constructions, "the initial constituent is relational rather than nominal in character, i.e., it profiles a relationship instead of a thing" (p.26). Again, only locative inversions are given as examples, but the understanding of a profiled relationship, which "functions as [...] the locative expressions' search domain" (Langacker 1993:26) could be extended, for instance, to *AdjP-inversion*: if, in (73), the locative evokes a range of possible locations, (74) could evoke a set of entities that have the property specified by the AdjP:

(73) On the table sat a nervous calico cat. [= Langacker 1993:(21a)]

(74) Equally nervous was the dog, sitting next to it on the chair.

A construction with a presentative function should also have a bearing on subsequent discourse: after a discourse entity is presented, it usually becomes the new focus of attention. Birner (1992:105) objects to this that not all postverbal NPs in an inversion are necessarily relevant in subsequent discourse, especially not if they have been evoked before. An example of hers is (75):

(75) McPherson proffered the cigar and a fat hand reached forward and accepted it. The round face was expanded in a grin of anticipated pleasure, and <u>into the wide mouth went half the cigar</u>, to be masticated by strong but tobacco-stained teeth. [= Birner 1992:(26a), p.105]

(75) certainly fits Drubig's "visual impact-reading", but it is true that no necessary claim about the topicality of *half the cigar* can be inferred from its introduction by way of inversion. Vice versa, this implies that the presentative function is no discourse function as such, but achieves various effects depending on the context.

Finally, I briefly consider the presumed functional properties of FI that underlie the claim that it is a *defocussing* device (Penhallurick 1984; Erdmann 1990). Focus is then identified with prominence and is attributed to the subject position, signalling the property of being *in-focus*: "[initial position] is a position of prominence, because the hearer is maximally ignorant at that point, and so is likely to be paying attention there" (Penhallurick 1984:46). FI, which removes the subject out of this position, therefore defocusses the subject (Penhallurick 1984:47; Erdmann 1990:5). Apart from the difference in the notion of focus, Penhallurick raises an important point about FI in discourse-initial position: in his view, what inhibits inversion in that position is that it would be "odd to defocus [...] entities who will continue to occupy the discourse focus" (Penhallurick 1984:47); hence, according to him, the lack of an inversion in the first sentence of (76):

(76) A girl and an older woman were walking along a metalled pathway. <u>To their left, beyond a strip of grass, was the front of a large high building in grey stone.</u> [= Penhallurick 1984:(26)]

Birner (1994:240), by contrast, claims the opposite; cf. her examples (77) and (78):

(77) <u>In a little white house lived two rabbits.</u>*It/*The house was the oldest one in the forest, and all the animals worried that someday it would come crashing down. [= (15a)]

(78) In a little white house lived two rabbits. They/The rabbits were named Flopsy and Mopsy, and they spent their days merrily invading neighborhood gardens. [=(15b)]

(Birner 1994)

This looks as if inversion is not exempted from discourse-initial position, and (78), as opposed to (77), shows that it focusses, rather than defocusses, an entity for the following discourse. Penhallurick's example given in (76) very much reads like the beginning of a story, and, for that purpose, *along a metalled pathway* is probably not "scene-setting" enough for presenting the main characters. Nonetheless, the discourse-initial position of an FI, such as in (78), is the exception rather than the rule. Stories are much more likely to begin like (79), in which the scene actually precedes the presentative inversion:

(79) Once upon a time there was a lake in the mountains, and in that lived a huge crab. (Rouse, *The Giant Crab*, p.1)

What has become apparent from the discussion of FI in terms of a focus-marking and a presentative function is that the discourse potential of the construction is not sufficiently explored by these functions. On the one hand, these claims are too general to account for the work of the individual FI types (e.g., *AdvP-* vs. *PP-* vs. *AdjP-inversion*), for instance, as concerns their reference-point constructions. On the other hand, their functions have not yet been appropriately described in a larger discourse context; inversion is a focussing, rather than a defocussing, device, but it has various discourse tasks and certainly carries further components of meaning.

3.4.2 *The information-packaging claim*

Birner's (1992, 1994) work is, to my knowledge, the most recent and the most unified functional account of full inversion in Modern English, based on a large corpus of naturally-occurring tokens. Her hypothesis derives from Chafe's (1976) notion of *information-packaging*, a metaphor which stresses that certain linguistic phenomena "have to do primarily with how the message is sent and only secondarily with the message itself" (p.28). The main claim about the discourse function of FI is that it serves an information-packaging function [...], linking relatively unfamiliar information to the prior context via the clause-initial placement of information which is relatively familiar (typically evoked or inferrable) in the current discourse. (Birner 1992:127)

This function has also a *connective* component: for instance, Green's (1980) practical, introductory, and emphatic functions, put forward for various FI types, "can be subsumed under the connective function" (Birner 1992:110); in fact, most previous functional work on inversion focusses, in one way or another, on information-packaging (e.g., Hartvigson/Jakobsen 1974; Green 1980; Penhallurick 1984). A summary of these can be found, e.g., in Birner (1992:107ff.).

The advantage of Birner's results lies in the fact that she has not treated *givenness* as a phenomenon measurable in an all-or-nothing way. Instead, she uses Prince's (1981b) scale of *assumed familiarity*, whereby discourse entities are ranked from most to least familiar: in order of decreasing assumed familiarity, these are *evoked > unused > inferrable > containing inferrable > brand-new anchored > brand-new* (cf. Prince 1981b:245). With this scale at hand, Birner posits a "pragmatic constraint" as outcome of her analysis of 1778 full inversions: "the preposed element in an inversion must not be newer in the discourse than the postposed element" (1994:245).

The prototypical distribution of information in an FI is therefore one in which the initial constituent and the postposed subject differ in status. In example (80), for instance, the initial element has been *evoked* in prior discourse, while the subject is *brand-new*:

(80) For example, "What's Hot", a magazine published by General Foods for children aged 4 to 14, is sent to households that are known to be responsive to ad promotions. The "message from the sponsor" is subtle, with brand names worked into activities such as games and quizzes. <u>Accompanying the magazine are cents-off coupons.</u> [= Birner 1992: (2b), p.130]

Furthermore, in case both elements seem to have equal information status, recency of mention and thereby *salience* of a discourse entity are also "relevant to the speaker's decision about whether to use an inversion" (Birner 1994:246).

The intermediate categories from the familiarity scale, however, apparently behave in a way opposite to their ordering in Prince's scale, in particular *inferrable* (including *containing inferrable*) and *unused* information. Birner therefore takes into account that assumed familiarity can have two origins: it arises either from "(the speaker's beliefs about) the hearer's beliefs" (Prince 1992:301), or from "the discourse-model being constructed during discourse processing" (Prince 1992:303); by way of this distinction, Birner's results suggest that inferrable information is treated as discourse-old and "pattern with evoked information with respect to inversion" (1994:251). For this reason, an example such as (81) is natural because "mention of labor savings renders inferrable that something (labor) has been eliminated" (Birner 1992:159):

(81) Labor savings are achieved because the crew is put to better use than cleaning belts manually; <u>also eliminated is the expense of buying costly chemicals</u>. [= Birner 1992:(17b), p.158f.]

By contrast, there are no tokens in Birner's corpus with, for instance, an unused element preposed and an inferrable element postposed.

The results of this study thus stress the relevance of *discourse*-familiarity as having priority over *hearer*-familiarity:

> [...] there is no single token in the corpus wherein the element represented by the initial constituent is discourse-new (i.e., unused or brand-new) while that represented by the final constituent is discourse-old (i.e., evoked). That there do exist felicitous tokens [...] containing a hearer-new initial constituent with a hearer-old final constituent suggests that it is not the (assumed) familiarity of the information to the hearer that is relevant, but rather familiarity WITHIN THE DISCOURSE of the information represented by the preposed and postposed constituents. (Birner 1992:148; her emphasis)

These findings constitute a crucial starting-point for my analysis of FI in chapter 4. In particular, I want to take up a question which Birner (1994) herself raises in her conclusion: if inferrable information is treated as discourse-old, this could also mean that "the use of an inferrable in a position reserved for discourse-old information cues the hearer to evoke it" (p.255). Front-shifting, like in (81), of a constituent which is not explicitly evoked in the context would then be more a coding, rather than a reflection, of the assumed familiarity status of a discourse entity or predicate. In this way, the information-packaging function of word order gets re-interpreted as an *instruction*, a device by way of which the reader's focus of attention is managed within an ever-changing discourse model.

The same interpretation can apply to the case of evoked entities, if these nevertheless occur postverbally: their felicity could also be due to purposes of reintroduction, to instructions of being re-focussed. Evocation in prior discourse means hearer-old and discourse-old status at that point of the discourse, but what an entity *remains* is only hearer-old: "hearers are assumed to remember the entities we have told them about, at least for the duration of the discourse" (Prince 1992:309). The discourse-old status, by contrast, gradually *diminishes*, which forms of reference cannot sufficiently reflect; a hearer-old entity, due to its "uniquely identifiable" status (cf. Gundel et al. 1993:275), is most likely to be a definite NP, but no further indication about the current state of discourse-familiarity is provided. FI could therefore be one device whereby a speaker signals reintroduction of, i.e. new focus of attention on, a hearer-familiar entity.

3.5 Related phenomena

Inversion shares with some other syntactic patterns the property of being a *non-canonical sentence* (cf. Kaplan 1989:230ff.), a status which derives from English as a grammatical word order language. Another implication (cf. Thompson 1978:25) of this word order type is that there are also special *varieties of canonical sentences*, such as passives, indirect object movement, or cleft constructions:

> [they] fit the NP-VP template for canonical sentences, but [...] are slightly unusual internally. [...] Their existence alongside their basic counterparts allows speakers additional options for expressing emphasis, focus, and other nuances of meaning. (Kaplan 1989:223)

In contrast to these canonical varieties, inversion concerns the relative order of the *major* constituents of the sentence. Their movement *within* the clause itself has a substantial effect, which, e.g., passives and cleft-constructions, although possibly carrying comparable pragmatic meanings, do not have. Instead, they maintain the canonical syntactic form. In the following, I shall discuss only the non-canonical patterns related to inversion, because they produce a similar effect of being "unusual" or deviant forms. They are also functionally closer to each other, in particular *there*-insertion (3.5.1) and preposing (3.5.2), which could superficially be considered a first step towards an inversion. Left-dislocation (3.5.3) is at first sight similar to a preposing (cf. Prince 1985) and in fact shares much of its discourse function with inversion. However, both differ strongly in their preferred mode of discourse.

3.5.1 *There*-insertion

Frequently, *there*-insertion is treated as an inversion (Hartvigson/Jakobsen 1974; Penhallurick 1984) or, alternatively, FI following a locative constituent is considered a presentative construction in which *there* has been optionally left out (Coopmans 1989; Rochemont/Culicover 1990). The range of alternative presentative constructions is, however, even broader and has been systematised as follows: Drubig (1988:84f.) distinguishes "existential" or "stative presentational" *there* (with *be*), "presentational" *there* (with any other verb), and a "preposed existential/presentational" construction, in which a locative is preposed and occurs before the *there*. It is the last option, in particular, which might be taken for an inversion, as can be seen from examples (82)-(87):

existential/stative presentational *there*:

(82) There were fields with vines outside the villages. [= (10)]

presentational *there*:

(83) There appeared a mysterious figure out of nowhere.

preposed existential/presentational construction:

(84) Outside the villages there were fields with vines. [= (13)]

(85) Out of nowhere there appeared a mysterious figure. [= (71)]

full inversion:

(86) Outside the villages were fields with vines. [= (15)]

(87) Out of nowhere appeared a mysterious figure. [= (70)]

(Drubig 1988)

Both FI and *there*-insertion dislodge the subject from preverbal position, which is why *there*-insertion in the literature equally emerges among focus constructions (Creider 1979; Rochemont/Culicover 1990) or defocussing devices (Penhallurick 1984; Erdmann 1990). Apart from that, however, constructions such as (82) and (83) are not inverted constructions, according to my approach. First because the *there* is not a locative constituent, i.e., it is not "a copy or anticipation of adverbials of place, direction etc." (Erdmann 1990:60). It does not necessarily have the meaning of "location" at all (cf. Bolinger 1977:91).[23] From a synchronic perspective, the existential/stative *there*-construction "simply postulates the existence of some entity or entities" (Quirk et al.1985:1406) and may contain no locative information at all, as in (88), or locative information following the clause, as in (82) above:

(88) There was a moment's silence. [= Quirk et al. 1985:p.1406]

Secondly, there is syntactic evidence, namely, in that "dummy *there* participates in subject-auxiliary-inversion [...], while the preposed locative of a locative inversion does not" (Birner 1992:38); cf. (86b) as opposed to (82b):

(82b) Were there fields with vines outside the villages?

(86b) * Were outside the villages fields with vines?

The most substantial criterion, however, to distinguish *there*-insertion from FI is by intonation: one can distinguish a "weak" from a "strong", which is a "local", *there* (Hartvigson/Jakobsen 1974:62), and only the local *there* justifies talk about inversion. In examples (89) and (90), in case of oral production, the *there* would be stressed, it is cataphoric to the following locative constituent and hence has itself locative meaning:

(89) There, outside the villages, were fields with vines.

(90) There, out of nowhere, appeared a mysterious figure.

The unstressed *there*, by contrast, introduces a distinct type of presentative construction, "which neither serves to set up a specific location in the addressee's model (in contrast to SVI [= FI]), nor points to a real or imagined location (in contrast to the demonstrative deictic)" (Drubig 1988:93). The contrast becomes apparent in an instance such as (91), which cannot have both adverbs as providing locative information:

(91) A large part of the KWV's role is to deal with the annual grape surplus, selling it off as bulk wine, grape concentrate, or distilled spirit. Here, too, there is a good dose of protectionism. (Guardw, 3 Jan.93, p.7)

From this difference between stressed (= "deictic") and unstressed (= "expletive") *there*, there finally also derives a basic functional difference:

> [..E]xpletive *there* cannot by definition carry focus and effect a shift in the center of attention [...]. Therefore, expletive *there*, much like a definite anaphoric pronoun, can only pick up its reference from the context: it refers back to whatever has been established as the relevant scene or reference situation in the preceding context, possibly further narrowed down by a fronted scene-setting adverb. (Drubig 1988:93)

By this criterion, the preposed variants of the existential/presentative construction in (84) and (85) are not inversions: instead of bringing something to a new centre of attention, they refer back to an already prominent scene, which is specified again by the fronted adverbial. FI, by contrast, initiates a scene-setting process of its own and therefore also allows for constituents that would not take *there*-insertion at all: only when no *there* is used does the scope of the initial constituent reach "from literal location through state to mere location in the text (topicalized prior context)" (Bolinger 1977:112). (92) and (93) are perfectly natural inversions, but would not be acceptable with a *there* inserted:

(92) Booked were several prostitutes and a few of their clients. [= (298)]

(93) Green with envy at his good fortune were several of his companions. [= (301)]

(Bolinger 1977)

It is thus a figurative conception of *location*, in the sense of location *within the text*, that accounts for the range of possible FIs, and by far most of them do not permit *there*-insertion. Only VS order following demonstrative uses of *here* and *there*[24] has therefore been treated as inversions in my corpus study, while *there*-insertion, with expletive, unaccented *there*, is a separate construction.

3.5.2 Preposing and initial adverbial placement

If *there*-insertion shares with FI the dislodging of the subject from preverbal position, preposing is related to FI in that it also has a non-canonical constituent in sentence-initial position. Syntactically, preposings are "those sentences in which a phrasal constituent is moved leftward to sentence-initial position" (Ward 1988:2). The discussion of preposing phenomena is extended here to adverbial placement, since the factors underlying initial placement in general are in principle quite the same. In the case of adverbials, however, there is less discussion about non-canonical position, since the canonical sentence patterns mainly specify the relative position of subject, verb (and object).

There is preposing with NPs, PPs, VPs, or AdjPs. Examples are (94) – (97), taken from Ward (1988):

> (94) Colonel Bykov had delivered to Chambers in Washington six Bokhara rugs which he directed Chambers to present as gifts from him and the Soviet Government to the members of the ring who had been most co-operative. <u>One of these rugs Chambers delivered to Harry Dexter White</u>. [= (2), p.3]
>
> (95) "With better jobs and more education," he writes, "women are also moving forward on the dollar front." <u>For that last bold assertion there are no statistics</u>. [= (3), p.3]
>
> (96) At the end of the term I took my first schools; it was necessary to pass, if I was to stay at Oxford, and <u>pass I did</u> [...]. (= (4), p.3]
>
> (97) In the early days, our productions were cheap and cheerful," says producer John Weaver of London-based Keefco. [...] Today's tapes may still be cheerful, but <u>cheap they are not</u>. [= (5), p.3]

(Ward 1988)

As can be seen from these examples, inversion and preposing[25] share the fronting of some constituent that would canonically stand behind the verb, but differ in the relative placement of the subject and the verb.[26] However, none of the examples could be turned into an inversion merely by further changing the relative order of subject and verb. Thus, while some inversions have a preposed counterpart, most preposings are constructions that could not be subject to inversion: for instance, they occur with transitive verbs (as in (94)), with negation (as in (95) and (97)), or with pronoun subjects (as in (96) and (97)). VP-preposing such as (96) is different from *VP-inversion* in that it only follows participle forms. Preposing is therefore also a separate construction, rather than an underlying, derived, or direct alternative to FI.

In fact, the discourse conditions of preposing are much more restricted than those for inversion:

[...] preposing serves two simultaneous discourse functions: first, it marks the entity represented by the preposed constituent as being anaphorically related to other discourse entities via a salient (partially ordered) set relation [...]; and second, preposing involves the instantiation of a salient OPEN PROPOSITION [...]. (Ward 1990:760; his emphasis)

The front-shifted items thus establish a link to previously established discourse units and thereby mark a whole proposition as salient or shared knowledge at the given point of the discourse.[27] The latter part of these discourse conditions is in clear contrast to the function of FI, which requires no shared knowldege in the sense of an open proposition in order to be felicitous (cf. Ward/Birner 1994).

A preposed constituent may nonetheless constitute the informational sentence-focus, in which case it is (potentially) realised with nuclear accent. Ward (1988) calls such instances *"focus preposing"*, while "topicalisation" — *topic preposing* for terminological consistency — applies to those cases where it is not the focussed part of the sentence that is preposed. Instances are (98) and (99), which thus have different open propositions:

focus preposing:

(98) I made a lot of sweetbreads. A couple of pounds I think I made for her. [= Ward 1988:(203), p.113]

topic preposing:

(99) I made two minor mistakes. One apparently everyone in the class made. [= Ward/Birner 1994:(9)]

In (98), the open proposition (*I made X amount of sweetbreads*; cf. Ward 1988:113) foreshadows the focus of the sentence. Since it is the informational focus of the sentence that appears initially, focus preposing has an *emphatic* focus: it signals "not the difference between shared and new information but rather the relative weight that a speaker wants to attach to a particular element" (Enkvist 1980:135). Topic preposing as in (99), by contrast, establishes a link between topic entities that are salient at that point of discourse. The open proposition is *X made some subset of the set of mistakes*, and the fronted element undergoes *topicalisation*: it "evokes a presuppositional set recoverable from an earlier portion of the text" (Enkvist 1980:149).

In sum, preposing is a comparatively local phenomenon that links a new proposition to prior discourse. The requirements in terms of discourse-familiarity are absolute rather than relative, with consequences for its discourse positioning: a preposing such as (100) could not stand discourse-initially, while an inversion as in (101) could, but only if the postposed constituent is also discourse-new (cf. 3.4 above):

(100) * In a little white house two rabbits lived. [= (13b)]

(101) In a little white house lived two rabbits. [= (13a)]

(Ward/Birner 1994)

What inversion and preposing nonetheless share is how they exploit the sentence-initial position: both FI and topic preposing are concerned with discourse-familiarity. Ward/Birner (1994) conclude "that fronting in general serves to place discourse-old information in clause-initial position" and that FI and preposing are "particularly well-suited to inferrable information, i.e. information that is neither discourse-new nor explicitly evoked" (p.164). This is in line with results from a study carried out by Virtanen (1988, 1992a) on the placement of adverbials of time and place: using the same *assumed familiarity* scale (Prince's 1981b) as Ward and Birner in their work, she finds that clause-initial adverbials, too, "typically represent entities that are situated in the middle of the scale, rather than at either of its extreme ends" (Virtanen 1992a:108).

Virtanen also touches upon the information status of initially placed adverbials in relation to the discourse structure. Their function is described as *strategy-markers*, because they "signal boundaries between different textual units [...] and also contribute to the marking of textual shifts as minor or major" (Virtanen 1992a:108). Strategy-markers in Virtanen's corpus are followed by CWO or by FI; thus, in her study, FIs are said to initiate major or minor textual shifts, depending on the relative distance from the source of familiarity as well as on the degree of assumed familiarity itself (cf. Virtanen 1992a:108). For instance, the first inversion in (102) signals a major textual shift, and the second a more local, minor shift of attention:

(102) <u>Opposite the path entrance on Lanark Road is Slateford Aqueduct</u>, carrying the Unio Canal over the Water of Leith on 8 arches, by Hugh Baird, 1822. <u>Behind it is the railway viaduct</u> (John Miller,

1842) carrying the former Caledonian Railway from Edinburgh to Carstairs on 14 segmental arches. [= Virtanen 1992a:(26b)]

Without an inversion, adverbials that mark major shifts do not create the impression of non-canonical initial placement: compare (103), where the temporal adverbials mark major shifts, to the PP-preposing in (95) and repeated here as (104). The initial PP is perceived as preposed since it directly relates to previous discourse, it thus only marks a very local topic shift:

(103) Then one day, winter came. All of a sudden, it snowed and the wind was wild. The man and woman stayed indoors, warm and snug. [= (24b)]

(104) "With better jobs and more education," he writes, "women are also moving forward on the dollar front." For that last bold assertion there are no statistics. [= (95)]

(Virtanen 1992a)

FI as a discourse marker is an issue that will be taken up in more detail in chapter 5, but it can be noted from this discussion that the potential comes from the sentence-initial position. In addition, there is a plausible iconic relation between the strategy-markers and the level of text organisation:

> [...] the text structure seems to some extent to be reflected in the size and information status of the material used for signalling textual units at different levels. Hence, more and informationally newer material may be used to indicate the starting point for a major textual unit, while the more local shifts seem to be associated with elements of lesser size that are also more given [...]. (Virtanen 1992a:109)

In that respect, FI, which is subject to only *relative* discourse-familiarity, is thus more flexible in introducing textual units of greater relevance than is preposing, i.e., it has the potential to signal *major* textual shifts. The shifts done by preposing, by contrast, are more "local" or *minor*, basically relating to previous discourse and the next proposition. Adverbials, however, that can be placed sentence-initially as well as -finally[28] perform major or minor shifts, depending on their information status, but do not create an impression of non-canonical placement.

Nonetheless, there are substantial differences in the discourse function between the initial and final placement of adverbials. Studies focussing on this issue are, for instance, Thompson (1985) on purpose clauses, Ramsey (1987) on conditional and temporal clauses, and, more recently, Ford (1993) on temporal, conditional, and causal adverbial clauses in conversation. The results give good reasons for a general claim that initial adverbials "function as a guide to the reader's attention" (Thompson 1985:61) and "do guiding and shifting work in the development in discourse" (Ford 1993:12). Placed finally, by contrast, adverbials "tend to work more locally in narrowing main clause meaning without creating links or shift points in a larger discourse pattern" (Ford 1993:146). It is also being claimed that only the initially placed adverbial clause operates "simultaneously at the ideational and the *textual* levels" (Thompson 1985:61; my emphasis).

This textual work of initially placed adverbials is not restricted to the linking function, but is even more related to subsequent discourse: while initial adverbial (purpose) clauses can be closely related to the preceding discourse, as in (105), they may in fact also be quite unrelated. (106) is one of Thompson's (1985) examples where "the initial purpose clause is as unrelated as could be to the preceding context" (p.80); rather, "position has to do with whether a discourse-organizing chain of expectations is being established" (p.81):

(105) The valve springs can be installed in or removed from most engines with the cylinder head in place. <u>To do this,</u> the spark plug is removed from the cylinder that requires valve-spring service and a threaded compressed-air adapter is inserted. [= (38)]

(106) <u>In order to ensure economical and smooth running engines,</u> some control of the amount of gas present in the gas-air mixture is necessary. [= (39)]

(Thompson 1985)

This is not accidental, in contrast to the more "local" discourse functions that front-placement has when constituents are perceivably moved leftward. There is certainly a connection between a "preposing effect", where a constituent is still felt as belonging canonically somewhere else, and its strong, but local, effect at that point. The canonically filled sentence-initial position otherwise hosts larger-scope points of departure for discourse-organisational anchoring and grounding mechanisms.

In conversational language, the textual function of initial adverbials has also been found to have an interactional component (cf. Ford 1993:146ff.): initially placed adverbials introduce extended turns, modify speaker-recipient roles, or present background information. This serves as overall support for the turn-taking system, as do sentence-initial elements as *points of departure* in general (cf. Lowe 1987):

> [they] give *interpersonal* information on the ensuing discourse, such as indicating its illocutionary force [...], or setting the mood [...] or giving an evaluation of the importance or reliability of the information in the ensuing discourse; [...]. (p.7; my emphasis)

In the same vein, it will be argued in more detail below that inversion, while it in principle maintains its ideational content, gains additional textual and interpersonal meaning.

3.5.3 *Left-dislocation*

The last non-canonical construction to be briefly discussed here is left-dislocation. It "consists of a sentence with a pro-form, preceded by a noun phrase which has the same reference as the following pronoun" (Geluykens 1992:18). Typically, the pronominal element is the subject or the object of the clause, as in (107) and (108), but it may also be, for instance, a locative, as in (109), or a possessive, as in (110):[29]

(107)   Steve, he likes beans. [= (1), p.1]

(108)   Beans, Steve likes them. [= (23), p.20]

(109)   This cupboard, Steve put the beans there. [= (24), p.20]

(110)   Steve, his mother likes beans. [= (25), p.20]

(Geluykens 1992)

Two important issues are raised in Geluykens' study: first, the predominant feature of left-dislocation is *semantic*, rather than syntactic: there is coreferentiality[30] between "a 'bare' NP, i.e. an NP which is not the argument in another clause" and "a complete clause — 'complete' in the sense that all the argument slots of the verbal predicate are filled" (Geluykens 1992:19). Second, left-dislocation is basically *interactional* in kind, "a typically conversational phenomenon" (Geluykens 1992:153): the construction is not only more frequent in conversational as opposed to spoken/non-conversational and written discourse (cf. p.140), but "its functioning in other discourse types is to a large extent a reflection of its conversational functions (p.153). These conversational functions are summarised as follows:

> [..T]he main function of LD [= left-dislocation] in English conversation is the collaborative introducing of a new (and topical) referent. This introduction is the result of a cooperative effort between speaker and hearer. [...] LD is the result of a (usually) three-stage, interactional process by which new referents are first introduced by the speaker, then acknowledged by the hearer, and finally elaborated upon by the speaker. The grammatical construction LD is thus the result of a conversational strategy which gets 'syntactisized'. (Geluykens 1992:33)

Constructions such as exemplified in (107) – (110) are thus basically put down to the same mechanism as found in a turn-sequence such as (111):

(111)   A: now, the last paragraph

            B: yes

            A: I seem to remember it being different from what's printed [...]. [= Geluykens 1992:(2), p.35)][31]

The intervening turn is of course not obligatory, it may also be realised by just a pause. But the claimed discourse function of left-dislocation is *referent-introduction*, and this implies the following for the discourse status of the majority of referents introduced:

> From the point of view of the preceding discourse, LD is shown to be a device for introducing *irrecoverable* referents into the discourse, i.e. referents which are not derivable from the previous discourse record. This explains why their introduction is something which has to be negotiated. [...]
> From the point of view of the subsequent discourse, LD mostly introduces referents which become *topicalized* [= are recurrent], i.e. which are developed in the following context. (Geluykens 1992:154f.; his emphasis)

This quote stresses again the linking, i.e. backward-looking, function of the sentence-initial position, as well as the creation of expectations for subsequent discourse. Furthermore, Geluykens' analysis makes an important point about the assumed information-status of discourse entities: this status does not in fact follow any absolute standard, but rather reflects the speaker's assumptions about the need for topic negotiation, for focussing or re-focussing. The same claim is made in Prince (1985): what counts is that a discourse entity

> is not currently 'in focus' [...]. Whether this entity was formerly evoked and has moved out of focus or has not yet been evoked and is new in the discourse does not seem to matter. (p. 74)

There are still instances of left-dislocation which cannot plausibly be related to referent-introduction. Geluykens analyses them in terms of "contrastiveness" or — in case of oppositions between more than two elements — "Listing-LDs [= left-dislocations]" (Geluykens 1992:89). An example from his corpus is (112):

(112) A: I mean we write down symptoms. <u>Signs you know I mean they're they're so different</u>. [= Geluykens 1992:(8), p.87]

Ultimately, there is a common functional denominator of *irrecoverability* as well as *contrast* expressed by the construction: some kind of highlighting is always achieved by exploiting the salient sentence-initial position; in other words, "the main function of LD in conversation is referent-highlighting" (Geluykens 1992:158). What this basically conversational phenomenon thereby emphasises is that reference in discourse is a primarily interactional phenomenon, worth considerable effort when necessary. In written monologue discourse, even more costly constructions may be expedient to this end, because not only do they have to negotiate the next topic entity, but also they have to locate it within the discourse world established. It is in this sense symptomatic that left-dislocation is inherently conversational, while inversion has a strong affinity with written discourse.

Chapter 4

The semantics of inversion

As a first step of the analysis, the range of inverted constructions as defined and classified so far are investigated as syntactic alternatives to their canonical counterparts, which have the same truth-conditional or *ideational* meaning. Following the terminology introduced in 2.1.3, the difference in meaning created by an inversion is considered to affect the clause at the message level, i.e. its thematic structure, and as such it is a *textual* kind of meaning. In addition, it will be shown below that the positions of the individual front-shifted and postposed constituents fulfil an interpersonal function beyond the proposition expressed, so that, ultimately, inversion is a carrier of *interpersonal* meaning. It is these two aspects that together constitute the *semantics of inversion*.

As spelled out in the preliminaries, there are two structural prerequisites for the creation of extra-meaning by means of word order variation: first, as discussed in 3.1, there must be a real choice on the part of the speaker between this and an alternative ordering, which could be used in its place. The types of inversion considered in this study in principle all have a CWO counterpart, despite their differences in automatisation of VS and AuxSV order entailed by the front-position of the respective constituents. Second, the word order variants resulting from inversion have a marked status as against the grammaticalised, unmarked word order pattern of Modern English (cf. 2.2). Under these circumstances, one can assume a semiotic process at work whereby extra-meaning is created following a principle similar to Grice's (1975) maxim of quantity: if a speaker or writer chooses to use a more marked word order pattern, the hearer or reader will be licensed to infer that something that goes beyond the meaning of the unmarked (canonical) word order is "meant" by the speaker.[1]

This semiotic process, which I call the *semantics of choice*, is analysed in detail in section 4.1, where, after some preliminary remarks (4.1.1), I compare FI and CWO (4.1.2) and SAI and CWO (4.1.3) respectively in terms of the overall meaning conveyed. In these two sections, it will also be discussed to what extent, compared to earlier stages of English, certain inversion types have become obligatory, syntacticised constructions, the semantics of which are now bleached and replaced by a grammaticalised kind of discourse meaning. Those aspects of meaning inherent in the ordering phenomena themselves, by contrast, are treated in a second step of the analysis in section 4.2. This part is concerned with the meaning of reversed positions of discourse entities (or predicates), which, in English, is a semantic potential to be exploited only if the existent word order norm is overridden. FI constructions, in particular, are of interest here because they affect the whole clause. Their meaning consists of expressing a speaker's point of view and, under the conditions of a grammaticalised word order system, has a substantial subjective component (4.2.2). This kind of analysis is foreshadowed by the restrictions at work as regards the occurrence of inversion in embeddings on the one hand, discussed initially in 4.2.1, and accounts for the actual use of FI as a focus management device on the other, which will be the topic of 4.2.3. The meaning of SAI constructions, by contrast, has to be approached differently since they affect, above all, the position of only one constituent of the clause. Originally, they meant to give additional prominence to that constituent (cf. 3.2.1), and, in the course of their history, SAI constructions have thereby come to display a direct interrelationship between the semantic nature of the constituents involved, their grammaticalisation and the creation of extra-meaning. Today, SAI occurs obligatorily with semantically heavy or affective constituents; these are grammaticalised prominence- or affect-marking constructions. In the case of constituents optionally followed by SAI, a special meaning effect is created, i.e., additional prominence is given to them, by virtue of being followed by inversion. This interrelationship in SAI constructions and their overall emotive meaning are the topic of 4.2.4. In the summary, it will have become apparent that it is a truism to derive semantic or functional homogeneity from a unitary formal feature such as VS or AuxSV order. That is why, as an outcome of this chapter, a functional classification of English inversion is introduced in 4.3 on the basis of the types of meaning identified.

4.1 The semantics of choice: inverted vs. canonical word order

4.1.1 *On the nature of the semiotic process*

At the heart of the semiotic process to be discussed in the following lies the choice between inverted and canonical word order. It should be noted, first, that this approach puts an obligatory nature of the construction into question and, in particular, does not tie inversion to preposing phenomena (cf. Green 1982:150). In fact, as the discussion of the diachronic evidence has shown (cf. 3.2), at least three different situations must be distinguished: in fully grammaticalised constructions, inversion is obligatory, in others it has remained an option, while what Stockwell (1984) considers to be an innovated type of inversion is obligatory again, but due only to the nature of the copular-*be* construction. The first class has been said to consist of those SAI constructions that have a negative or affective constituent in front-position, the second of most FI types with a component of locativity, while the innovated class seems to have had the second as its model, but extending the possibility of FI to nonlocative predicates and occurring with *be* exclusively. An example of each case is repeated in (1) – (3):

inversion obligatory after preposing:

(1) Never before have fans been promised such a feast of speed. (LOB, rep.)

inversion in principle optional after preposing:

(2) With greater individual freedom should come greater individual responsibility. (Times, 15 Dec.92, p.29)

inversion obligatory after preposing due to copular-*be* construction:

(3) Most disturbing is conservationists' willingness to spend money to appease local government honchos. (NW, 12 Apr.93, p.47)

As these examples show, for only a subset of inversions does mere front-shifting constitute a potential second paradigm. Furthermore, as discussed in 3.5.2, the preposing of core constituents in Modern English fulfils a basically different, and more local, discourse function, while initially placed adverbials not followed by inversion do normally not become part of the predication proper, but remain scene-setting sentence adverbials.

Second, for the kinds of extra-meaning produced by the semiotic process, the natural or *cognitive* aspect of ordering phenomena and the matter of grammaticalisation must be held apart: what previous studies of inversion have attributed to FI as an information-packaging — and thereby linking — function (cf. 3.4.2), and to most SAI constructions as the highlighting of initially-placed, individual constituents on the basis of diachronic evidence (cf. 3.2.1), are factors of the former kind. From a cognitive viewpoint, both functions ultimately have a common origin: natural prominence of the sentence-initial position. In the case of FI, this position is used to link information, i.e. to provide *anchoring* for what is to follow, if this is considered expedient or an "urgent task" (cf. 2.3). Alternatively, it may be, not the relative discourse-familiarity of discourse entities that is considered urgent to express, but the relative prominence directly given to a constituent by the speaker. Such "subjective speaker-oriented" prominence corresponds to Enkvist's (1980:135) notion of emphatic focus and is, for instance, expressible by the fronting of a constituent followed by AuxSV order. Due to an equal exploitation of the sentence-initial position as underlies the linking effect of FI, SAI thereby comes to carry *emphatic* meaning.

These kinds of meaning that rather naturally arise from sentence-initial placement interact with the issue of grammaticalisation in my analysis. Grammaticalisation reduces the speaker's choice, so that, only when there is still optionality to meaningfully deviate from the word order norm, are those meanings of a speaker-based, hence subjective, nature (cf. Stein 1995). Only then can they be attributed to a Gricean mechanism, as suggested above, and ultimately have the status of implicatures. By contrast, in various inversion types, this speaker-based meaning has become bleached and replaced by a *langue*-kind of meaning in the course of the history of English word order. The natural or cognitive principles underlying word order have been taken over by the language system. In addition to an increasing automatisation, it is especially the *limiting* of VS or AuxSV order to narrower domains that is symptomatic of a grammaticalisation process (cf. Stockwell 1984; Hopper/Traugott 1993). To a certain extent, this holds for all inversion types of Modern English in the form of various semantic and syntactic restrictions, so that all of them can be said to be affected by a relatively advanced degree of grammaticalisation, at least compared to earlier stages of English.

Finally, as already stated above (cf. 3.4.2), my notion of a semantics of choice also implies that I do not identify the function of inversion with a *reflection* of information-structure (Birner 1992, 1994), or with emphasis expressed within the clause (Schmidt 1980). It is, rather, the reverse that is postulated here: information-structure and other kinds of meaning are *encoded* by means of word order variation. Therefore, an inversion in my understanding not only expresses, for instance, "a speaker's assessment of assumed familiarity in discourse" (Birner 1992:174), but expresses how the speaker intends to *instruct* the reader about his or her current focus of attention, or about the emphasis to be attached to individual discourse items. Since this active instruction via word order choice implies that "the speaker or writer [is] doing something to the listener or reader by means of language" (Halliday 1985:53; cf. the complete quote in 2.1.3), the semantics of choice are a combination of textual and interpersonal meaning.

4.1.2 Full inversion vs. canonical word order

4.1.2.1 A deictic presentative prototype

The discussion of the various full inversion types and their CWO counterparts starts with the most advanced instance of automatisation within this group, on the basis of one crucial criterion: in the case of *AdvP-inversion* following deictic adverbs, inversion cannot really be said to be still truth-conditionally equivalent with the unmarked word order pattern. Instead, the construction itself has absorbed a discourse meaning, it has "de-subjectivised" what is originally a speaker-based meaning.

This holds for FI following deictic adverbs, and most clearly so when these adverbs perform real situational or *exophoric* reference (cf. Halliday/ Hasan 1976), i.e., when they are used in their basic function of locating in real (physical) space or time (cf. p.57). In non-conversational contexts, situational reference of this kind is normally not very specific, but it can nonetheless refer to a concrete location, as illustrated by (4) and (5):

(4)   Here comes a time of great challenge for this country. [= Green 1982:(20a)]

(5) <u>Now is the time</u> to consider the future of how Britain should be governed. (Guardw, 20 Dec.92, p.2)

The distal counterparts would be FI following *there* (if stressed) and *then*. Taken together, these represent the kind of FI which earlier functional literature on inversion has claimed to perform a basic presentative function (cf. 3.4.1) and to constitute the "central deictic prototype" (Drubig 1988:91). Since the use of such a construction is subject to the restriction that there must be a perceptual field shared by both speaker and hearer, it is plausible that inversion following deictic adverbs is a typical "oral language construction", as Green (1982:130) has claimed. Nonetheless, one easily finds occurrences in written discourse as well, such as (6) and (7), which both contain the deictic *here* followed by FI:

(6) Some of the evocations of even the recent past deserve to be recalled. <u>Here is Ward Thomas on Ben Hogan at Carnoustie</u>, 1953: [...]. (Guardw, 27 Dec.92, p.24)

(7) The economy, Berlin, the Common Market — <u>here are three issues</u> whose gravity has during the past few days led to regretful sighings over the impracticability of a National Government. (LOB, ed.)

What these instances of the central deictic prototype of FI indicate is that deictic reference can also be made to the text itself. A text has its own deictic dimensions and thereby offers an alternative perceptual field available to both writer and reader. The adverbs are then used *endophorically*: anaphorically in (7), where *here* refers to the preceding text, and cataphorically in (6), in which an FI introduces what is to follow. Similar uses are FI following *next, first* and the like; they also locate something within the speech event itself and constitute deictic textual reference. Therefore, (8) is another example of an endophoric deictic adverb followed by FI:

(8) After the reposed and subdued work of the Nabis we suddenly come face to face with the agitated, violent chromatic paintings of the Fauves [...].
<u>Next come the German Expressionists</u> and the paintings of Nolde and of Munch, in particular, have been carefully selected to indicate the important role that this School played in the formation of 20th-century art. (LOB, sc.writ.)

Endophoric reference is a device of textual cohesion (cf. Halliday/Hasan 1976), which is the basic function shared by all types of FI with the deictic prototype. Other than with *here* and (stressed) *there*, *AdvP-inversion* has therefore been said to be, no longer typically oral, but typical of "colloquial writing" (Green 1982:140). Written discourse generally needs more cohesive constructions; it mostly takes place under conditions of *displacement* (cf. Chafe 1992, 1994), i.e. tends to deal with events which are not part of — are *displaced from* — the immediate environment of both writer and reader, so that deictic reference to location and time must rely solely on information provided by the text. This can be done, not only by referring to the deictic dimension of the text itself (as in (6) and (7)); most cohesive links in written discourse are created by reference to what is here most often the focus of attention, a displaced *universe of discourse*. The adverb *next* in (8), for instance, performs this kind of deictic reference to a discourse world established by the text. The function is even more evident when a deictic adverb is followed by a past tense form, because past tense "means" focussing on a displaced discourse world, and no longer on the immediate experience of the speech event itself (cf. Chafe 1992:240). An example for this is (9): here, the deictics *first* and *then* no longer function like the prototypical instances exemplified by (4) and (5), pointing to the text as a shared *perceptual* field, but perform a linking and thereby cohesive function within a displaced (= *conceptual*) universe of discourse:

(9)   This year has seen the literary battle of the G men. First came Gooch, then came Gower. (Guardw, 3 Jan.93, p.24)

One can summarise the instances discussed so far by a first class of FI, namely inversion after adverbs of local or temporal meaning, which perform *deictic* reference. In their most prototypical usage, they point to a spatial or temporal location of shared perceptual access. Once the addressee's attention is directed towards this location, he can be made to focus an object within it. This process is basically *presentative*, which is why I label this type of FI *deictic presentative inversion*. The object presented is a discourse entity in displaced discourse. The adverbs as the starting-point of the construction embody in their meaning "an instruction to retrieve from elsewhere" (Halliday/Hasan 1976:33) the information for locating discourse entities, information which may be situational or textual. Under the conditions of written discourse, reference to a shared field is normally restricted to the text itself, either to the — physically present — co-text, or, more frequently, to the — mentally evoked — universe of discourse.

In Modern English, this deictic presentative form of inversion is a fairly syntacticised construction, notably because there is often no real truth-conditional equivalence with comparable CWO sentences. The CWO counterparts of the instances used above provide the following kinds of relations between FI and CWO: first, as in (4b) – (7b), the version in unmarked word order may not be a grammatical sentence at all, which is, significantly, the case with the directly perception-based (situational or textual) uses of deictic adverbs:

(4b) * A time of great challenge for this country comes here.

(5b) * The time is now to consider the future of how Britain should be governed.

(6b) ?? Ward Thomas is here on Ben Hogan at Carnoustie, 1953: [...].

(7b) ?? The economy, Berlin, the Common Market — three issues are here whose gravity has during the past few days led to regretful sighings over the impracticability of a National Government.

Second, if one leaves aside the context of the inversion in (6b), as in (6c), CWO is acceptable, but not necessarily with the same meaning anymore. The same is true of the FIs from (8) and (9), their CWO versions are formulated in (8b) and (9b):

(6c) Ward Thomas is here.

(8b) The German Expressionists come next.

(9b) Gooch came first, Gower came then.

Finally, a CWO version of the deictic presentative type of FI can undeniably have a truth-value different from that of the inverted form. This arises if the speaker is separated from the textual context itself, whereby, for instance, (10a) and (10b), in an email context, would come to express two different things:

(10a) <u>Here is the paper</u> I promised you last week.

(10b) The paper I promised you last week is here.

On the basis of these observations, deictic presentative inversion must in fact be considered a construction in which the *presentative* discourse function has become grammaticalised. The meaning of the deictic adverbs in these cases is an extension of situation-based reference, which indexical expressions by definition perform.[2] In that respect, what has become grammaticalised is a *textual metaphor* of the originally situational presentative prototype. As a result, an inversion can be grammatical where the CWO version is not, or it can specify a different location, and thereby different truth-conditions, than a corresponding CWO sentence. That is why (4b) – (7b) are unacceptable: in each of them, reference to the speaker-based situation is averted or implausible and only textual reference makes sense. In other cases, textual as opposed to situational reference can relate to different situations, as in (10a) and (10b).

The textual, metaphorical usage of deictic adverbs in a presentative construction also means that there is an *internal*, as opposed to an *external* (cf. Halliday/Hasan 1976:241), kind of conjunctive relation which these adverbs create with respect to preceding text. They do not so much express relations between objects, phenomena or events in the outside world, in which case they would mainly function on an ideational level, but, rather, they link "linguistic events" and belong to "the speaker's organisation of his discourse" (Halliday/ Hasan 1976:239). Their meaning is therefore mainly interpersonal and textual, and, since it is speaker-based, it is also subjective.

This external-internal opposition also makes the truth-conditional effect of FIs following deictic adverbs, in opposition to adverbs in final position, more explicit: where both orderings are in principle grammatical, the adverbs in fact refer to different locations. In a CWO sentence like in (6c) above, *here* specifies a physical location of the subject or a property belonging to the outside world: "a relation between meanings in the sense of representations of 'contents', (our experience of) external reality" (Halliday/Hasan 1976:240). The meaning of *here* in CWO depends on the location of the speaker, but it nonetheless performs an objectively given, situation-based, reference. In deictic presentative inversion, by contrast, the *here* is anchored within the text, within the speech event itself. It expresses "a relation between meanings in the sense of representations of the speaker's own 'stamp' on the situation" (Halliday/Hasan 1976:240). The same applies to other deictic adverbs: in (8b) and (9b), *there, next, first* and *then* express external properties of the outside world, while they "mean" a location within the text if followed by FI, as in (8) and (9).

It is in this sense that the presentative construction is not only a textual metaphor, but can also be considered an instance of subjectivisation, or "subjectification", as defined by Traugott (1995) as a process whereby "meanings become increasingly based in the speaker's subjective belief state/attitude toward [...] what the speaker is talking about" (p.31). This is exactly what holds for deictic presentative inversion, which expresses speaker-based discourse organisation and produces a meaning of deictic adverbs that is only subjectively given. An indication is that, while a CWO sentence containing a deictic adverb can be attributed a truth-value, i.e. can be unequivocally true or false, a comparable FI is "made true" solely by virtue of being used by the speaker. That is why not only deictic presentative inversion, but FI in general, can normally not be negated. More on this will be said in 4.2 below.

A useful way to summarise the difference between a CWO and a comparable presentative construction is by dynamic semantic functions as developed in the theory of functional sentence perspective (= FSP) by the Prague School linguists (Firbas 1979, 1986, 1992). The approach distinguishes two basic types of sentences, an "existential scale"[3] and a "quality scale" type.[4] In an existential scale sentence, the following dynamic semantic functions occur:

> The verb [...] performs the dynamic function of expressing appearance/ existence [...], and the adverbial elements perform the dynamic function of expressing the setting [...]. The subject, on the other hand, performs the dynamic function of expressing a phenomenon that appears or exists on the scene. (Firbas 1986:48)

By contrast, under a quality scale reading,

> the verb ascribes a characteristic to a notion that has already been introduced into the flow of communication; it performs the dynamic function of expressing a quality [...]. Consequently, the subject performs the dynamic function of expressing a quality bearer [...], and the adverbial element performs the dynamic function of expressing a specification [...]; [... it] completes the development of the communication within the sentence. (p.48f.)

Under these two scales, adverbs thus function "either as situational settings or as temporal/local specifications" (Firbas 1979:42f.), and which function holds is determined by word order interacting with what FSP defines as "context-dependence" or *communicative dynamism*:

> [A]n adverbial of time/ place can serve as a specification only if context-independent [... and] if context-dependent it can only serve as a setting. (Firbas 1979: 43f.)

Since deictic meaning is by definition always context-dependent, it is not surprising that deictic adverbs can alternatively refer to the context (the situation) as a given setting, or can use deictic meaning as a specification, i.e., to complete a predication. In this case, the setting/specification assignment cannot be made on the basis of context-dependence; instead, it must be from word order alone that the language user derives that in *Here is Ward Thomas*, *here* functions as the setting, whereas in *Ward Thomas is here*, the adverb represents a quality, presupposing the existence of a quality bearer (cf. Firbas 1979:55).

In this way, word order in presentative constructions affects the discourse status of the subject as well. It is not necessarily by the semantics of the verb that it is determined whether a sentence gets an existential or a quality scale reading, but ultimately by the context-dependence of the subject. As pointed out in Firbas (1979), even a verb of existence/appearance on the scene can represent a — transient — quality if assigned to a subject of a clearly discourse-familiar status. Thus, even an example such as (11), if occurring in a context where *John* has been previously evoked, would express a quality ascribed to the subject:

(11) What happened to John next? John appeared on the scene.

Vice versa, "the semantic content of a subject cannot fully function as a quality bearer unless it can be regarded as already introduced into discourse, i.e. as having already appeared on the narrow scene" (Firbas 1979:42). As discussed above (cf. 3.4.2), being introduced into the discourse — i.e. relative discourse-familiarity — is a property which a discourse entity only temporarily assumes and which is a gradient phenomenon. Word order contributes to the creation of a quality or an existential scale reading of a sentence and thereby affects the very discourse status of the subject.

Reconsidering, in this light, (7) from above, this is exactly what the inversion performs:

(7) The economy, Berlin, the Common Market — here are three issues whose gravity has during the past few days led to regretful sighings over the impracticability of a National Government. (LOB, ed.)

In principle, *issues* is a noun which summarises the three previous ones and thus implies givenness, one would now expect it to be further specified. By inverted word order, however, an existential scale reading is created and thereby an impression of a re-introduction of this discourse entity. The intended effect is that expectations for subsequent discourse are raised: the presentative construction, by virtue of introducing an entity by (subjective) reference to the text itself, in fact suggests some higher-level topic status, raising expectations of further elaboration in the subsequent discourse.

4.1.2.2 *The lexical presentative type of FI*

Compared to the remaining types of FT, deictic presentative inversion as discussed so far plays something like an archetypal role. This is strongly supported by the historical facts: as noted in 3.2.1, there was obligatory, at least very common, V-2 order after deictic adverbs (such as *nu, her, tha* and *thaer*). Certainly, a deictic presentative process must therefore be said to have been pre-existing prior to the grammaticalisation of the textual metaphorical usage. In that respect, it is interesting to note that the temporal adverbs *nu* and *tha*, and even longer temporal phrases, are more frequently followed by inverted order in Old English than is, significantly, preposed *her*. In one of Schmidt's (1980) Old English corpora, for instance, only 36% of preposed *her* are followed by inversion, which is a much lower rate than the ones she finds for longer temporal adverb phrases, as well as for all other locatives (cf. p.84f.). Seemingly, temporal reference, due to the automatic temporal progression of a text, has always been more directly prone to internal conjunctive work.

In Modern English, the context of a rigidified word order system, which sets apart an inverted sentence from a CWO one as a separate constructional choice, has thus created the metaphorical usage of locative reference, meaning text-internal, in place of external, situation-based, deictic reference. As illustrated, for example, by (7), this need not be reference to the concrete linguistic event itself, but, in written discourse, it is more likely to be a location within the discourse world established. In exactly this way, FI after locative, directional, or temporal prepositional phrases is related to deictic presentative inversion: the deictic element as starting-point of the presentative process is replaced by fully specified, lexical information. Drubig (1988) explicitly takes this relationship into account and distinguishes a *lexical* type of inversion in opposition to, and in complementary distribution with, the *deictic* type. His distinction now serves me to establish a second class of FI, *lexical presentative inversion*: in them,

> [...] instead of referring the addressee to the shared perceptual field, the speaker must provide him with all the lexical information necessary to construct a mental model of the reference situation [...]. (Drubig 1988: 91)

Deictic reference to the speech situation can thus be replaced by lexical information which specifies the reference situation, it is then part of the universe of discourse mentally established. And while deictic adverbs followed by FI are interpreted relative to the point in discourse at which they occur, lexical information in fact *constructs* a new setting as a physical stage or *ground* (cf. Drubig 1988:92), specifying also where the — local or temporal — relation to the previous, the old ground lies.

For a further subclassification of lexical presentative inversion, it is important to note that, minimally, the lexical information necessary for a change of ground specifies the location in relation to the previous ground. This is the case in those instances of *AdvP-inversion* in which the adverb is a mere directional particle. An example is the first FI in (12):

(12) Out came the journal and in it went Ann's own description of the scene. (BRW, bbe.)

In (12), the addressee is invited to start from the introductory lexical information as the physical stage or the ground, and then something is brought literally or figuratively before his eyes. The effect has been shown to be one of "staged activity" (Bolinger 1977:94), which is especially prominent because only the direction is lexically indicated: the location of the observer is implied due to the absence of a more concrete specification. As a result, we mentally conceive of (12) as an event, which is the reason why directional adverbs cannot occur with static copular *be*. The reference point itself from where the event is viewed is created, since an FI always signals a change of ground.

Due to the absence of an explicit reference point, which could be interpreted as context-dependent, a directional adverb initiating an FI is not even potentially a setting in the above-mentioned sense. Adverbials of place in general already have higher frequencies as specifications than adverbials of time (cf. Firbas 1979:43), but a directional adverb alone never switches to a setting function, even when fronted. It must therefore be considered a rather marked kind of departure for an existential scale sentence. These instances of FI create a considerable meaning effect, and, due to the staged activity effect, produce a rather drastic change in perspective. Since the fronted adverb can only represent entirely new information, the "given" part being the implicit reference point, the construction is a focus-movement in Prince's (1981a) sense, in that it has moved the former informational focus to the front. At the same time, the subject, which has also not been in focus before, becomes the new, now marked, focus and is thereby put "onstage".

A CWO version of (12), such as (12b), by contrast, signals the quality-bearer of the sentence as to some extent context-dependent. It then attributes to the subject a (transient) quality, with the adverb as a specification and at the same time the unmarked sentence focus:

> (12b) The journal came out and Ann's own description of the scene went in it.

(12b) is a version with the same propositional content as (12), but is much less tension-creating and involves much less dynamism. The whole event is presented as a property or quality, which is a mere specification ascribed to the subject. In either front- or end-position, the directional adverb attracts the focus of the predication, but only an FI turns the subject into the marked focus of the sentence and thereby emphasises the process of emergence on the scene.

This is a device which typically and almost exclusively occurs in fictional discourse, more generally speaking, in contexts in which a strong effect of displaced immediacy is intended (discussed in detail in chapter 5.3). A more common and more widely used type of FI, by contrast, is the second inversion in (12), repeated here, or an occurrence like (13). In both instances, the FI follows a directional adverb plus a prepositional phrase and thereby explicitly states the location of the observer:

> (12) Out came the journal and <u>in it went Ann's own description of the scene</u>. (BRW, bbe.)

> (13) <u>Off to the United Nation forces in the Congo goes a load of 1,000 lb bombs</u> sent with the compliments of the British taxpayer. (LOB, ed.)

In these two inversions, the change of ground is made explicit by introducing the referent which constitutes the new location or centre of attention, i.e. the setting in relation to which a new discourse entity is located. Prepositional phrases combine relational information of time or place with an absolute indication of reference point, and it is only the latter part which fulfils Birner's (1992, 1994) condition of relative discourse-familiarity. Compared to CWO, a switch from a specification to a setting interpretation of the PP takes place, attributable to a combined effect of word order and context. *PP-inversion* is therefore a second subtype of lexical presentative inversion, and it is more closely related to archetypal deictic presentative inversion, since it involves, in the PP, the same switch from specification to setting which deictic adverbs undergo. This becomes even more explicit in an instance such as (14), where a deictic combined with a PP refers to a displaced, previously established, universe of discourse:

(14) [...] at Hamley's. <u>There, on the fourth floor, was a rocking chair</u>. (Times, 15 Dec.92, p.13)

Quite commonly, however, it is the prepositional phrase alone that yields the setting of a lexical presentative construction. In the absence of deictic reference, through the mere use of inverted order it becomes clear that the prepositional phrase has to be located somewhere in relation to an old ground, that it thereby constitutes a textual reference. This textual link is of course often supported by anaphoric items, such as in (15) and (16):

(15) The klondikers and the trawlers pursued the fish round the Scottish coast, stopping at the tiny port of Ullapool, going to Ireland, to Donegal and Cork. <u>In their wake sprouted a service industry of second-hand goods</u> — everything from clothes, televisions and microwave ovens to fridges. (Guardw, 3 Jan.93, p.5)

(16) Besides the implacable momentum which renders it likely that all Euro-summits will end in a version of success, the fists of those who oppose it look puny indeed. <u>On the one side are ranged 12 governments</u>, each staffed by 12 times 1200 expert officials whose very lives are dedicated to the pursuit of compromises that will make the project work. [...] <u>On the other side are forces</u> whose time came, if ever, long ago. (Guardw, 20 Dec.92, p.7)

In these instances, the prepositional phrases provide a reference point by means of explicit lexical introduction, on the basis of which new or out-of-focus subjects are introduced. Accordingly, constructions such as in (15) and (16) are most likely to occur in longer stretches of text, particularly in "extended narratives" (cf. Green 1982:137), where they do cohesive work and at the same time fulfil their information-packaging function. In these cases, word order and context-dependence can be said to be in line: both signal a setting function of the PP, inversion by suggesting what is considered the "basic distribution of communicative dynamism" (Firbas 1979:49), or discourse-familiarity, and the PP itself by virtue of being equipped with overt signals of givenness. Under these circumstances, the prepositional phrase, if occurring sentence-finally, would not be a specification either; consequently, inversion merely *underlines* the existential scale reading.

However, there is not always sufficient linguistic indication of the actual discourse-familiarity status of discourse items. In this case, the use of an inversion, as opposed to a CWO sentence, is meaningful in itself and virtually *encodes* whether the sentence receives an existential or a quality scale reading. An instance is (17a), as opposed to (17b):

(17a) The senior official said the statement was part of a concerted American campaign to nurture and develop an Iraqi resistance. Among the covert action options that Saudi Arabia is promoting is the formation of arms-supply and guerrilla-warfare networks organized by allied intelligence services [...]. (IHT, 20 Jan.92, p.6)

(17b) The formation of arms-supply is among the covert action options.

In (17a), the front-shifted PP has not been overtly evoked by prior context. Furthermore, the use of the definite article in both the PP and the subject NP signals "uniquely identifiable" status (Gundel et al. 1993:275) for both of them, probably because they are inferrable from prior discourse. As shown above (cf. 3.4.2), inferrable entities have been found to be treated as hearer-old, but they can also be treated as discourse-old. Due to this similar discourse-status of both NPs in (17a) and (17b), the proposition could therefore form an existential or a quality scale sentence. In (17a), it is the inversion which induces the addressee to "understand" a presentative process, with the PP as setting and the subject signalled as relatively less discourse-familiar, hence newly or reintroduced.[5] CWO as in (17b), by contrast, signals to the reader to take the subject as somehow inferrable and to consequently interpret the PP as a specification. The choice between a lexical presentative inversion and CWO can thus indeed carry a discourse meaning of its own and goes beyond the mere reflection of information-status.

4.1.2.3 *The lexical predicative type of FI*

So far, those FI types have been dealt with that can plausibly be ascribed a presentative discourse function. They have been shown to consist of a bi-focal construction, whereby a scene is set and a discourse entity subsequently introduced.[6] This presentative mechanism goes for a deictic and for a lexical subtype of FI. Now, I turn to those cases of FI which cannot be said to be exclusively presentative, because, in them, the grounding mechanism is more than, or not at all, a mere location. For instance, there is a broad variety of PPs that give rise to *PP-inversion*, illustrated in (18) – (21):

(18) On the walls of his office hung pictures of sporting celebrities signed in "many thanks" terms. (LOB, rep.)

(19) In the loss of focus on the central bilateral relationship with Japan lies the real misfortune of the Bush trip. (IHT, 13 Jan.92, p.4)

(20) Within reach is a package of trade reforms that would raise real incomes everywhere — [...]. (Econ, 4 Jan.92, p.12)

(21) Of greater concern to many proliferation experts is the political braindrain of thousands of former Soviet nuclear scientists. (NW, 13 Jan.92, p.12)

These occurrences show that a fronted PP can in principle be followed by a lexical verb or by copular *be*: (18) and (19) are lexical-verb-inversions, (20) and (21) are *be*-inversions. However, the static nature of the verbs in (18) and (19) would not create much difference in meaning, if these were in fact *be*-inversions; vice versa, (20) could equally well contain a static lexical verb such as *lie*. Only (21) is unequivocally restricted to copular *be*. This is of course due to the fact that (18) – (20) contain fronted locative information, with a meaning of *existence*, and not *appearance*, on the scene. It is the kind of information that typically initiates the presentative process and, accordingly, lexical verbs of appearance or existence have a natural affinity with these existential scale sentences. Nonetheless, copular *be* can in principle do the same work.[7]

There is a corresponding correlation between static locative information and copular *be*. Since a static locative predicate, however, is ultimately a property or a quality assigned to the subject, other predicates can in principle play the same role in a parallel construction. This is also implied by the conditions stated above for an existential as opposed to a quality scale interpretation of a sentence: transient phenomena, which naturally have existential or presentative meaning, can possibly function as transient qualities if ascribed to a subject that is context-dependent. Vice versa, permanent phenomena, mostly, but by far not exclusively, expressed by adjectives (cf. Firbas 1979:49), have a natural meaning of quality, but they do not carry this function unless "a quality bearer [...] can be regarded as already introduced into the discourse" (Firbas 1979:42).

Static locative PPs, as in (18) – (20), and so-considered "abstract" PPs (Green 1982:127), as in (21), may therefore have a presentative function as well, departing, however, from a permanent property assigned to the subject. While part of the effect of these inversions is still that they focus the subject for further treatment in subsequent discourse, they nonetheless express a proposition of an inherently ascriptive character. As a consequence, the function of providing a new setting or ground is supplemented by an effect of contrastiveness. Long and complex predicates, in particular, if lacking any linguistic indication of discourse-familiarity, will be understood as being "shifted" to sentence-initial position for reasons beyond matters of information-status. The motivation will rather have to be sought in some kind of prominence that the speaker wants to give to these properties (cf. Enkvist 1980:135), stressing the validity of this, and no other, point of departure. The effect amounts to an evocation of a "presuppositional set" (Enkvist 1980:137): (19), in contrast to the CWO version in (19b), is likely to receive a contrastive interpretation as in (19a):

(19a)   In the loss of focus on the central bilateral relationship with Japan — and in nothing else — lies the real misfortune of the Bush trip.

(19b)   The real misfortune of the Bush trip lies in the loss of focus on the central bilateral relationship with Japan.

In view of this additional semantic effect, such *PP-inversions* following long and heavy PPs, attributable to the subject by static verbs or copular *be* only, therefore constitute, in terms of their function, a separate type of FI.[8] This is not to deny that the presentative function is also present: as discussed in section 3.4.1, Cognitive Grammar (e.g., Langacker 1993), for instance, acknowledges the aptitude of a profiled relationship, which can be a location or a property, to form the starting-point of a presentative construction. But it is more appropriate to speak of a *lexical predicative*, in contrast to a *presentative*, *inversion* type, if the ascriptive aspect dominates. This terminology follows Rapoport (1987), who defines predicative sentences as those in which "a quality or property specified by the post-copular phrase is attributed to the NP subject" (p.29). *PP-inversions* fall under this lexical predicative inversion type if, in addition to the use of a static verb or copular *be*, there is a combined effect of complex lexical information provided by the PP (as in (19)) and of apparent absence of discourse-familiarity (as in (20)), and most clearly so in cases of abstract, at best nonlocative, meaning (as in (21)). Admittedly, there remains a fuzzy borderline between instances of *PP-inversion*, which could be either presentative or predicative, but this is plausible in the light of my assumption, formulated in 3.3, that nonlocative and locative *be*-inversions are ultimately related.

An unequivocal representative of lexical predicative inversion is *AdjP-inversion*, most symptomatically because it exclusively occurs with copular *be*. To illustrate the relatedness to instances of predicative *PP-inversion*, a variation of (21) is produced in (21b), while natural instances of *AdjP-inversion* are (22) and (23):

(21b) <u>More important to many proliferation experts is the political braindrain</u> of thousands of former Soviet nuclear scientists.

(22) These are shocking figures, but <u>even more shocking is the fact</u> that at least half the people behind these crimes will go undetected. (LOB, ed.)

(23) <u>More troublesome to German planners is the country's inflation rate</u>, which last month crept above the 4% annual pace tolerated by the Bundesbank, prompting the sharp interest-rate hike. (Time, 20 Jan.92, p.9)

One crucial component of meaning created by predicative FI in opposition to CWO is that the subject is marked as non-salient at that point of discourse, even where the context could yield an opposite inference, and that it is then newly put on stage. However, referent-introduction is here no longer the only or dominant function of inversion, which is reflected by the common occurrence of definite subjects in *AdjP-inversion*. What most clearly distinguishes predicative from presentative inversion is a more complex function of the preposed constituent, often reflected by substantial formal complexity. The marked focus which these constituents carry no longer singles out a location from a set of all possible locations, but, rather, it identifies a property which is particularly attributable to the discourse entity that follows as subject. For example, this property may be *more* or *most* attributable to the discourse entity introduced; hence the fact that inversion after fronted AdjPs largely improves as a comparative, or if accompanied by *also, especially, as...as* etc. Earlier accounts of this observation (Penhallurick 1984:43; Birner 1992:64ff.) have been that these items underline the discourse-familiar status of the AdjP, but in my view this is not the whole story: in addition to a *change* of topic, which a presentative construction initiates by virtue of focussing a new discourse entity, inverted predicative sentences mark a topic *contrast*. They single out one referent out of a set of potential referents, which all have the property assigned, but to a more negligible extent than the entity that is the subject of the FI. This contrast among topic entities is also reflected by the fact that *AdjP-inversion* is frequently found paragraph-initially. The inversion represents an instruction for topic change, but it also singles out a topic entity of higher-level relevance, one which often deserves treatment within a textual part of its own.

The effect, which is again suitably described as evocation of a presuppositional set, is not produced by the respective CWO versions, as in (22b) and (23b):

(22b) These are shocking figures, but the fact that at least half the people behind these crimes will go undetected is even more shocking.

(23b) ?The country's inflation rate, which last month crept above the 4% annual pace tolerated by the Bundesbank, prompting the sharp interest-rate hike, is more troublesome to German planners.

(22b) is acceptable, but only because the set of candidates, against which the contrast is marked, is overtly named in the preceding clause. The sentence, however, does not mark a topic contrast. In (23b), by contrast, the comparative is hardly acceptable, due to the lack of an overt mention of the basis of comparison. In inverted form as in (23), it is the inversion itself which evokes a given status of the property fronted, and it thereby signals the existence of a set of candidates which have the same property: (23) thus evokes a set of *troublesome issues in economic policy*.

Not surprisingly, there are also *AdjP-inversions* with locative meaning, since there are many adjectives which express a locative property or even have a meaning of "impact and high visibility" (Bolinger 1977:108). Significantly, in these cases, a comparative or other givenness-marking item is less obligatory, as illustrated by (24) – (26):

(24) Also present will be the bride's children, Joan, 13, and Kirkland, 11. (BRW, rep.)

(25) Noticeable were two dark-clad figures in the background. [= (235)]

(26) Visible were many traces of their occupancy. [= (236)]

(Bolinger 1977)

This again stresses the fact that the presentative and the predicative inversion types are ultimately related. What, at best, holds them apart is the distinction between dynamic as opposed to static meaning and, accordingly, the verb type used. However, although static verbs have a meaning of "existence", they nonetheless express "emergence" within the text. Lexical predicative inversion is therefore always presentative as well, which emphasises what fully inverted word order always "means": regardless of the point of departure, it is fore and foremost an instruction to focus a new discourse entity.

Quite a clear symptom of a predominantly static and predicative function, however, is the non-acceptability of *there*-insertion, illustrated by the following (c)-versions of some of the examples used above:

(18c) On the walls of his office there hung pictures of sporting celebrities signed in "many thanks" terms.

(19c) ? In the loss of focus on the central bilateral relationship with Japan there lies the real misfortune of the Bush trip.

(25c) ?? Noticeable there were two dark-clad figures in the background.

(21c) * Of greater concern to many proliferation experts there is the political braindrain of thousands of former Soviet nuclear scientists.

(23c) * More troublesome to German planners there is the country's inflation rate, which last month crept above the 4% annual pace tolerated by the Bundesbank, prompting the sharp interest-rate hike.

By this criterion, there is another kind of FI, *NP-inversion*, which is entirely static, never accepts the insertion of *there*, and which thus without doubt belongs to the predicative type. *NP-inversion* consists of two NPs linked in a copular construction and creates the difficulty, noted in the beginning, that a mere syntactic sequence NP-*be*-NP makes it hard to identify one NP as the subject and the other as the complement of the clause. Possibly on the basis of an indefinite article in the initial NP, such as in (27), or by a lack of article, such as in (28), certain NP-*be*-NP sequences can nonetheless be considered instances of FI; they represent inverted ascriptive constructions very similar to predicative *PP-* and *AdjP-inversions*:

(27) <u>An exception to this rule are the wealthy merchants, Ministers, and senior Government officials</u> who have invested in cattle. (Guardw, 3 Jan.93, p.23)

(28) [...], the crews come to Lerwick more frequently and are no longer restricted to the centre. <u>First stop is still the second-hand shops</u> where the men intently rifle through the racks of children's and women's clothing. (Guardw, 3 Jan.93, p.5)

The reason why *NP-inversion* is often excluded from studies of inversion, despite obvious similarities with other *be*-inversion types, is that, formally, this category comprises "characterisation" as well as "identification" predicates (Quirk et al. 1985:742). By classifying as *NP-inversion* only those sentences with a fronted characterisation attribute, they become recognisable by an indefinite article, or by no article at all, both cases signalling a "type identifiable" discourse-status of the fronted NP (Gundel et al. 1993:275). Another criterion is lexical meaning which must also suggest "characterization rather than naming" (Garcia 1979:32). These criteria are necessary components of an ascriptive proposition; hence, they can be taken as evidence that an NP-*be*-NP-sequence, if an inversion at all, belongs to the lexical predicative type.

By contrast, identification predicates apparently allow for a free reversal of subject and complement. Nonetheless, an instance such as (29a), compared to (29b), produces a difference in terms of the grounding mechanism as well: by means of word order, the first NP is signalled to constitute the ground, which is somehow, here overtly, linked to prior discourse. The post-verbal NP is subsequently singled out from the presuppositional set and becomes the new focus of attention at the end of the sentence:

(29a) [...] he has continued to insist that certain forms of armed struggle remain incontrovertibly legitimate; and the most legitimate, indeed noble, of them is that which is directed against Israeli soldiers. (Guardw, 27 Dec.92, p.10)

(29b) [...] he has continued to insist that certain forms of armed struggle remain incontrovertibly legitimate; and that which is directed against Israeli soldiers is the most legitimate, indeed noble, of them.

Instances like (29a) and (29b) have been called *equative* sentences (cf. Rapoport 1987), as opposed to predicative ones, which still create a perceivable inversion. If all NP-*be*-NP sentences express "set membership" relations (Longacre 1983:235), equative sentences refer to the special case of one-unit sets. In the absence of any difference between the preverbal and the postverbal constituent as concerns their likelihood to serve either as ground or as new focus of attention — both are equally definite — it is no longer possible to identify either of the orderings as an inversion. Nonetheless, the word order chosen determines a perspective in that it chooses one of the NP constituents as the ground, from where the other is subsequently presented and focussed.

Finally, there is *VP-inversion* as the last lexical predicative inversion type to be considered here. It can have a strong presentative component again, since the fronted present and past participle groups followed by FI form a heterogeneous group: first, because participles have an inherent action-state duality (cf. Sundby 1970:12), which gives rise to a rather fuzzy transition from verbal to adjectival uses. Clear-cut adjectival instances are found in (30), which is very similar to an *AdjP-inversion* due to the comparative construction, and in (31):

(30) [...] but almost as disturbing as the national complacency is the apparent lack of any real sense of national unity. (LOB, ed.)

(31) "Not recommended" according to the BHF are the "8-Week Cholesterol Cure" diet, since "dietary changes causing plasma cholesterol reduction must be long-term for benefit to accrue", [...]. (Times, 15 Dec.92, p.12)

It is not necessary here to draw the exact borderline between adjectival and verbal uses of participles, since front-shifted AdjPs and participle forms in fact behave quite similarly. Svartvik (1966:132ff.) suggests that there is a *scale* from "passive" to "equative" (here: predicative) clauses, in which the key feature at the passive end is "expressed animate *by*-agent and expressed inanimate *by*-agent" (p.133). In a CWO sentence containing a past participle, a *by*-agent can always be added, at least potentially, but it cannot occur if the participle is fronted; this is a clear clue that the verb in *VP-inversion* has lost part of its verbal meaning and is in principle *predicative* in kind.

In line with this is a claim made by Ward/Birner (1992) that fronted present participles do not carry the same implicatures as their CWO counterparts: they suggest that, due to the absence of a competing preterit form, the fronted version lacks "the implicature of imperfectiveness" (Ward/Birner 1992:578) at work in CWO progressives. In front-position, participles seem to become aspectually neutralised. This is evidence for another loss of meaning typically expressed by the verb which takes place in *VP-inversion*, and constitutes further support for its predicative nature. At the same time, neutralisation of aspect is indicative of a certain degree of grammaticalisation in *VP-inversion*, compared to the CWO syntactic pattern. Vice versa, as Ward/Birner also argue, some progressives anomalous in CWO become acceptable in inverted order: in instances like (32), even though the direct object still supports the verbal character of the fronted VP, the progressive meaning is lost, leaving a rather static, property-like meaning, which could be paraphrased by an abstract PP such as *in search of*.[9] By contrast, when a non-progressive counterpart exists, as in (33), the implicature of non-completion re-arises, due to a real choice which can be made in favour of the progressive form:

(32) Seeking this two-year term are James Culbertson, Dwight M. Steeves, James C. Piersee, [...]. (BRW, rep.)

(33) Also being treated are Houston, Bleckley, Tift, Turner and Dodge counties, Blasingame said. (BRW, rep.)

The second reason why *VP-inversion* is a more heterogeneous type of FI is that fronted participle groups are frequently accompanied by local or directional PPs. These VPs could in fact be analysed as premodifications of the PPs, the construction then comes close to a *PP-inversion*. Examples are (34) and (35):

(34) Applauding on the river banks at Leningrad were thousands now told that in 20 years they will have free food, housing, light, heat, transport and medical treatment all for a working week of 34 to 36 hours. (LOB, rep.)

(35) Forty-seven of these ageing vessels [...] are anchored off Lerwick in Shetland. <u>Packed into them are about 3,000 seamen</u> earning L40 a month processing fish caught by British trawlers. (Guardw, 3 Jan.93, p.5)

The combination of a fronted participle with one or more PPs also causes a reduction of information units (cf. Sundby 1970:79): (34) and (35) consist of two informational units, while, in a CWO version such as (35b), the verb attracts the informational focus and is followed by the PP, a further specification:

(35b) (The) 3,000 seamen (working on these vessels) are packed into them.

The presence of PPs in *VP-inversion* emphasises that these are basically static, ascriptive constructions: it is rather the location contained in the PP which dominates and which is the main property ascribed to the subject. If a PP is lacking, however, the acceptability of *VP-inversion* is not self-evident; it depends on whether the verb itself can express a "lasting effect" or "locative consequences" (Bolinger 1977:106), like, for instance, in (36). In (37), by contrast, a modifier that refers more to an event than to a lasting effect makes a *VP-inversion* almost unacceptable:

(36) Rudely (painfully) shaken were several of the passengers. [= (198)]

(37) ? Abruptly (suddenly) shaken were several of the passengers. [= (199)]

(Bolinger 1977)

All this is evidence for a reduction of the verbal, activity semantics to a static, locative predicate in *VP-inversion*. It also sheds more light on the general difference between lexical-verb-inversion and *be*-inversion. Comparing (35c) to the constructed inversions in (38) – (40), it is (38) which is almost unacceptable because it involves an *activity* sense of the verb, with the subject as a real *agent*:

(35c) Into them are packed about 3,000 seamen [...].

(38) Into the vessel ran three members of the crew.

(39) ?? In the vessel danced three members of the crew.

(40)   In the vessel slept three very tired members of the crew.

FI accepts an activity verb only with directional PPs, as in (38), because it then expresses the inherently dynamic, presentative process of "appearance on the scene". Otherwise, i.e., when the speaker uses a pre-existing location, or a predicate, to put the subject onto the scene, this subject is in fact treated as a *patient*: in locative-state case frames, full verbs only contribute "an indication of the shape, size or posture of the patient" (Longacre 1983:204). This is typically the case with inanimate subjects, because "if an animate subject is standing, lying or sitting [or dancing] somewhere this is an activity" (Longacre 1983:204). It is exactly this that makes inversion unacceptable in (39). (40), by contrast, is acceptable because the attribute *tired* allows for the verb *sleep* to contribute a property to the then patient, it thereby blocks the activity reading.

There is thus plenty of evidence that the participle in *VP-inversion* is an ascriptive quality rather than an activity and that, consequently, *VP-inversion* is a lexical predicative inversion type. In the scene-setting process that is part of FI, verbal meaning is least prominent; what is needed to locate a referent in a displaced universe of discourse is the location as the ground plus the item to be located. Apart from directional semantics, the process can in principle always be taken over by *be*.[10] The relative negligence of verbal meaning in FI also explains why, as noted by Birner (1992:20), there are cases of *VP-inversion* which do not have a felicitous CWO counterpart at all. The meaning of (41a), for instance, is either equivalent to scene-setting by a directional PP, such as in (41b), or by a location as a static predicate, as in (41c). The verbal semantics, however, is least important, which explains why the verb in the inversion does not need to subcategorise for the verb contained in the fronted VP:

(41a)   Coming up the street rode a body of men in blue. [= Birner 1992:(9a), p.20]

(41b)   Up the street rode a body of men in blue.

(41c)   Coming up the street was a body of men in blue.

To summarise, it should have become apparent that lexical presentative and lexical predicative inversion do not on principled grounds consitute separate classes. What they do is stress different aspects of meaning by fronting different kinds of lexical predicates, which are assigned to the subject and thereby become the departure of an existential scale sentence: if a transient property, or an activity, is expressed, the process of putting the subject in focus is dynamic and event-like, while a permanent property assigned by static verbs or *be* serves to locate a discourse entity within the text, within the universe of discourse. Since locations, however, are also properties of the subject, the "innovation" (cf.3.2.2) of *AdjP-inversion*, *VP-inversion* and predicative *PP-inversion*, available in Modern English, must in fact have derived from the pre-existing locative, inherently presentative, type of full inversion.

4.1.2.4 *The anaphoric/cataphoric type*

Quite the opposite of the lexical grounding mechanism displayed by the majority of FI types are full inversions following a pronominal adverb, as well as those occurring in comparative or correlative constructions. Both build up different kinds of complex constructions (for the details cf. 3.1.2.2) and mainly occur with SAI, but they can invert the entire VP as well. Formally, a *pro-inversion* is an instance of FI if, as illustrated by (42),[11] *as*, *thus* and *so* occur with full verbs,[12] or when, in case of *be*, the subject ends up in sentence-final position. This can be tested by adding other auxiliaries, as in examples (43) and (44):

(42) So wrote Mr. Julius Nyere, the Chief Minister of Tanganyika, in last Sunday's Observer, and [...]. (LOB, ed.)

(43) But the main elements have been retained and so, most importantly, has been the standard. (Times, 15 Dec.92, p.35)

(44) Thus was born the Barbados Coup, a variation of the Grosvenor Gambit, in which [...]. (Guardw, 3 Jan.93, p.8)

Alternatively, *so* and *thus* in the sense of *in this way* or *in this manner* can also be followed by SAI, in which case some sentence constituent other than the subject ends up in final position and attracts the informational focus. In that case, the adverb is not really a pro-form, but a sentence adverbial, which receives additional prominence by way of SAI, as in (45):

(45) Thus does Mr Karadzic provide a timely reminder of why he is high on U.S. Secretary of State Lawrence Eagleburger's newly announced list of war criminals. (WashP, 27 Dec.92, p.15)

The same goes for the *corr-inversion* types, which, apart from the fronted constituent, can either focus the subject, and are then an FI, as in (46) and (47), or focus the verb by means of AuxSV order, as in (48) and (49):

(46) So great is the apathy that the Government could probably go in or stay out without vitally offending either its own followers or the country. (LOB, ed.)

(47) [...] less willing than were the West European countries to regard American economic aid as part of a pattern of political and military co-operation. (LOB, ed.)

(48) So wholly desperate do they seem, indeed, that it comes as something of a shock [...]. (LOB, bbe.)

(49) [...] the more often a trial is repeated, the more exactly can the probability of ignition by an individual shot be stated. (LOB, sc.writ.)

There is a big difference between these pronominal and correlative constructions and the other FI types as dealt with so far: pro-forms and correlative connectives are primarily grammatical devices, which perform a linkage of clauses, and they have a mainly grammatical, their anaphoric or cataphoric, meaning. This is why they constitute a clearly separate class of FI constructions, which I call the *anaphoric/cataphoric inversion* type.

Some of these pronominal elements are also possible with CWO, in opposition to which the effect of the inversion is again that it puts the subject into focus.[13] At the same time, an inversion following a pronominal adverb in front-position has a stronger connective force than its CWO counterpart; hence the fact that, for example, pronominal *so* in end-position requires a conjunct which supports the connection, as in (43b):

(43b) [...] and, most importantly, the standard has so, too.

Pronominal adverbs followed by inversion thus bear a high functional load: they refer back to an entire predication and attribute to (as with *so*) or exclude another referent (with pronominal *nor/neither*) from the same predication. The result is a bi-focal construction like all other FIs, but pronominal and correlative elements nonetheless construct an especially close, syntacticised unit. Despite their bi-focal nature, they are therefore in general realised as a single tone unit (cf. Quirk et al. 1985:1381).

4.1.3 *Subject-auxiliary-inversion vs. canonical word order*

In contrast to FI, which puts the subject into focus, an SAI construction is present "whenever a constituent other than the subject is selected as focus" (König 1988:63). Formally, this correlates with the fact that the subject does not move out of its usual position, but remains in its unmarked place, to the left of the lexical verb. It is therefore the constituent which is least affected by the deviation from CWO.

Front-shifting of an individual sentence-constituent which would be canonically placed elsewhere in the clause does not primarily have to do with matters of information-status. As has been shown, these give rise to reorderings that affect the whole clause. By contrast, a marked position of an individual item will rather be taken to derive from the relative importance which the speaker subjectively attaches to that part of the predication. Following Enkvist' s (1980) definition of *emphatic focus*, such speaker-based weight or prominence creates an *emphatic* kind of meaning (cf. p.135). The difference between obligatory and non-obligatory SAI constructions in Modern English arises because many, especially the negative, constituents involved gain so much emphasis by the very fact of sentence-initial placement that they are today obligatorily followed by SAI order. Others, however, can unemphatically occur in that position, so that additional emphasis is created only by the inversion itself.[14]

An exception to this, however, are *nor* and *neither*, the main representatives of the above-established *add-inversion* category (cf. 3.1.2.2). They show obligatory fronting plus obligatory SAI, probably because, in them, there is both a connective (anaphoric) and a negative component of meaning. They thereby give rise to SAI instances in which AuxSV order is grammaticalised; there is no more real semantics of choice. Nonetheless, these negative additive adverbs combine the semantic components of the anaphoric/cataphoric inversion type and of real constituent-focussing SAI, to be discussed below.

Out of the *add-inversion* category, *nor* is by far the most frequently used adverb. Moreover, Kjellmer (1979), for example, claims that it is a very "subtle" and "refined" device of textual cohesion,

> by means of which different parts of an argument or an exposition can be held together, and which can allow a writer insertions and deviations without jeopardising the stringency of his argument. (p. 292).

This suggestion is confirmed by natural occurrences of SAI following *nor*, such as in (50) and (51):

(50) It was faintly ridiculous to find John Major, [...], suddenly informing the Commons that the couple "will from time to time attend family occasions together".

[13 lines later, starting a new paragraph]

<u>Nor, indeed, was the statement itself without curiosities</u>. (Guardw, 20 Dec.92, p.1)

(51) When Britain tried to make clear that something else was in prospect – [...] – Ribbentrop was dismissed. <u>Nor did Hitler seem to need much persuading</u>. (Guardw, 20 Dec.92, p.28)

(50) and (51) both illustrate that the text preceding a *nor*-clause does not need to contain an overt or explicit negative element; instead, "what matters is the positive/negative equivalence between pre-context and *nor*-clause" (Kjellmer 1979:291). In (50), this equivalence is achieved through the second negative element *without curiosities*, which turns the entire clause into an affirmative in line with the previous text, while (51) contains an only implicit negative component in the lexical meaning of *dismiss*. Moreover, *nor* is able to refer back to an element in the previous text over quite considerable stretches of text, as is the case in (50). This flexibility in anaphoric reference further expresses itself by the creation of links which are not self-evident from a semantic point of view: in (51), there is nothing in the previous text to which the *nor*-clause can refer back because it introduces a hierachically higher passage, a comment, following a narrative part. One may therefore conclude that "when a *nor*-clause is used, the reader or listener will try to force even a recalcitrant context into some kind of meaningful relationship with the *nor*-clause" (Kjellmer 1979:288).

Thus, in the case of *nor* as negative additive adverb, a connective (discourse) meaning as well as negative semantics have become grammaticalised in an obligatory SAI construction, which brings both meaning components into prominent front-position and thereby achieves a considerable effect in discourse. Functionally, the category *add-inversion* therefore combines the *anaphoric/cataphoric* plus a *constituent-focussing* aspect of inversion. By contrast, what could be considered a corresponding CWO version, coordination with *and...not*, does not possess the same potential. Instead, in (51b), some kind of cohesive link is missing:

(51b)   ?When Britain tried to make clear that something else was in prospect – [...] – Ribbentrop was dismissed. And Hitler did not seem to need much persuading.

Since (51b) does not achieve the same effect as the inverted version in (51), the cohesive work of the *nor*-construction cannot be put down to a mere combination of additive and negative semantics. It must instead be a syntacticised function which arises out of the construction as a whole. Compared to *nor*, SAI following *neither* seems to have this discourse function to a much weaker extent: Kjellmer (1979:295) notes that it "is a less refined instrument, picking up a content element and a negation in the preceding sentence in an almost mechanical fashion". In my view, this is most clearly reflected by the fact that, while *nor* can normally not be preceded by *and*,[15] *and neither* is acceptable.

The primary function of the remaining SAI constructions is to focus on an individual constituent. Accordingly, I subsume them as a *constituent-focussing inversion* type. This class, in particular, includes the semantically defined *neg-inversion* type, which is, of course, not unrelated to *nor*, in view of their shared negative semantics. Non-negative fronted adverbs, by contrast, are in general optionally followed by SAI, but, in that position, gain a stronger connective, hence anaphoric, force. If pro-forms can be used as additive adverbs, such as (45), discussed above and repeated below, the meaning of other adverbs can plausibly be enriched by an anaphoric effect, as soon as these occur in front-position. At the same time, however, adverbs such as those in (52) – (54) are semantically too complex to be taken as mere anaphoric items; primarily, they gain emphatic meaning by virtue of being perceivably fronted. In addition to a cohesive effect, the front-position of non-negative adverbs thus represents a real speaker-based choice and thereby also adds prominence to them:

(45)   <u>Thus does Mr Karadzic provide a timely reminder</u> of why he is high on U.S. Secretary of State Lawrence Eagleburger's newly announced list of war criminals. (WashP, 27 Dec.92, p.15)

(52)   [...] it merely wished to minimize subjective views of officials who wielded public authority.
<u>Particularly was this true</u> as laissez-faire capitalism became the dominant credo of Western society. (BRW, sc.writ.)

(53) [...] <u>in this small way do the leaders of a city, or of a nation, inure the masses</u> to watching, [...]. (BRW, ed.)

(54) <u>Truly are the tax gatherers an unbeloved people</u>. (LOB, ed.)

In (52) and (53), the adverbials represent a connective device, but the use of SAI at the same time marks them as the focus of the predication, an *emphatic* focus in the sense defined above. As opposed to canonical, sentence-internal, placement, a reduction of these adverbials to predication or minor scope reading is avoided: for instance, *particularly* is a degree adverb in (52b) and has scope only over the complement, while, in (53b), *in this small way* is almost obligatorily fronted due to its anaphoric meaning; it is a conjunct and not a sentence adjunct as with subsequent SAI. Front-shifting of *particularly*, by contrast, makes SAI almost obligatory, probably because its meaning is not apt to function as a disjunct or stance adverb. T*ruly*, as in (54), is not necessarily followed by SAI: here, it is the function of the inversion to signal closer integration into the predication itself. By contrast, placed sentence-initially without SAI, as in (54b), it becomes a mere disjunct:

(52b) This was particularly true as laissez-faire capitalism became the dominant credo of Western society.

(53b) [...] in this small way, the leaders of a city, or of a nation, inure the masses to watching, [...].

(54b) Truly, the tax gatherers are an unbeloved people.

Thus, the effect of *optional* constituent-focussing SAI is that it produces emphatic meaning; and the more emphasis is expressed, the less prominent is the connective potential of the front-shifted item. As a consequence, there is an emotional flavour to all of these clauses, since a position — and a meaning — normally reserved for speaker's comments and links, for disjuncts and conjuncts, becomes more closely integrated into the predication itself. Fronting of adverbials plus subsequent SAI is therefore a further instance of subjectification in language: the meaning of these adverbials, which nonetheless remain part of the predication itself, becomes increasingly based in the speaker's own attitude.

Basically the same mechanism is present in the syntax of those adverbs that are followed by SAI *obligatorily*, such as instances (55) – (58):

(55) At no stage in the match was Stich seriously threatened. (Guardw, 20 Dec.92, p.32)

(56) Little could he have imagined that one of those who overheard this conversation would make it public at the Nuremberg trial. (Guardw, 20 Dec.92, p.28)

(57) Only in wartimes does it add some value as a focus of national unity. (Guardw, 20 Dec.92, p.5)

(58) [...] agree that rarely has trade union loyalty faced a more baffling test. (LOB, ed.)

Most of this group consists of adverbials and object phrases "of negative form or meaning" (Quirk et al. 1985:1382). Not restricted to explicit negation of constituents by *not* and *no* (as in (55)), it also includes implicit negators, such as downtoners (e.g., *barely*), negative frequency adverbs (as in (58)), restrictive focussing adjuncts (as in (57)) and restrictive determiners (as in (56)) (cf. König 1988:56).

However, negative or restrictive expressions also occur clause-initially without subsequent SAI. Accounts for the difference have previously been formulated in terms of the "scope" of the negative or restrictive operator (König 1988:59) or of "sentence negation" vs. "constituent negation" (Rudanko 1982:349), a classical example being (59a) as opposed to (59b) (quoted from König 1988:59). The difference is also exemplified by natural occurrences such as (57), given above, as opposed to CWO, as in (60):

(59a) With no job would John be happy.

(59b) With no job, John would be happy.

(60) A left-wing organ recalled that only the previous year Tagliabue had received a scroll. (LOB, bbe.)

If no SAI follows a constituent containing *not* or *only*, such as in (59b) and (60), its meaning is not really negative (cf. Rudanko 1982:356): the restrictive constituent in (60), for example, is appropriately paraphrased as *as early as the previous year*. In other words, the position of the auxiliary itself "correlates with and in fact identifies the scope of the negative operator" (König 1988:59).

What is important, however, is that the negative or restrictive meaning does not need to be explicit in the fronted constituent itself; it is also created by an inversion. Thus, in (61), SAI marks a more subjective, emotional meaning, which leads to an interpretation of the *now* phrase as *only now...* or *finally*, while, if followed by CWO, as in (62), *now* expresses an objectively given, temporal framework:

(61) Now that our future king is a man responsible for a one-parent family [...] can we assume that the establishment, not least the Tories, will finally stop blaming one-parent families for violence, crime, and all society's other ills. (Guardw, 20 Dec.92, p.2)

(62) Now that we have a mass of regular statistical information, on a standard international classification, about this trade, we can examine its pattern and structure in great detail. (LOB, sc.writ.)

Similar as in the case of positive adverbs, SAI in (61) identifies the function of the adverbial in front-position as a predication adjunct; it is a specification, which attracts the focus onto the predicate. In (62), by contrast, the adverbial functions as the setting of the clause and is not integrated into the predication. Syntactically, it therefore remains a sentence adjunct.

To summarise on the kind of meaning involved in constituent-focussing inversion, one can ascribe a dual function to the constituents followed by SAI: as part of the predication of the clause, they in fact express part of its experiential content, while, by assuming the point of departure position, they gain an additional interpersonal meaning. Similar to "real" point of departure elements, integral parts of the predication thereby become enriched by interpersonal meaning components: by elements such as "setting the mood", "giving an evaluation of the importance or reliability of the information in the ensuing discourse" (Lowe 1987:7), and the like. It is in this sense that the constituent-focussing type of SAI creates emphatic and subjective meaning: it singles out the focus of the predication as the speaker-based point of departure of the clause, and thereby adds to it interpersonal meaning.

4.2 Viewpoint and subjectivity in inversion

In the previous sections, the semantic potential of both FI and SAI has been investigated, on the basis of which various functional categories of the phenomenon have been introduced. One basic assumption has underlain the procedure of comparing the individual inversion types to their CWO counterparts: namely, that it is in fact a matter of choice whether an inversion is preferred to a canonical sentence pattern. This was possible because, *structurally*, almost all inverted inversion types considered here have a corresponding CWO version. What has been neglected, however, is that the actual *use* of an inversion is often far from being a choice; under many contextual conditions an inverted sentence is almost unacceptable, while only others, quite specific ones, make the choice in favour of an inversion really preferable. It is the aim of the remainder of this chapter to subsume the semantics of inversion phenomena in more general terms in order to identify the contextual conditions of its usage. What the previous discussion has shown is that subjectivity plays a particularly important role in the semantics of the construction; contextualised, this kind of meaning will now be shown to establish point of view in discourse. As a start, those contextual conditions are taken up which represent the strictest limitation for the occurrence of an inversion: its apparent restriction to main clauses, or, put differently, the putative inability to occur in an embedded construction.

4.2.1 *Inversion in embedded constructions*

In section 3.3.1, it was already noted that, for inversion, the structure-preserving constraint in the strict syntactic sense of Emonds (1976) does not hold. Its status as a root transformation is more than questionable, at least if the evidence is sought in a principled incapacity to occur in an embedded clause. Attempts to replace the putative structural constraint by semantic and/or pragmatic factors (Hooper/Thompson 1973), or to assume a complex interaction of syntactic, semantic and pragmatic factors have not yet let to any unified account, let alone to a "simple answer" (Green 1976:397). Nonetheless, the conditions that affect the acceptability of inversion in embeddings give an important indication of the overall meaning of the construction.

From previous attempts to get hold of the semantic and pragmatic factors that determine inversion in embeddings, a common core of arguments can be identified, less for a formal status as a root transformation, but for justifiably characterising it as a "main clause phenomenon" (Green 1976). There is in fact much more freedom to invert in a main clause, so that this is, following Givón's (1979:46) "completeness argument", the *basic* or *default* case. In the same vein, Hooper/Thompson (1973:472) argue for a restriction of inversion to "asserted" clauses, a similar claim like the one made by Green (1976):

> It seems that the more the embedded clause *looks like it could be* a direct quotation which could stand alone, where anything goes, the more easily it embeds. (p. 395; my emphasis)

Apparently, what one has to look for is a feature which makes inversion typically occur in a main clause, but which, alternatively, can be maintained in an embedded clause as well, provided certain contextual conditions are fulfilled. Given these, the embedded clause "looks like" a matrix clause.

A first pattern of acceptability can be noted on the basis of some constructed examples, such as discussed in previous literature.[16] To these, a natural occurrence is added in (66), which I encountered by chance in the linguistic literature:

(63) * Harry was annoyed that even more corrupt was the Republican Party. [= Hooper/Thompson 1973:(105)]

(64a) John says that standing in the corner is a man with a camera, and I think he's right. [= (34a)]

(64b) * John says that standing in the corner is a man with a camera, and he's wrong. [= (34c)]

(Green 1976)

(65) He has forgotten that over the fireplace hangs a picture of his late wife. [= Birner 1992:(8), p.87]

(66) Van Dijk (1982), for example, argues that <u>between the unit of the sentence and the unit of the text or conversation exists a further unit of analysis</u>, which he calls the episode: [...]. (Ehrlich, Point of view, p.27)

Hooper/Thompson (1973) claim that the main function of root transformations is to produce *emphasis* and "emphasis would be unacceptable in sentences that are not asserted" (p.172f.); hence the fact that they are not applicable in a presupposed sentence such as (63). However, at least (66) looks very unemphatic to me, nor does the assertion criterion explain the acceptability of (65), one of Birner's (1992) examples where the embedded clause is presupposed and inversion nonetheless acceptable. A related suggestion, put forward by Green (1976), is *speaker's agreement* as exemplified in (64a) and (64b): presumably, "the embeddability of main clause phenomena in general correlates with the strength of the speaker's agreement with the content of that clause" (p.387). In the absence of explicit indicators, however, this criterion is hardly operable; Green tries to use the matrix verb's expressing or implying agreement as a criterion, but a corresponding hierarchy of verbs which she establishes does not reflect decreasing tolerance for main clause phenomena. The contextual conditions for speaker's agreement therefore lack reliability and measurability, even though it is probably right to assume that they "will form part of an ultimate theory" (Green 1976:394) of main clause phenomena.

The notion of agreement can be refined by some insights provided by theories of *point of view* (Banfield 1982; Reinhart 1983; Ehrlich 1990). Developed mainly to analyse free indirect discourse in literature, some of them are equally applicable to less literary styles, and to indirect or reported speech in particular, contexts in which embedded inversions, like in (66), seemingly prefer to occur. Point of view analyses of indirect discourse distinguish between the *speaker* of the discourse itself and the *subject* of an utterance or thought reported. For instance, in a sentence such as (64c), the parenthetical could be *speaker-oriented* or *subject-oriented*, two readings out of which, however, only one is possible, given a specific parenthetical (cf. Ehrlich 1990:12):

(64c) Standing in the corner is a man with a camera, John says.

Sentences with an embedded *that*-clause, by contrast, potentially have both readings: one in which the speaker's point of view is represented and one in which the subject's point of view is represented (cf. Reinhart 1983:170). Which reading is the more likely to be understood is the outcome of an interplay of the context on the one hand and of the nature of the matrix verb on the other. In (64a) and (64b), the speaker's attitude towards the proposition is explicitly mentioned in the context, while the matrix verb *say* is neutral with respect to speaker- or subject-orientation. By contrast, *forget* in (65) semantically blocks subject-orientation, while *be annoyed* in (63), though not prohibiting speaker-orientation, at least strongly favours subject-orientation. In (66), at last, the embedded clause does not receive only one orientation assigned by the verb; as a consequence, speaker- and subject-orientation can coincide.

It thereby becomes apparent that the acceptability of an embedded inversion depends on the possibility at least that there is speaker-orientation; hence (64a), (65) and (66) are acceptable. And while speaker-orientation is in fact the only possible reading of (65), real indirect quotes as in (64a/b) and (66) always receive subject-orientation in the first place. They can additionally have speaker-orientation, if, like in (66), an author uses an indirect quote for the development of her own line of thought. The matrix verb *argue*, however, is no open signal of a possible speaker-orientation; nonetheless, the inversion in (66) is perfectly acceptable. This suggests that there is an even stronger correlation between inversion and speaker-orientation: not only does the felicity of an inversion *depend on* the plausibility of speaker-orientation in a given context; context permitting, what it does is to *create* it, i.e., it signals that it is the *point of view* of the speaker which is also being expressed. Adding the speaker-based, hence subjective, meaning component of an inversion to an embedded clause makes it evident to the hearer or reader that the speaker himself, though not overtly the subject of the discourse reported, does at least not dissociate himself from the content expressed.

Accordingly, in analyses of point of view phenomena in discourse, one finds that the occurrence of root transformations, notably of inversions in embedded *that*-clauses, is used as one kind of evidence (e.g., in Ehrlich 1990). It is further noted that, due to the point of view present in an embedding, their matrix clauses are "reduced in terms of semantic force and their accompanying clauses are interpreted as dominant" (Ehrlich 1990:45).[17] This also accounts for the case of presuppositions, insufficiently explained so far by the usual distinction between presupposition and assertion:[18] (67a) and (68a), for instance, illustrate that inversion is not in principle excluded from presupposed sentences (cf. Green 1976:391), but their variations in (67b) and (68b) are much less acceptable:

(67a)   We can support the claim that standing in the corner was a black umbrella. [= Green 1976:(56b)]

(67b)   ?? He supports the claim that standing in the corner was a black umbrella.

(68a)   John pretended that standing in the corner was a Tiffany lamp. [= Green 1976:(57a)]

(68b)   ?? John pretends that standing in the corner is a Tiffany lamp.

If, as assumed here, the acceptability of an inversion requires a context in which the speaker can identify with the subject of a reported utterance, this explains the acceptability of (67a) as opposed to (67b): in a first person matrix clause, speaker and subject naturally coincide, so that the speaker can easily adopt a subjective attitude towards the embedded proposition involved.[19] In counterfactive complements narrated in the past tense as in (68a), by contrast, there is an overall distance of the narrator towards the event of the utterance itself. Perhaps this allows the speaker to return to a more subjective presentation without contradicting the subject's own perspective, who, at the time of uttering it, knew the proposition not to be true. In (68b), utterance and quote are simultaneous; here, it is harder for the speaker to identify with the subject and at the same time present a counterfactive proposition from his own point of view.

The examples discussed so far have illustrated the behaviour of FI in embedded constructions, with a more detailed analysis of the viewpoint expressed by FI to follow in the next section. SAI is in principle subject to similar restrictions, even though these arise out of the more directly speaker-based meaning of it, associated with the focussing of an individual constituent. Nonetheless, expressing a speaker-based, emphatic focus equally calls for a context that is compatible with speaker-orientation. This is illustrated by examples (69a) as opposed to (69b), and (70a) as opposed to (70b):

(69a)   I regret that never before has such a proposal been made. [= (40a)]

(69b) * Nixon regrets that never before have prices been so high. [= (1b)]

(Green 1976)

(70a)   We cannot be hungry because not a bite would he eat.

(70b) * (Why is he hungry?) He is hungry because not a bite would he eat. [= Green 1976:(63b)]

For SAI to be acceptable, the predication must again be one made from the speaker's own perspective: in (69a), a first person factive makes embedded SAI acceptable, in contrast to a third person factive as in (69b). What is interesting about (70a) is that SAI in a causal adverbial clause is acceptable only if this represents an external reason, i.e. is non-restrictive. An internal or restrictive causal adverbial clause, by contrast, does not permit neither an SAI, as in (70b), nor an FI, as in (71b):

(71a)   Something must have happened because in came my father.

(71b)   * I had to hide the book because in came my father.

Despite many obvious differences between FI and SAI, which will constitute the focus of the following sections, both kinds of inversions thus share the basic mechanism underlying their acceptability in embeddings.

A final remark remains to be made on the whole discussion about inversion in embedded constructions: judgements of acceptability are a particularly vulnerable issue here. This is confirmed by all treatments in the literature quoted, best illustrated by Hooper/Thompson's (1973) observation that "a few speakers allow RTs [= root transformations] in all *that*-S complements" (p.479). The distinction between speaker-orientation and subject-orientation accounts for these uncertainties: context permitting, it remains up to the speaker's choice — or to the judger's imagination — to shift an embedded predication into the perspective of the subject and to thereby background the embedded material in relation to the speaker (cf. Hooper/Thompson 1973:496).[20]

4.2.2 *Viewpoint analysis of main clause full inversion*

In the previous section, it has been claimed that the embedding of an inversion depends on the compatibility with a speaker-orientation of the embedded clause. In other words, the clause must contain a viewpoint or perspective that belongs to the speaker himself and that cannot be projected to the subject only; if this perspective is unacceptable, so becomes the embedded inversion. This issue of a speaker-orientation is also relevant for the basic or default case of inversion occurrence, which is the main clause. In a main clause, the speaker-orientation inherent in inversion establishes a *viewpoint* and determines a *perspective*.

For this kind of meaning involved in FI, two examples drawn from Langacker's work on subjectivity (1990) are illustrative:

(72a)   The tree is in front of the house.

(72b)   In front of the house is a tree.

Langacker (1990) claims that a sentence like (72a) is "appropriate only if the tree is in the viewer's line of sight" (p.6), i.e., if the location is defined in relation to the viewer. Depending on the context, it may remain unclear, however, whether the side where the tree stands is in fact the front or the back side of the house. With FI, as in (72b), no such potential ambiguity arises: the viewpoint from where the phenomenon is seen is moved to the house, the location of the tree defined in relation to it. By using an FI, the speaker thus moves his own position from where he views a phenomenon to the location designated by the referent of the NP in the fronted constituent.

In a lexical FI, this referent is part of the universe of discourse established and serves as reference point from where relational information can be interpreted. Relational information thereby becomes what Langacker calls a *profiled* relationship; it forms the starting-point of a presentative construction. A starting-point is static if it expresses temporal or locative relations, as in (72b), but it may also be dynamic, in the case of directional relations. Not all directional relations, however, can be profiled: (73a) and (73b) are from Bresnan (1994), and she notes that only certain PPs with subsequent FI are acceptable:

(73a)   *   Toward me looked a drunk. [= (16b)]

(73b)   Toward me lurched a drunk. [= (16a)]

(Bresnan 1994)

This kind of evidence has been discussed as "split intransitivity" (Bresnan 1994:78), but, semantically, it can be accounted for in terms of point of view and speaker-orientation: an FI is acceptable if there is movement of the discourse entity in relation to the viewpoint adopted, which is why directional PPs require a dynamic verb. The event is perceived by the speaker as a participant on the scene; he may be named explicity, as in (73b), or merely assume the viewpoint of the discourse entity referred to, as in (72b).

Viewpoint differences are also covered by Kuno's (1987) theory of *empathy*, in which the metaphor of a "camera angle" (p.203) treats similar effects. Empathy is "the speaker's identification, which may vary in degree, with a person/thing that participates in the event or state that he describes in a sentence" (Kuno 1987:206) and has been used to account for a range of linguistic phenomena. Some of them, notably the difference between reflexive and non-reflexive pronouns, reflect similar conditions for the interpretation of locative, thus relational, information and thereby carry meanings of perspective such as the ones demonstrated by (72b) and (73b). For instance, the difference in empathy and viewpoint between the classical examples (74a) and (74b), here from Kemmer (1995:67), can also be expressed by an FI, such as in (74c):

(74a)   The women were standing in the background, with the children behind them. [= (12a)]

(74b)   The women were standing in the background, with the children behind themselves. [= (12b)]

(Kemmer 1995)

(74c)   The women were standing in the background. <u>Behind them were the children</u>, who were [...].[21]

(74a) is ambiguous as to where the children are standing: farther from the camera, or behind the women's backs. By contrast, the reflexive pronoun in (74b) signals that it has to be interpreted from the point of view of the antecedent, *the women*. In both, however, the vantage point from which the whole event is presented remains the same for the entire sentence — the camera stays out of the picture, so to speak —, while only (74c) induces what was above called an effect of "staged activity" (cf. 4.1.2.2) and what is equally well described as "camera movement": the speaker starts from the viewpoint of the fronted PP, i.e. of the referent which it contains, and from this new vantage point focusses *the children*. This takes place in accordance with Kuno's empathy principles: first of all, the beginning of a new sentence in principle allows for a new viewpoint or empathy relation (cf. Kuno 1987:207). And, second, the "syntactic prominence principle" is at work (Kuno 1987:232), not in terms of the assignment of subject role, but following the other manifestation of syntactic prominence, the "word order empathy hierarchy" (p.232).

That the speaker in fact performs a shift in his position or viewpoint can be illustrated if one combines some of Kuno's examples, quoted in (75a) and (75b), with an inversion as in (75c):

(75a) (?)   A boy sneaked into the room and was immediately hit on the head by John. [= (8.5a)]

(75b) ??   A boy sneaked into the room and was immediately hit on the head by me. [= (8.5b)]

(Kuno 1987)

(75c)   Into the room sneaked a boy and was immediately hit on the head by me.

(75a) is considered marginally acceptable due to the pressure of the parallel subjects. It is in any case considered more acceptable than (75b), because (75b) not only violates the "topic empathy hierarchy" (Kuno 1987:212), but, more important, the "speech act empathy hierachy" (p.212), i.e. the strong tendency of the speaker to empathise with himself. An FI as in (75c) makes this constructed example more acceptable, which means that speaker empathy must have become more likely. The effect of the inversion is that the speaker "has moved his camera closer", due to his having adopted a reference point from the discourse world established and in relation to which he then focusses a new discourse entity.

4.2.3 Focus management through point of view

In ongoing discourse, the viewpoint established by FI becomes a device of *focus management*, focus being understood here in its discourse sense as the listener's/reader's current focus of attention or interest (cf. 2.1.2). The metaphor of a "camera movement" introduced above describes a change in focus: a move from a lexically specified ground at the beginning to a new focus of attention at the end of an inverted clause. Such changes of perspective or viewpoint are also *topic change markers* (cf. van Dijk/Kintsch 1983:204) and structure a discourse into separate units or episodes. Focus management thus has an effect on the structure of a discourse: the ground represents a new scene "set", which is defined in relation to previously established topics, while the discourse entity that is focussed becomes the potentially new topic for subsequent discourse. The focus management work of inversion therefore already implies that it also contributes to building up a discourse structure, hence is a *discourse marker* (cf. 5.4).

Of the conditions of information-status noted for FI (cf. 3.4.2), one constraint for the preposed element was that it "must not be newer in the discourse than the postposed element" (Birner 1992:151). It is therefore the one which is the more accessible and thus the more salient in the reader's mind. Due to this, it can serve as what Cognitive Grammar calls a cognitive *reference point*. The instruction for a change in focus performed by FI corresponds to the dynamic process of a reference point *construction*:

> [A] reference point has a certain cognitive salience, either intrinsic or contextually determined. It is [...] owing to some kind of salience that an entity comes to be chosen as a reference point in the first place. [...] To serve as a reference point, a notion must first be activated and thus established as an entity currently capable of serving in that capacity. [...] However, when this potential is exploited [...] it is the target thereby reached that now becomes prominent in the sense of being the focus of C's [the conceptualiser's] conception. (Langacker 1993:6)

The fronted constituent of an FI in most cases has *contextually determined* salience, in general decidedly more salience than the subject of the inverted clause. However, where both are inferrable entities, and thereby linguistically underspecified in terms of their relative salience, it is the "natural" salience of the sentence-initial position that makes a constituent placed there apt to serve as the reference point of the construction. Due to this salience, which arises independently of actual discourse-status, FI can focus and re-focus any discourse entity: "any – known or unknown – referent may be put on stage" (Stein 1995:136).

As stated above, these are necessary conditions for a potential topic change. In cognitive terms, a topic is

> a prominent conceptualization which acts as a kind of cognitive anchoring point; other [...] conceptualizations are brought into the discourse by virtue of their perceived ties to the reference point. (Kemmer 1995:58)

In an inversion, however, not always — in fact rarely — are the points of departure mere entities, i.e. mere cognitive anchoring *points*. Rather, inversions depart from non-nominal categories (cf. 3.3), i.e. from constituents that are relational rather than nominal in character. It is therefore more precise to speak of a *frame* of reference, which serves as a "search domain" (Langacker 1993:26), in which a new element is subsequently integrated. Nonetheless, a frame of reference must contain a reference point, which links the new to the old ground, and by reference to which a new discourse entity can be anchored and *construed*.

This topic construal process can be performed *subjectively* or *objectively*. In Langacker's (1990) work on subjectivity, a *perspective*, or a point of view, in discourse subsumes *orientation* and *vantage point* (cf. p.6). He introduces a subjective-objective dichotomy in a technical sense, which allows for a treatment of any viewing arrangement, or of any construal of discourse entities, in terms of this perspective or viewpoint involved. The basic idea is that discourse entities as elements of conception are accessed or *conceptualised* by the language user, who is the *subject* of conception. In what Langacker terms the "optimal viewing arrangement" (Langacker 1990:7), this subject, i.e. the speaker or viewer, is only implicit, he is non-salient and "offstage" and hence subjectively construed. The perspective is compared to the wearing of glasses which "fade from my conscious awareness despite their role in determining the nature of the perceptual field" (p.7). By contrast, the discourse entities, which are placed "onstage" in this viewing arrangement independently of the ground of the language user, are objectively construed.

In this sense, the construal of discourse entities by means of inverted predications at first sight looks as if the mechanism were entirely objective. With the exception of exophorically used deictic adverbs, the reader's focus of attention is directed to new topic entities by mere reference to the conceptual scene expressed via language, to the universe of discourse established. The speaker or viewer, by contrast, remains maximally subjective, with the result that "the inherent asymmetry between a perceiving individual and the entity perceived" (Langacker 1990:7) is maximised. In (76) and (78a), for instance, the speaker remains subjective and "offstage"; instead, he assumes the viewpoint of the fronted constituent which is a part of the conceptual scene. By contrast, if, as in (77) and (78b), some part of the ground, e.g. the speaker and/ or the hearer, is put "onstage" or *profiled* (cf. Langacker 1990:10), the ground itself becomes salient, objectively construed and the asymmetry diminishes:

(76) Next come the German Expressionists and the paintings of Nolde and Munch, in particular, have been carefully selected to indicate the important role that this School played in the formation of 20th-century art. (LOB, sc.writ.)

(77) And then we come to the British section which is very revealing (for the French public anyway) in that the accent is much more on arts and crafts than on painting and sculpture. (LOB, sc.writ.)

(78a) These are shocking figures, but even more shocking is the fact that at least half the people behind these crimes will go undetected. (LOB, ed.)

(78b) These are shocking figures, but even more shocking I consider/ you will find/... the fact that at least half the people behind these crimes will go undetected.

An alternative objective construal of the ground is (78c), since explicit reference to the ground by use of a personal pronoun represents "a more detached outlook in which the speaker treats his own participation as being on a par with anybody else's" (Langacker 1990:20):

(78c)   These are shocking figures, but even more shocking to me is the fact that at least half the people behind these crimes will go undetected.

The increase in objectivity as displayed in (78c) supposedly has iconic reasons: "the formal distinction between overt and covert reference to the ground [...] iconically reflects its being construed with a greater or lesser degree of objectivity" (Langacker 1990:20). (78c) is nonetheless much less natural than (78a), given that FI inherently departs from a vantage point which is that of the speaker. Consequently, only if the comparative is not to be anchored to the speaker himself, as in (79), is explicit reference to the ground really necessary:

(79)   More troublesome to German planners is the country's inflation rate, which last month crept above the 4% annual pace tolerated by the Bundesbank, prompting the sharp interest-rate hike. (Time, 20 Jan.92, p.9)

Since a fully inverted clause uses as ground the predicate of the sentence, and not the subject, the access or conceptualisation of discourse entities takes place through reference to *frames* that belong to the conceptual scene established by the discourse. These frames contain their reference *point* implicitly or explicitly. In the latter case, the fronted constituents become particularly long and complex, as, for instance, in (79). By contrast, in (78a) above, the reference point is only implicit. In both cases, empathy with the reference point is established via word order; from this vantage point, the speaker shifts his focus of attention to a discourse entity newly or re-introduced.

It is typical of written texts that the reference point underlying topic construal is less likely to be a part of the real ground itself. Rather, the conceptual scene of the universe of discourse has a "surrogate" (Kemmer 1995:78) ground of its own. Without overt intervention of the speaker, a text can thereby manage its own topic supply. It may thereby look entirely objective, but the perspective involved is nonetheless more subjective than are CWO clauses: similar as in free indirect discourse, this is a kind of "non-speaker subjectivity" (Brinton 1995:173), which the speaker expresses by adopting the viewpoint of an entity from the discourse world established. It will be shown in chapter 5 that this is a characteristic of discourse under conditions of *displacement* (Chafe 1992, 1994) and produces an effect of *displaced immediacy*.

Different types of FI constructions display different forms of focus management and topic entity construal. Deictic presentative inversion does not really possess the topic change potential of lexical predicates, because the ground from where the shift in focus takes place is in fact construed beforehand: it is the — always present — *here and now* of the speaker. Hence, deictic adverbs followed by FI lack a reference point of their own and are mere cataphoric or anaphoric devices. What they do is fulfil functions of *topic supply*, such as topic announcement or summarising. (80), for instance, serves the introduction of sub-topics, (81) provides a specification of the main topic; in both, however, the frame or location to which attention is directed relies entirely on what is accessible by *perception*:

(80) Sadly, the forceps and C-section stories are part of a continuum. [...] Here are some examples. (WashP, 3 Jan.93, p.16)

(81) Back to punch. Here is a standard recipe. (Guardw, 27 Dec.92, p.22)

In terms of subjectivity, reference to *here* and *there*[22] comes closest to an objective construal of the speaker's own ground (cf. Langacker 1990:10).

The lexical inversion types are different in that respect. Their primarily presentative function in discourse rests on a directional, local, or predicative constituent, which anchors a location or frame to a reference point belonging to a previous, the old, ground. From here, a new entity is mentally perceived, either like a dynamic appearance, or the property expressed is static and the focus of attention shifted to its existence. Locating the new object of focus is always a matter of *conception*.

As regards the focus management effect of these constructions and their contribution to the structure of a discourse, different contexts and genres make different uses of the mechanism. First, there is quite a basic use, which I call the *procedural* use of inversion, whereby the speaker instructs the addressee to mentally reconstruct a certain lay-out of a place. The predicates are concrete locative relations, but, due to a displacement from the situation itself, a conceptual reconstruction in the mind of the addressee is required. Such uses of FI are found, for instance, in descriptions of apartment lay-outs, such as described by Linde/Labov (1975). Interestingly, the typical sequence is to start with an objective construal of the real (speaker/hearer) ground and to let a row of FIs subsequently follow. The reference point itself does then not need to be explicitly mentioned, but can consist of where the centre of attention currently is. An illustration is (82):

(82) <u>You</u> walk into a long, narrow foyer, leading into a smaller, squarer foyer, eating place, dinette-area. And <u>to the right is my kitchen</u>, and <u>to the left [is] my living room</u> [...]. [= Linde/Labov 1975:(5)]

It is symptomatic of this procedural use of FI that it displays several FIs in a row, whereby the whole sequence becomes something like an "imaginary guided tour" (Drubig 1988:87). The "camera movement" effect guarantees step-by-step acquaintance with the place described. Typical contexts of this kind of use are guidebooks or exhibitions reviews, in general any part of a discourse where a visual impact reading is desirable. From my corpus, an instance is the passage given in (83):

(83) I was very much aware of this as I stood, a few weeks ago, in the "Ring", the Market Place of the Old City.
The temptation to find "sermons in stones" was almost irresistible. <u>There, in the centre of the "Ring", stands a magnificent statue of Jan Hus</u>, the Bohemian reformer and martyr who, in 1406, went to the stake rather than renounce what the Council of Constance had judged to be his heresies. <u>On his left is the Tyn Church</u>, austerely Gothic, and a symbol of the Hussite reform movement of which it was the spiritual centre in the fifteenth century. <u>On the other side of the "Ring", stands one of the many Baroque Churches</u>, which in Prague bear witness to the Catholic revival of the seventeenth century.
But that is not all. <u>Linking the "Ring" with the south bank of the Ultava river is a splendid modern thoroughfare</u> cut towards the end of the nineteenth century through the heart of what was formerly the Prague Ghetto. And <u>at the far end, high on the north bank of the river, stands a colossal figure of Joseph Stalin</u>, forever looking down towards the Market Place [...]. (LOB, bbe.)

FIs in procedural use produce a rather "inflated" effect. Frequent shifts of attention or focus probably induce an addressee not to spend too much effort on, not to pay too much attention to, the individual discourse items. This makes sense, as in (83), as long as concrete locational settings are the concern of the discourse, so that all predications are of roughly equal relevance, and the topic entities introduced of roughly equal topicality.

A more sophisticated variant of the procedural use arises when FIs occur, not directly in a row, but at the beginning of separate textual units. In (84), for instance, they correspond to the presentation of a spatial unit each:

(84) This exhibition of 'Les Sources du 20ème Siècle' has been so well planned and displayed that one is continually startled and excited by the contrasting schools and groups of artists that confront one as one moves on from room to room. [...]
Next come the German Expressionists and the paintings of Nolde and of Munch, in particular, [...] Principal among the number of exhibits lent to the Museum of Modern Art by the Victoria and Albert Museum, is an enchanting tapestry, designed by Voysey and which was executed, in 1899, by [...] Nearby are hung a few small water-colours and drawings by Klee. This is [...]. (LOB, sc.writ.)

The structure of (84) follows the lay-out of the museum, which, like in a procedural sequence, is mentally reproduced by viewing from one section to the next. Each section is mentally located in relation to the previous one. The inversions in (84) therefore perform a real *topic change* function: they differ from the procedural use in that they exploit the shift in viewpoint not only for a visual impact reading, but to create cohesive links between textual parts. Deictic adverbs such as *next* or *nearby* create internal conjunctive relations, while the more complex fronted constituents such as *principal among the numbers of exhibits...* rely on lexical cohesion: the inclusive relation of *exhibition* and *exhibits*, the text-internal location expressed by *among*, as well as the contrastive relation implied by premodifying *principal*, which creates some kind of hierarchical text structure. Due to the frames of reference, to which inversion anchors the construal of topic entities, the nature of the links is specified by the relational information contained in them.

In genres that are not particularly prone to the special procedural usage, the majority of lexical presentative FIs have such a topic change function; they must thus be said to do more than direct the observer's view — or "move the camera" — from one location to the next. Like in (84), FIs in topic change use can still express what could marginally be considered a location, i.e. something which has a physical correspondence in external reality. In that case, external relations or ideational meaning gain additional textual and interpersonal significance, by virtue of being used as points of departure for the beginning of textual units.

However, the locative relations can also be "made up" by the speaker, i.e., in fact be internal relations merely claimed to exist among discourse entities. In (85), for instance, the inversion expresses an additive cohesive link which holds only discourse-internally. It thereby not only has a topic change function, but also contributes to the structure of the discourse:

(85) Several hundred thousand people have left the country to stay with friends or relations working abroad. <u>On top of this are thousands</u> who have fled the draft, the families of 36,000 Yugoslav army officers being moved from Croatia and Slovenia, [...]. (Econ, 11 Jan.92, p.24)

Thus, as soon as a text no longer focusses on concrete physical conditions of place, the discourse function of lexical presentative FI consists of a *topic change* plus a potential *structure-building* function. Locative relations contribute to structuring a text, by expressing more or less complex relations among topics and managing the reader's attention accordingly. The natural salience of the anchoring-point raises expectations that, on the one hand, the anchoring point is now put aside as topic and that, on the other, the discourse entity introduced will be subject to treatment in subsequent discourse. Finally, there must be a relation between those topics which is valuable enough to be explicitly expressed. This is typically the case with hierarchical relations, whereby the focus of attention is not only diverted, but directed towards a more prominent part of the discourse. An example for this is (86):

(86) [...] many other prominent contenders for the Premiership in the radical sector of the party.
Mr. Iain Macleod, [...].
Mr. Reginald Maudling [...].
Mr. Edward Heath, [...].
And Viscount Hailsham, [...].
Lord Home [...].
   <u>Over them all is Mr. Macmillan</u>, silent about his own future. In about 18 months or so he will have to make it clear to the Conservative Party whether he [...]. (LOB, ed.)

Both FI occurrences in (85) and (86) contain explicit mention of a reference point: by pronominal, meaning "in focus" (cf. Gundel et al. 1993:275), reference in (86), and by demonstrative, meaning "activated" (p.275), reference in (85). This supports the assumption that the discourse entity whose viewpoint is adopted is relatively salient, and it implies an "optimal viewing arrangement" in Langacker's (1990:7) sense quoted above: the speaker is entirely subjective and topic construal entirely objective. Alternatively, the reference point could be only implicit. This is frequently the case if the FI is following a directional adverb, such as in the beginning of (87), which has already been discussed in section 4.1.2.2:

(87)   Out came the journal and in it went Ann's own description of the scene. (BRW, bbe.)

(87) is an example in which the referential part of the text's surrogate ground is not explicitly put "onstage" and topic construal no longer entirely objective: in addition to the *topic change* and *structure-building* functions, what further takes place is the *creation* of a *reference point*. The point of view which the speaker adopts is subjectively constructed, induced by inversion which serves as an instruction to this end. The strong deictic effect which FI produces after directional adverbs is symptomatic of this mechanism.

The FI type which quite commonly involves an implicit, as opposed to an explicit, reference point is lexical predicative inversion. In lexical predicates, the frame of reference is not a mere location, which in principle has as "location for the camera" a place in the outside world, but a property assigned to the subject of the clause. One could thus speak of predicative inversion departing from *anchor predicates*. As noted earlier on examples (78c) and (79), repeated below, anchor predicates can contain overt reference to the speaker's own ground, as in (78c), or to the "surrogate" ground of some other character, as in (79):

(78c)   These are shocking figures, but even more shocking to me is the fact that at least half the people behind these crimes will go undetected.

(79)   More troublesome to German planners is the country's inflation rate, which last month crept above the 4% annual pace tolerated by the Bundesbank, prompting the sharp interest-rate hike. (Time, 20 Jan.92, p.9)

These thus represent objective departures of the topic construal process induced by lexical predicative inversion.

In the majority of anchor predicates, however, there is only an implicit reference point: either due to a local meaning of the predicate again, as in (88), or, more characteristically, due to the special semantics of most fronted AdjPs and predicative PPs. Predominantly, these are of a commenting or evaluating nature, whereby they are inherently — and mostly subjectively — anchored. Adjectives typically followed by FI are, for instance, *important, shocking, troublesome* and the like, which, as illustrated by (78a), repeated here as (89), have an underlying experiencer (*to X*) or gain an even more evaluating, subjective meaning by virtue of being fronted, as in (90):

(88) Also present [implied: at the event] is a London journalist who arrived two hours earlier [...]. (LOB, rev.)

(89) These are shocking figures, but even more shocking [implied: to the commentator] is the fact that at least half the people behind these crimes will go undetected. (LOB, ed.)

(90) Most charming [implied: to the reviewer] was his tongue-in-cheek "Unheimliche Geschichten" (1920), five ghost stories with a light touch, [...]. (LOB, rev.)

This supports my claim made above that there is more to the large share of comparatives, superlatives and otherwise modified predicates followed by FI than their being marked as relatively discourse-familiar. Rather, it is the viewpoint of an entity either of the ground (the speaker) or of the surrogate ground (some character) that is implied or explicitly mentioned in inverted comparative and superlative predications: in the end, it always takes an evaluating subject to judge *X as more... than Y* (= *to me* or *to Z*). Thus, (89) and (90) introduce topics subjectively, i.e. from the viewpoint of the speaker who remains "offstage", while reference to a character's evaluation, as in (79), can only be made objectively.

Ultimately, fronted predicates can even be said to have a twofold anchor, the second one being the presuppositional set evoked (cf. 4.1.2.3), responsible for a meaning of contrast. This second reference point is most of the time implicit, since it is the inversion itself which evokes the set of competing candidates: (91a), already discussed in section 4.1.2, automatically receives the contrastive interpretation of (91b). In principle, however, "likeness" is always a referential property (cf. Halliday/Hasan 1976): "a thing cannot just be 'like'; it must be 'like something'" (p.78). Comparatives thus always imply a form of reference, implicitly, as in (89) and (90), or explicitly mentioned, as in (92):

(91a) In the loss of focus on the central bilateral relationship with Japan lies the real misfortune of the Bush trip. (IHT, 13 Jan.92, p.4)

(91b) In the loss of focus on the central bilateral relationship with Japan — and in nothing else — lies the real misfortune of the Bush trip.

(92) More important than Japanese concessions, many business executives on the trip believed, was the event's symbolism — a point that even the disappointed Big Three chairmen underscored. (NW, 20 Jan.92, p.24)

One can conclude on lexical predicative inversion that it also performs topic change and structure-building functions in discourse and that the latter is even the predominant task. In addition, the creation of reference point is often implied by a predicative inversion: since ascribing a property to a discourse entity is an inherently speaker-based process and always has a component of evaluation or comment, there is an inherent proneness to implicit reference points only, hence to subjective grounding mechanisms.

Finally, the anaphoric/cataphoric types of FI, under which I have subsumed all inversions following a pronominal, correlative or comparative item, do not produce a comparable viewpoint effect. They do not have the same function of directing the focus of attention from one discourse item, or a ground, to the next. Instead, they merely focus the subject occurring at the end of a grammaticalised construction, and this is triggered by a grammatical function word. Topic construal in these cases is at most an aside, as in (93), a mere coordination, as in (94), or some kind of summary, as in (95):

(93) Czech and Polish musicology have fairly long traditions and very high standards, as indeed has Soviet musicology, [...]. (LOB, sc.writ.)

(94) Maitland as Superintendent of Airships appears to have been left on the fringes <u>as was Masterman</u> after he transferred from the Navy to the R.A.F. [...]. (LOB, sc.writ.)

(95) <u>Such, at any rate, is Mr Hartmann's opinion.</u> (LOB, bbe.)

Anaphoric and cataphoric adverbs represent a purely textual device and merely point back and forth. Therefore, they cannot involve a particular viewpoint, let alone produce a change in it, since the ground from where they depart is a textual link, an objectively given part of the discourse. There is no real choice in fronting them either, thus no subjective meaning attached to that position. The construal of discourse entities by means of anaphoric/cataphoric FI must therefore be considered an entirely objective process, during which the speaker remains entirely subjective. This explains, by the way, why anaphoric and cataphoric adverbs do not occur in free indirect discourse, as noted by Fillmore (1981). To use his examples, (96) can be interpreted from a speaker's or, alternatively, from a character's ("her") point of view, while (97) "has to be taken as the speaker informing the addressee that he perceived both persons as angry" (Fillmore 1981:161):

(96) He looked into her eyes. He seemed angry. [= (43)]

(97) He looked into her eyes. He seemed angry, and <u>so did she</u>. [= (44)]

(Fillmore 1981)

4.2.4 *Markedness, unexpectedness and emotive meaning*
The viewpoint meaning of FI as described so far directly derives from the relative ordering of discourse entities, whereby the speaker attaches a perspective to them. The process of reordering itself, however, produces a further effect, which arises from the status of inversion within the English language system: almost all inverted structures bear a component of emotivity. Since most of them have a CWO counterpart, they involve the breaking of expectations about the use of an unmarked sentence pattern and, accordingly, concerning "normal" discourse conditions. There thus has to be something newsworthy about the use of an inversion to justify this departure from the norm. This may be a topic change, entailed by an instruction to produce a change in focus, or the particular prominence of a discourse item, requiring an instruction which attracts special attention to it. In any case, it is plausible to assume that "the cost of an extra, perceptible [...] signal is indeed worth

incurring only when there is a need to prevent the hearer from coming to a likely — but erroneous — conclusion" (Garcia 1994:334).

This has several consequences for the overall discourse meaning of the construction. First, the grammaticalised word order system of Modern English has an unmarked sentence pattern which usually correlates with discourse expectations such as continuity of discourse participants (cf. Fox 1985) or referential predictability (Givón 1988). By contrast, inversion, which deviates from this pattern, will be used when normal discourse expectations fail to be met. As has been shown for word order systems of different languages (e.g., Givón (ed.) 1985), relative unmarkedness tends to identify topic continuity and foregrounded material, while relative markedness points to topic shifts, backgrounded material, digressions or turns within the structure of the text. The same goes for a change of perspective: while sameness in form usually reflects a constant perspective (cf. Garcia 1994:337), any deviation from a norm is apt to signal a departure from it, and is thereby a natural symptom of topic change, subjective viewpoint, or change in focus of attention.

As argued in Stein (1995), the breaking of normal discourse expectations furthermore has "a clear affectual component" (p.137). The same idea is put forward by Garcia (1994:338): presumably, the use of marked forms "jointly reflects a property of the ‚scene' described and the speaker's concern with that property". This is implied in the speaker-based, hence subjective, meaning inherent in reordering and adding to the ideational content of a clause. FI thus combines a presentative function, which is "naturally" realised by inverted word order, and an expectation-breaking and thereby emotive function, which arises from its marked status. SAI, by contrast, in particular the constituent-focussing type, is more exclusively emotionally expressive: it reflects the concern of the speaker with the relative weight or prominence of a single element from the clause.

A further aspect whereby inversion creates emotive meaning arises from the component parts of it, notably of FI. On the one hand, FI shifts those types of constituents to the front of the clause which, in English, are exempt from subject status and are thereby unexpected in their discourse role of departure for topic construal. On the other hand, the referent of the subject, due to its marked position, is signalled to be unexpected as well, which means that in principle some other potential referent should have been more likely or expected. This is what prepares the reader for a change in focus and underlies the "camera-movement" explicated above, and it thereby makes it possible to shift (back) to topics that are already known, to focus discourse entities anew.

Finally, the analysis of inversion as expressing emotive meaning is supported by what has been said elsewhere on expressive syntax in general. Banfield (1982), for instance, attributes exclusion from embedded clauses to an "E-node",[23] reflecting "syntax of expression" (p.37ff.). This status is attributed not only to structure-preserving transformations, including inversions, but also to addressee-oriented and exclusively expressive linguistic items, such as exclamations, subjectless imperatives, addressee-oriented adverbials and the like. The status of expressive syntax brings up several syntactic properties that clearly apply to FI. Most importantly, there is the lack of a truth-value and its formal correlate, the incapacity to be negated: where "subjectivity is expressed [...] nothing is asserted or denied" (Banfield 1982:41). As stated earlier, FI, in contrast to CWO, is indeed generally not acceptable with a negated predication. Instead, the truth-value of a presentative, an existential scale (cf. 4.1.2.1), sentence must be understood to constitute its reference, i.e., reference in fully inverted sentences is established, but not relied upon. Further symptoms of expressive syntax are the absence of compound tenses in inversions, which also "testifies to the 'presentative' or initiating nature of these constructions" (Stein 1995:138), and of transitive verbs, which "have too much content" (Schmidt 1980:295) themselves. Of the restrictions that hold for embedded constructions, it is, in particular, the incapacity to occur in an internal causal adverbial clause that can be related to an expressive kind of meaning.

To sum up, inversions have been characterised in this and the preceding sections as a device of emotivity and subjectivity, the latter in Banfield's (1982) intuitive understanding as well as in Langacker's (1990) technical sense. By the use of an FI, the speaker does not need to appear "onstage", but can nonetheless adopt a viewpoint from within the universe of discourse and take a perspective of his own on the states and events which he describes. An SAI construction focusses a constituent by virtue of bringing it to the frontposition, thereby expressing directly that — and how — the speaker is affected by this item. There nonetheless remain substantial differences between the kinds of speaker-based meaning produced by FI as opposed to SAI, as can be seen from a divergence between them, as concerns the matter of their embeddability, noted by Green (1976). After negated first person matrix clauses, an FI, as in (98), is acceptable, while an SAI, as in (99) and (100), would be not:

(98)   I didn't realise that standing in the corner was a black umbrella.
        [= (71b)]

(99)   *   I didn't realise that not a bite had she eaten. [= (70c)]

(100)   *   I didn't realise that never before had prices been so high. [= (70d)]

(Green 1976)

This means that, in an FI, the speaker can be simultaneously the subject of the matrix clause, who is not aware of the fact expressed by the embedding, and nonetheless — as the speaker — adopt his own perspective. The subjective and emotive meaning carried by FI is attached to the discourse world established. SAI, by contrast, directly expresses how the speaker himself is affected by the negative focus of the predication.

4.3 Summary: a functional classification of English inversion

The different types of inversion as discussed so far can now be summarised in a functional classification. In this classification, the FI types behave more like a continuum than as distinct categories according to the criteria used; therefore, they are subclassified only on the basis of prototypical functions, such as identified in the course of the analysis. However, this does not mean that there are no "squishy" transitions between them.

Figure 1 identifies six functional prototypes of inversion, which come about through the combination of two basic features:

(a)   The horizontal axis of the matrix gives the different kinds of *anchoring mechanisms* which occur as departures of an inverted clause. Full inversions have points of departure which are either *deictic* (including text-internal reference), in that they rely on a situation of *perceptual* access (which can also be the text itself), or *lexical*, in which case a reference situation is provided from the universe of discourse, i.e. is *conceptually* accessed. Anaphoric/cataphoric FI as well as those SAI types that combine an anaphoric/cataphoric plus a constituent-focussing function exploit the sentence-initial position following the same principle, though with a different effect: they also constitute linking mechanisms, "deictic" in a somewhat broader sense, but their primary effect is not in all cases to place the subject in end (focus) position. Constituent-focussing SAI, by contrast, has a (lexical) part of the predication fronted, which thereby gains additional prominence.

(b) The vertical axis contains the different *predication types*, reflecting the various distinctions brought forward as existential vs. quality scale readings of sentences, or presentative statements vs. "real" predications. Basically, this difference is determined by the context, and only partly encoded by linguistic signals of relative salience of the constituents involved. In the case of unambiguously local (deictic or lexical) points of departure, which prototypically introduce non-salient discourse entities, a predication is predominantly *presentative*, which corresponds to an exclusive existential scale reading. For this, the possibility to occur with lexical verbs is the clearest indicator. The *predicative* inversion type, by contrast, combines an existential scale reading with a statement inherently ascriptive in kind. Finally, *non-subject-focus* predications are sentences which are not concerned with a presentative process at all; they have a clear quality scale reading and focus the fronted items as well as the constituents following the verb.

The different types are numbered in the order of treatment under 4.1. One example of each type is repeated in the following:

I. deictic presentative

(7) The economy, Berlin, the Common Market- here are three issues whose gravity has during the past few days led to regretful sighings over the impracticability of a National Government. (LOB, ed.)

II. lexical presentative

(15) The klondikers and the trawlers pursued the fish round the Scottish coast, stopping at the tiny port of Ullapool, going to Ireland, to Donegal and Cork. In their wake sprouted a service industry of second-hand goods — everything from clothes, televisions and microwave ovens to fridges. (Guardw, 3 Jan.93, p.5)

III. lexical predicative

(23) More troublesome to German planners is the country's inflation rate, which last month crept above the 4% annual pace tolerated by the Bundesbank, prompting the sharp interest-rate hike. (Time, 20 Jan.92, p.9)

IV. anaphoric/cataphoric

(43) But the main elements have been retained and so, most importantly, has been the standard. (Times, 15 Dec.92, p.35)

V. anaphoric/cataphoric + constituent-focussing

(51) When Britain tried to make clear that something else was in prospect — [...] — Ribbentrop was dismissed. Nor did Hitler seem to need much persuading. (Guardw, 20 Dec.92, p.28)

VI. constituent-focussing

(54) [...] tax than you need." Truly are the tax gatherers an unbeloved people. (LOB, ed.)

The link in *figure 1* between types II and III indicates the close connection between lexical predicative and lexical presentative inversion, static locatives being also properties of the subject and real (ascriptive) predicates also serving a presentative purpose if followed by FI. Historically, one can assume a pre-existing locative, inherently presentative, type of inversion, from which predicative FI has later emerged as an innovation, probably as an extension of it. The joint mechanism underlying both types of FI can be explained in the

predication \ anchoring	deictic	lexical
presentative	I deictic	**II** lexical presentative see *figure 2*
predicative	**IV** anaphoric/ cataphoric	**III** lexical predicative
non-subject-focus	**V** anaphoric/ cataphoric + constituent-focussing	**VI** constituent-focussing

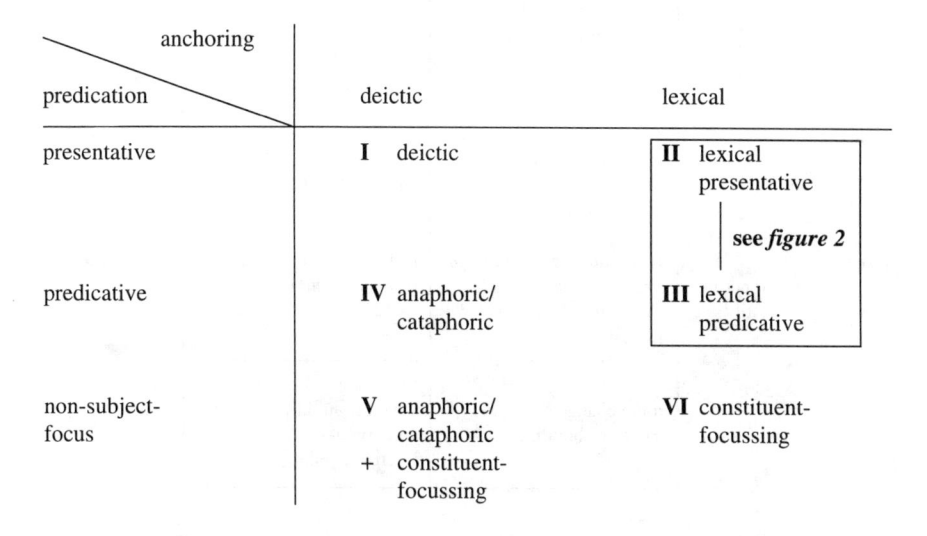

Figure 1. *A functional classification of English inversion*

light of those contexts in which both constructions typically occur, namely in discourse under conditions of displacement. Topics which do not arise out of the immediate environment of both speaker and hearer can be construed by FI following lexical constituents, permitting the speaker to stay out of the text and to nonetheless adopt a perspective from within it. The process can take on different forms, discussed in section 4.2 and summarised in *figure 2*.[24] There are again two axes of variation:

(a) The vertical axis reflects semantic alternatives of the fronted constituents, which basically reach from real *frames of reference* (directions and locations) to *anchor predicates* (properties). The transition is symptomatically accompanied by decreasing tolerance — and importance[25] — of full

frames of reference	(surrogate) grounding	objective	subjective	
direction	verbal-dynamic	*Off to the United Nations in the Congo goes a load of 1,000 lb bombs sent with compliments [...]* [= (13)]	*Out came the journal [...]* [= (12)]	increasing
location		*On the walls of his office hung pictures of sporting celebrities [...]* [= (18)]	*On the other side are forces whose time came [...]* [= (16)]	relevance for discourse
property	adjectival-static	*Of greater concern to many proliferation experts is the political braindrain [...]* [= (21)]	*[...] even more shocking is the fact that [...]* [= (22)]	structure
		topic change + structure-building	topic change + structure-building + creation of reference point	

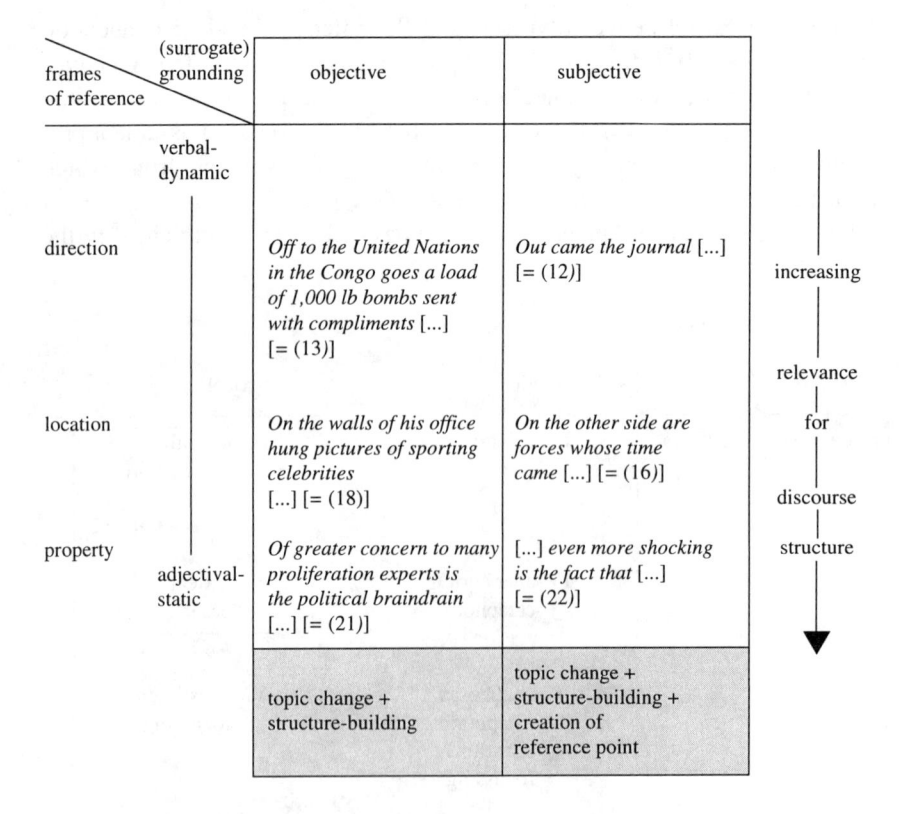

Figure 2. *Mechanisms of topic construal through full inversion*

verbs, and increasing exclusiveness of copular *be*. In these terms, topic construal can be more *verbal-dynamic* or more *adjectival-static* in kind.

(b) The horizontal axis distinguishes between *objective* and *subjective* departures from the new ground, which, in displaced discourse, is most often a "surrogate" ground of the universe of discourse, belonging to a location or character. In addition to the *topic change* function inherent in both presentative and predicative lexical inversion, and adding to the *structure-building* function that the relational information contained in the fronted constituent performs, subjective topic construal involves the *creation of a reference point*.

In contrast to the lexical types illustrated in *figure 2*, which have more complex discourse functions, deictic inversions depart from the speaker's own ground and anaphoric/cataphoric inversion from a purely textual, grammaticalised device. They have therefore been characterised as mere *topic supply* devices.

Finally, *figure 3* illustrates the relation of the formal types of inversion, such as introduced in 3.1.2, and the functional classification developed in this chapter:

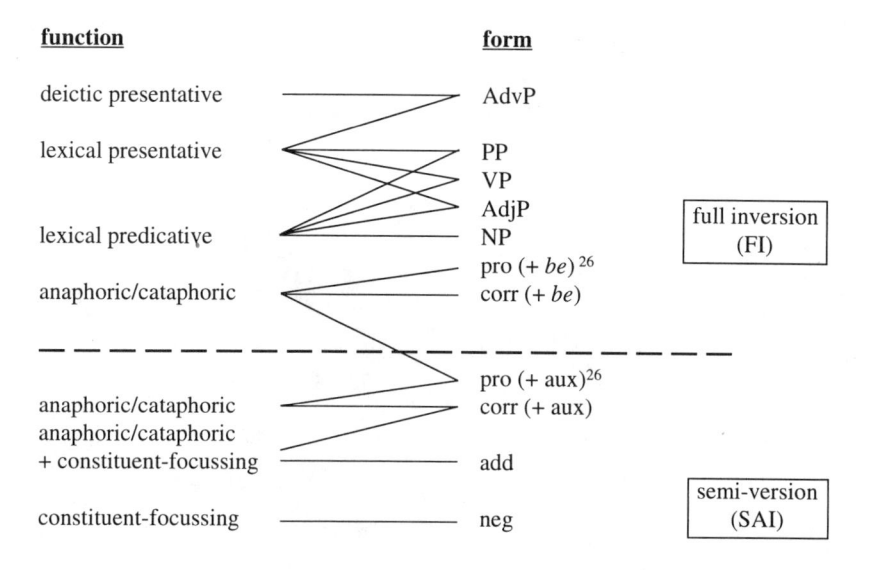

function		form	
deictic presentative	———————	AdvP	
lexical presentative		PP	
		VP	
		AdjP	full inversion
lexical predicative		NP	(FI)
		pro (+ *be*)[26]	
anaphoric/cataphoric		corr (+ *be*)	
		pro (+ aux)[26]	
anaphoric/cataphoric		corr (+ aux)	
anaphoric/cataphoric + constituent-focussing		add	
			semi-version
constituent-focussing	———————	neg	(SAI)

Figure 3. *From a formal to a functional classification*

Chapter 5

Inversion in discourse

This chapter presents the outcome of the previous semantic analysis as tested against the linguistic reality of inversion, i.e. against its actual usage in discourse. It is based on a corpus of naturally-occurring texts, of which the patterns of occurrences of inversion are described and interpreted. On the one hand, it will be shown that there are clear affinities of inversion with certain types of written texts, which allow, though not for predictions, but for a narrowing down of those kinds of contexts in which the construction is more likely to occur. On the other hand, the meaning and discourse function carried by inversions also varies with the context; consequently, a more detailed analysis of the work that inversions do in individual contexts is also necessary. This is undertaken by an illustration of its various usages in political news reporting, based on a selection of texts, in the latter part of this chapter.

In general, the texts that I have used are written, non-fictional discourse only. This may appear to be only a small part of linguistic reality, but discourse or texts[1] vary quite systematically in certain well-defined respects: they are "related along particular situational or functional parameters, such as formal/ informal, interactive/non-interactive, literary/colloquial, restricted/elaborated" (Biber 1988:9). Following Biber, these functional or situational parameters have been called *textual relations*, they find their expression in continua or *dimensions* of linguistic variation. One may, as Biber does, take linguistic co-occurrence patterns as defining textual relations, because "linguistic co-occurrence reflects shared function" (Biber 1989:5), but one can also tackle the issue from the other end: since the focus here is on a single linguistic phenomenon, and since much has already been said about what is presumably its core meaning and function, the semantic claims made so far are directly related to those functional or situational parameters which can be assumed to be particularly relevant. Some of them come from earlier works on inversion, also taken into account in the beginning of section 5.1.

The present chapter has two main objectives: one is to determine a dimension of linguistic variation along which the use of inversion in a limited number of categories of discourse can be shown to vary (5.2). In that context, I shall also touch upon some general issues of text typology and the notion of genre in particular. Classifying discourse is a topic in text linguistics that has some theoretical tradition (cf. Gülich/Raible 1975; Werlich 1976; Isenberg 1978), but it also possesses considerable complexity. My approach is to circumvent the more theoretical intricacies, and to use only a basic distinction between *types* of discourse in terms of structural and functional characteristics on the one hand, and more conventional patterns of usage, i.e. *genres*, on the other. What has furthermore been mentioned as a crucial factor at several points above are the particular conditions of displacement in a text. It is therefore the other aim of this chapter to relate the use of inverted constructions to texts dealing with displaced discourse worlds, using political news reporting as an example (5.3). These aspects of a discourse function have been gained from analyses of individual occurrences, which were more difficult to subject to a strict classificatory scheme. Instead, the point of the discussion is to spell out the typical contributions that inversion makes to building up the structure of a discourse. In 5.4, the overall function of full inversion is summarised as a discourse marker, while, as an outcome of the entire chapter, inversion as a whole is suitably called a marker of subjectivity.

5.1 Inversion and other textual relations

The textual relations named above in Biber's quote have all, more or less, been put into question as regards their validness in systematically accounting for linguistic variation (cf. Biber 1988:24f.). Nonetheless, the following are, by intuition or on the basis of previous works, worthy of consideration as potentially relevant for the usage of inversions: spoken vs. written mode (5.1.1), colloquial vs. literary style (5.1.2), as well as potential differences between British and American English (5.1.3). In sociolinguistics, the former two have the status of registers, i.e. of *intraspeaker* variation, while variation between British and American English constitutes *interspeaker* variation (cf. Bell 1984). Inversion is a phenomenon that comes about through choice; hence the dominance of potentially relevant varieties available to one single speaker. By contrast, the relevance of interspeaker variation gives an idea of the extent to which its usage is also determined by convention.

5.1.1 *Spoken vs. written mode*

Technically speaking, speech and writing differ in *mode*, which does not have to have any a priori functional relevance. Biber (1988:24) claims that "the variation among texts within speech and writing is often as great as the variation across the two modes". Nonetheless, sets of features have repeatedly been developed for summarising the characteristic differences, for instance, by Olson (1981). According to him, speech and writing differ in the following characteristics:

1. permanence
2. detachment
3. absence of feedback
4. nonspecificity
5. tellability
6. organisation
7. formality
8. economy
9. greater precision and detail
10. greater complexity and abstractness of subject matter

(cf. Olson 1981:285)

It is evident that this list includes aspects of speech variation which cannot necessarily be attributed to a difference in mode. In particular, there is considerable overlap between features 6 and 7 and other textual relations, such as genre and style. Nonetheless, organisation and formality, which correspond to an *unplanned/planned* and a *formal/informal* distinction put forward by other authors (e.g., Tannen 1982), are among the properties most frequently referred to in this context. In addition, what is also important is that the spoken mode is generally considered more *interactive* and written discourse more *content-focussed* in kind (cf. Tannen 1982). These three features are thus quite widely accepted as characterising the differences between the spoken and the written mode, but, to account for linguistic variation proper, they are nonetheless not entirely appropriate:

(a) The *formal/informal* distinction also underlies Chafe's (1982, 1985) work on spoken and written English, whereby he identifies four styles of language: informal spoken, formal spoken, informal written, formal written. Thus, formality is not automatically triggered by the use of a certain medium and is in fact better considered a "stylistic" variety (Wardhaugh 1992:48).

(b) The *planned/unplanned* distinction, as a strict consideration of planning time, does not necessarily account for most speech variation phenomena either. Tannen (1982) argues that most linguistic features that are sometimes attributed to matters of planning time can indeed be shown "to be more a matter of register than planning" (p.6). At least, both factors can probably not be held apart in their effect; thus, while one can neglect here the question of planning *time*, planned *character* in terms of a more complex organisation must be taken into account under considerations of discourse structure.

(c) Finally, the *interactive/content-focussed* distinction touches more directly upon the function of a discourse, in particular upon its hearer-orientation and audience involvement. There are in fact some affinities between these properties and some typical forms of speech and writing, such as conversation as opposed to intellectual argument. But audience involvement — or the creation of "subjective knowing" (Tannen 1982:2) — is found in written language as well, for instance in imaginative literature. There is thus no direct correlation between interactive and content-focussed linguistic properties and the spoken and the written mode. Nonetheless, this distinction comes close to providing a parameter whereby a discourse can be characterised as more or less subjective and inducing more or less hearer involvement; it is therefore referred to later again, in 5.2 and 5.3 below.

What is it then that remains to be said about a direct relevance of spoken and written mode in the present context, i.e. for the usage of inversion in discourse? Previous work on inversion creates the impression that the construction in fact mostly occurs in written discourse,[3] this is also confirmed by some glances at, for instance, the London-Lund Corpus.[4] By contrast, Green (1982) "take[s] pains along the way to show that it is not on the basis of spoken vs. written language that speakers discriminate contexts for inversions, but on the basis of colloquial vs. literary language" (p.120). Yet, in the same article, she comments on her experience which made her abandon "natural speech as a primary source of inversions for syntactic studies" (p.123). Equally, Birner's (1992) corpus contains only about 6.5% inversions from spoken sources.[5]

There is a basic situational property that sets apart writing from speech and that better explains the use of most inverted constructions in one rather than the other mode. It is brought up, in particular, in Chafe's (1992, 1994) work on discourse and consciousness. According to him, speech and writing differ in the factors "copresence" and "interaction" of language producer and receiver, which together define the property of *situatedness* (cf. Chafe 1994:44f.): it reflects "the closeness language has to the immediate physical and social situation in which it is produced and received" (p.44). Written discourse is usually *desituated* (cf. Chafe 1994:45), with an important bearing on the relative irrelevance, not only of the location of both writer and reader, but also of their identity.[6]

It is important to note, however, that "it is not that writing is devoid of a context, but that the immediate context in which it is performed is seldom the focus of attention" (Chafe 1992:241). Instead, the primary focus of attention in written discourse is usually a universe of discourse of its own, which is probably the most fundamental reason for an affinity of lexical FI with the written language. In general, focus management and the construal of discourse topics are needed in both modes, but they can be performed either by reference to a shared perceptual field or to lexical information yielding conceptual frames of reference. Presentative constructions as such are thus nothing peculiar to either of the two modes: inversion after *here* (and *there*) is common in conversational discourse as well and is in fact a very unmarked — or "almost invisible" (Green 1982:129) — device there. It reflects conditions of reciprocity where the speaker has to be least explicit about the scene he wants to direct his audience's attention to and is therefore the only FI type that has its origin in discourse conditions typical of oral communication. What is typical of written communication, by contrast, is to let the text perform its own focus management, to supply and change topics by mechanisms of its own. The presence of the author thereby becomes less direct and the focus of attention remains on displaced matters, on the actual universe of discourse that is being dealt with.

This is not to say, however, that non-deictic FIs cannot be found in spoken discourse. Written texts are not in principle more explicit, but, as do all texts, balance "the respective concerns of the writer for expression and the reader for comprehension" (Nystrand 1986:95). A discourse that deals with displaced events by definition has conditions of reciprocity requiring a high degree of explicitness, which lexical FI, among other linguistic devices, can provide. But there is spoken discourse as well that is very similar in that respect, for instance "play-by-play sportscasting" (cf. Green 1982:131f.).

Apart from what are ultimately differences in style or register, what remains to be said about inversion as related to the mode of communication has to do with the complexity or "integrated" character (Chafe 1982) of the constructions. Chafe suggests that, due mainly to matters of speed, "written language tends to have an 'integrated' quality which contrasts with the fragmented quality of spoken language" (Chafe 1982:38), an idea which corresponds to Olson's feature 6, organisation. Birner's (1992, 1994) information-packaging function of FI, as well as Green's functional explanation of inversion after participles as "a manner of sparing words and space" (1982:146), would confirm the idea that the written mode is indeed a more integrated way of language use, taken that these inversions dominate in the written mode. In oral communication, by contrast, discourse organisation makes use of one further important device: intonation. Orientation or anchoring tasks, relative salience of discourse entities, topic changes, prominence of individual constituents as well as the expression of emotions and attitudes can all also be performed by intonational patterns, by prominence, pauses, etc. It is only writing that has to rely solely on linear ordering and syntactic constructions.

As regards the emotive meaning of most inversion types, there might seem to be a contradiction, at least if Green (1982) is right that "trafficking in emotions is generally impossible or taboo in written materials" (p.146). Since FIs, however, are devices that reflect a point of view of the speaker without his overt intervention or comment, they are even particularly well-suited for expressing subjectivity in writing. Historically, they have in fact emerged and expanded within a stylistic ideal that allowed for the intrusion of devices of intensity and emotionality into literary styles (cf. Stein 1995:144f.). Similarly, SAI constructions, especially the quite formal and slightly archaic-sounding types of constituent-focussing SAI, have become characteristics of certain forms of emotional writing. There is thus justification enough to restrict the corpus work to written discourse, and to non-fictional discourse on top of that. Although writing is "hospitable to fiction" (Chafe 1992:241), and fiction thereby in principle hospitable to the use of inversions, fictional texts carry the complexity of an additional, fictional, speaker, which it seemed advisable to avoid. In the present corpus, there is thus in principle only one (non-fictitious) speaker, operating invisibly in the immediate context and dealing with matters displaced from this context. In this basic situation of written non-fictional discourse, by the use of inversions the speaker nonetheless makes his subjective presence felt.

5.1.2 *Colloquial vs. literary style*

This section rests on the findings presented in Green (1982), who, drawing on a collection of more than 360 inversions from various sources, classifies a broad range of inversion types as either belonging to *colloquial* or to *literary* language, or at least to "sound" as such. I use her results and further interpret them here in the light of the semantic and functional claims made so far. It is most important in this context that the distinction of colloquial and literary language constitutes, on the basis of whatever notion of *style*,[7] intraspeaker variation and is therefore variation as to the *uses*, and not to the users (cf. Bell 1984:146).

The same has held for the distinction between spoken and written mode, which is why the issue of style is a direct continuation of the previous discussion. In particular, Green (1982) takes typical or exclusive occurrence in written texts as an indication of *positively literary* inversions (cf. p.123), and occurrence in colloquial speech, dialects or reported speech as an indication of *perfectly colloquial* inversions (cf. p.128). By contrast, her intermediate categories *literary speech* and *colloquial writing* comprise "minority" contexts" or usages "out of the ordinary", i.e. are less directly related to mode. It is in such minority contexts that inversions produce a "literary tone in speech" or a "colloquial tone in writing" (Green 1982:133).

Positively literary inversions occur predominantly in the following types of discourse used in Green's study: memoirs, academic prose, scientific writing, formal essays, legal prose, formal letters, novels, short stories with invisible, omniscient author, journalistic essays. Three of the inversions types assigned to this category also form part of my taxonomy of the phenomenon: two of the constituent-focussing SAI type, exemplified by (1) and (2); and one that has, in 4.1.2.3, been considered the "least locative", or unambiguously predicative, *PP-inversion* type, namely FI following "preposed abstract prepositional phrases"(Green 1982:127), as in (3):

(1) Thus sharply did the terrified three learn the difference between an island of make-believe and the same island come true. [= (5c)]

(2) Bitterly did we repent our decision. [= (10b)]

(3) Of more probable concern to Crane's followers is a feeling Crane didn't come off too well in the first debate. [= (12a)]

(Green 1982)

(1) and (2) belong to the class of those constituents which do not automatically trigger AuxSV order, but receive additional highlighting by virtue of being optionally followed by it. This produces an even stronger emotive colouring, since the marked word order evidently arises out of a speaker-based, subjective choice. In that, (1) and (2) have earlier been characterised as extensions, diachronically possible "re-rises", of the nowadays obligatory SAI type after negative constituents, i.e., after those which are inherently "heavy" or "inbuilt emotional" (cf. 3.2.1).

The literary FI type illustrated in (3) is another case of an extension of a diachronically older inversion type, namely of static locative properties. These have always optionally triggered FI and were argued above (3.2.2 and 4.1.2) to have possibly underlain an extension of FI to nonlocative predicates. Interestingly, there thus seems to be an affinity of the positively literary character of inversions and their arising as extensions of more basic — and pre-existing — types, which are themselves less strongly stylistically marked. Possibly, in that non-obligatory constituent-focussing SAI and predicative *PP-inversion* less naturally derive from factors such as the fronting of inherently heavy items or of real locative settings, they make a speaker-based choice more markedly felt and thereby reflect a high degree of attention paid to linguistic expression. This can plausibly be assumed to be typical of literary language.

This hypothesis is supported by the fact that among the inversion types attributed to literary speech are the "more basic" SAI and FI counterparts of the positively literary ones. Contexts in which literary speech inversions have been found are the following: formal oral narratives and addresses, long re-told stories, pretentious speech, impromptu legal, administrative, academic, and bureaucratic speech. In this category, Green (1982:134ff.) subsumes inversion after negative adverbials, as in (4), and almost all remaining FI types, namely those following AdjPs, participles, as well as locative and directional PPs, as in (5) – (8):

(4) Not until The Book of Splendor (the Zohar) appeared in Spain in the thirteenth century did a formidable metaphysical text on cabalism appear. [= (34b)]

(5) Equally obvious, as pointed out on occasion by Matijevich, are the potential advantages for an incumbent to be able to send out congratulatory resolutions to their constituents. [= (37c)]

(6) Representing Mayberry in the arguments next week will be Stephen P. Hurley, court appointed appellate defender. [= (42c)]

(7) Under this belt, did they but know it, lay the Ruby Eye. [= (39e)]

(8) It burst open, and from it rolled a shining golden egg. [= (40d)]

(Green 1982)

If produced orally, instances like these are claimed "to have an especially strong literary tone in speech" (Green 1982:133), they are thus apparently less strongly marked as belonging to literary language in particular. That they produce a literary effect in speech contexts as those named above probably comes from a written language flavour which is nonetheless attached to them.

The following are typical colloquial writing contexts from which Green has drawn the next set of inversions: personal letters, stream-of-consciousness, indirect free style, 1st person narratives and essays, humorous essays, book reviews. Attributed to this style are SAI following negated NPs, as in (9), some correlative constructions such as (10), as well as FIs following temporal adverbs and PPs, as in (11) and (12), or directional adverbs, as in (13):

(9) 'You took the words out of my mouth,' I said. 'I hammered on the door for over half an hour, but not a tumble did I get.' [= (45a)]

(10) No sooner had I turned my back, a laborious and rather painful procedure these days, than some bright-eyed woman or other rises briskly from her escritoire [...]. [= (46a)]

(11) Now appears The Common Press. [= (51a)]

(12) In '70 came the Vega. [= (49a)]

(13) Up leaped the haggard husband. [= (53e)]

(Green 1982)

The first two types, according to Green, sound "emotional" or "particularly dramatic" (1982:140) and are not natural in formal literary prose; they may occur in writing, but only in rather personal narratives. I agree with the assessment of a strong emotional flavour of, for instance, (9), which can probably be attributed to the fact that by front-shifting negated *NPs* — in contrast to adverbs, which are more commonly found in that position — the speaker signals very immediate concern with this item and its negation. However, the construction is not, as were those exemplified by (1) and (2), a direct extension of another, already grammaticalised, SAI construction, which has itself a written language affinity. It is plausible that such subjective meaning is more typical of direct, emotional interaction.

The FIs in (11) – (13) are less "dramatic", they are colloquial for probably different reasons. On the one hand, as in (11) and (12), temporal adverbs and temporal PPs have above (cf. 4.1.2.1) been said to be more regularly, and from earlier stages of English onwards, followed by FI; this was attributed to the automatic temporal progression of a text, which makes temporal meaning more prone to the basic — and entirely colloquial (see below) — deictic presentative process and to internal conjunctive work. On the other hand, directional adverbs, as in (13), have been shown to produce an additional deictic effect, which is probably why Green characterises them as "even more" colloquial (1982:141) than the others and finds that they are "extraordinarily common in picture books for young children" (p.142). They are thus typical of a more oral style, and in particular of oral story-telling, because they create excitement and expectation.

Finally, perfectly colloquial inversions are classified to comprise inversions after *here* and (stressed) *there*, as well as SAI following pronominal *so* and *neither*, with the following typical contexts of occurrence: impromptu conversation, service encounters, relaxed, extended casual conversation. The colloquial character, or origin in interactive speech, of deictic presentative inversions is not surprising, taken that the reference they make is originally perception-based. However, it is my impression that the textual metaphorical usage discussed above has neutralised any stylistic effect of "sounding" particularly colloquial or oral, so that deictic presentative inversion occurs in virtually all kinds of contexts. That pronominal adverbs are considered especially "common in speech" (Green 1982:130), by contrast, probably has to do with their function of a purely textual and cohesive device (cf. 4.2.3); as such they are freely available independent of matters of mode or style. In contrast to *as* and *nor*, however, *so* and *neither* seem to have become particularly typical of interactive speech, as in (14):

(14) A: You never clear your dishes off anymore.
B: Neither do you. [= Green 1982:(21b)]

For all those stylistic characterisations, Green assumes a range of "functional", "circumstantial" and "conventional" (1982:145ff.) factors at work, which it is not necessary to repeat here. But the variety of factors that one may think of suggests a complex interplay of functional motivations on the one hand, and structural prerequisites arising out of diachronic developments on the other.

5.1.3 *British vs. American English*

Syntactic differences between the two interspeaker varieties British and American English have not been studied in the same detail as have, for instance, differences in vocabulary, pronunciation or intonation. Algeo (1988) attributes this to the fact that "they are the least numerous, the least salient, and the least confusing to speakers of one variety encountering a text composed in the other variety" (p.2). Moreover, there is reason to believe that "linguistic differences among genres [or styles] are likely to be larger than differences between British and American English of the same genre" (Biber 1987:116). In fact, syntactic constructions, as long as they are in principle acceptable in both varieties, are not likely to be perceived as Briticisms or Americanisms. Nonetheless, individual patterns may vary in terms of their frequency and likelihood of occurrence and form part of different registers within the stylistic competence of both speakers and hearers. That is what may be true of inverted constructions in British compared to American English: inversions occur in both varieties and do therefore not mark one variety as such, but they may of course differ in their frequency of usage or their contexts of occurrence.

On the basis of the corpus, however, no dramatic discrepancy can be stated for any of the text categories: as shown in *table 1*, an equal number of samples of British and American English from five text categories of the LOB and the Brown corpus[8] yields surprisingly similar frequencies in FI as well as SAI occurrences in the majority of text cases. In both varieties, based on an overall corpus size of 146 text samples or 292,000 words each, there is also roughly the same total density of inversions.

Table 1. *British and American uses of FI and SAI in five text categories of the LOB and the Brown corpus*

	rep. LOB	rep. BRW	ed. LOB	ed. BRW	rev. LOB	rev. BRW	bbe. LOB	bbe. BRW	sc.writ. LOB	sc.writ. BRW	**total LOB**	**total BRW**
number of texts	34	34	27	27	17	17	34	34	34	34	**146**	**146**
FI	35	36	14	28	23	23	49	42	23	29	**144**	**158**
SAI	8	7	35	26	15	15	42	21	31	32	**131**	**101**
total	**43**	**43**	**49**	**54**	**38**	**38**	**91**	**63**	**54**	**61**	**275**	**259**

The categories 'press: reportage' and 'press: reviews' provide particularly parallel results for both varieties. To a somewhat lesser extent, this goes for 'scientific writing' as well, while a more substantial discrepancy must be noted between the varieties in the categories 'press: editorials' and 'belles-lettres, biography, essays'. Both findings — a striking overall similarity in usage and minor differences in two out of five text categories — shall briefly be discussed, in particular in the light of the conclusions that come from Biber's (1987, 1988) work, based on his multi-feature/multi-dimensional analysis of the same corpora,[9] on differences between British and American English.

Testing out three functional parameters of linguistic variation, Biber has found that there are substantial differences between the two varieties for those linguistic features that set apart "interactive" from "edited text", as well as "abstract" from "situated content". Here is his conclusion on the peculiarities of British as opposed to American English:

> British written genres tend to have the surface characteristics of prescribed good writing to a greater extent than the corresponding American written genres. [...] British genres are characterized by fewer colloquial or interactive features than the American genres [... and] exhibit fewer features associated with a highly nominal and jargon-ridden style [...]. (Biber 1987:116)

By contrast, there is a third parameter of linguistic variation, the one distinguishing "reported" from "immediate" style, which is "apparently not important in distinguishing between British and American writing" (Biber 1987:116). Significantly, it is this parameter that "separate[s] the fictional genres, which refer to a reported, narrative context [...], from the other genres, which can refer to an immediate, physically present context" (Biber 1987:116).

The striking overall uniformity in the use of inversions across British and American writing suggests that inversions could belong to this dimension of linguistic variation as well. This would, in particular, account for the almost equal numbers of FI occurrences in four out of the five text categories: their usage would be less a matter of convention or interspeaker variation; instead, it is mostly determined by their function in reported as opposed to immediate style. This is in line with what has been said above, with the assumption that FI is a device typically found in discourse dealing with displaced events, and performing a natural focus management function in those contexts.

This is not to say that there may not be differences among genres within the two varieties in question, differing via convention in their need to exploit the discourse functions of inversion. But if the origins of a construction are functional, rather than conventional, there should be less interspeaker variation in its usage in the same categories of discourse than across them. And the same in principle goes for SAI constructions, also available in both varieties. Their actual usage, expressing grammaticalised prominence and clause linkage as well as emphasis, may nonetheless be determined to a considerable extent by (culture-specific) genre conventions about the degree of emotion and subjectivity that a text category permits. This could explain why in two out of five categories of British and American writing SAI occurrence is subject to interspeaker variation.

In the same respect, and supporting Biber's above-quoted claim for greater prescriptivism in British writing, one finds an explanation for the fact that reportages and reviews differ least in their numbers of inversions, and the other text categories somewhat more substantially. Out of the five text categories considered, reportages and reviews are the ones most clearly defined by a distinct textual function. More importantly, this primary function relatively clearly determines their proneness to overt subjectivity and speaker-based contents: oversimplifying a bit, subjectivity is least compatible with the intention underlying a press reportage, while reviews by definition express comment and evaluation and are inherently subjective. It is plausible that, in case of those clear-cut textual functions, cultural traditions or genre conventions play a less important role.

In the case of editorials and scientific texts, however, American writing shows a slightly stronger preference for FI uses; perhaps it accepts their marked status, their being departures from a norm, more easily. In particular, and this can be seen in more detail in *table 2*, American English more readily

Table 2. British and American uses of formal inversion types based on a corpus of 146 sample texts (= 292,000 words) each

	LOB	BRW	total
AdvP	31	24	55
PP	81	90	171
VP	14	27	41
AdjP	18	17	35
total FI	144	158	302
pro	39	29	68
corr	24	19	43
add	35	26	61
neg	33	27	60
total SAI	131	101	232
total inversion	**275**	**259**	**534**

employs *VP-inversion* and *PP-inversion*, which often involve the front-shifting of quite complex, conjoined or otherwise, constituents (cf. 4.1.2.3). This may be a correlate of the heavily nominal style noted by Biber (1987) about American writing and which, according to traditional writing prescriptions, is what "students and careful writers are admonished to avoid" (p.116). Thus, where genre conventions rather than natural necessities of focus management are at work, the use of FIs in American as opposed to British English indeed seems to confirm that "writing prescriptions appear to play a greater role in the British genres than in the corresponding American genres" (Biber 1987:116).

In the case of scientific writing, the differences between the two varieties are less distinct. Again, an explanation could be that a predominantly informative intention generally prohibits subjectivity and speaker point of view in most scientific texts. However, in this category, presumably there also remains a fair amount of variation, not only between the two varieties, but between, for instance, the usage in articles as opposed to the usage in monographs.[10] It may thus just be that, out of the five categories of the LOB and the Brown corpus, 'scientific writing' and, certainly, 'belles-lettres, biography, essays' are too heterogeneously composed to allow for any general statement in terms of genre conventions differing between British and American writing.

There is one further difference that *table 1* and, more distinctly, the splitting up of the results into the formal inversion types, presented in *table 2*, reveal: British English has a stronger preference for all types of SAI constructions, i.e. for the grammaticalised ones. Especially in editorials and scientific texts, British English uses anaphoric and cataphoric linkage as well as constituent-focussing through SAI to distinctly higher extents. This means that it must not be avoidance of marked word order in general, or of the emotive meaning thereby expressed, which characterises British writing, but that there is mainly reluctance to condense information through FI constructions. SAI constructions, by contrast, could even be part of a stylistic ideal of "good" writing. Such matters of *convention* nonetheless play the more negligible role; they probably operate within the confines that the functional factors leave, while, overall, the results presented here suggest that interspeaker variation of inversion is primarily determined by its *function*.

5.2 Inversion and categories of discourse

This section deals with the occurrence of inverted constructions in a number of selected categories of discourse, based on five sub-corpora from the LOB and the Brown corpus. Since the patterns of inversion usage are related here to relevant characteristics of the text categories, 5.2.1 casts a brief look at principles of discourse classification and how discourse typologies have traditionally been built up: on the one hand, this is to briefly clarify the terminology used, while, on the other, it will become evident that the structure of the LOB and the Brown corpus does not follow any homogeneous typological principle. 5.2.2 presents the quantitative results for the patterns of use of inversions in the five categories, and attempts an interpretation and illustration of the most typical cases of occurrence.

5.2.1 *Discourse types and discourse typologies*

Using the terms *text* and *discourse* as synonyms leads to some difficulties in classifying discourse. Many approaches to discourse analysis published in English draw the distinction between *discourse type* and *text type*: the former notion is "connected with the discourse function or the purpose of discourse", the latter is "the aggregate of prototypical surface features" (Virtanen 1992b:298). Although this distinction is in principle very useful, the terminology is misleading in view of the fact that there is no clear definition to set apart discourse from text.

German terminology distinguishes between *Texttyp* (discourse type) and *Textsorte* (text type, literally kind or "sort" of text). These terms carry less of the flavour of "folk-typology" (Biber 1989:5) than, for instance, the German word *Gattung*, quasi-equivalent of English *genre*. From German text linguistics, one can further adopt the distinction that discourse types are classified according to a basic — and limited — number of text functions or illocutions, while a more numerous and open-ended list of "sorts" of texts emphasises the conventional status of certain text forms and combines situational, functional and structural features (cf. Große 1976; Lux 1981; Brinker 1985). Such conventions are part of the linguistic competence within the larger context of the cultural competence of speakers (cf. Brinker 1985:124) and probably come closest to the English technical use of genre as "text categories readily distinguished by mature speakers of a language" (Biber 1989:5).

As shown in *Figure 4*, the two different terminological systems have created the following situation: first, the more neutral notion of *type* of discourse or text is used in English and German in a diametrically opposed way, with discourse type corresponding roughly to the concept that lies behind the established use of German *Texttyp*. Second, in English the notion of *genre* is a more established and general concept that comprises aspects of German *Textsorte* as well as of *Gattung*, which is still closely associated with literary theory. *Genre* in Biber's sense quoted above, by contrast, has lost much of this literary connotation if referred to in linguistics.

This is why it is advisable to establish the following conventions: *discourse* (or *text*) *types* are the outcome of any classification based on clearly stated typological criteria. In principle, there is no such thing as a fixed number of text types for a given language or human communication in general. Nonetheless, certain typologies are clearly preferred, not only in this study, but by many authors, probably because they have proved adequate for a number of purposes. This is especially true for basic functional and structural parameters, which are also used here, while, for instance, Biber's (1989) typology, based on linguistic co-occurrence, has a more specific and certainly less intuition-based justification. In contrast to text type, *genre* is understood in the sense quoted above, i.e., it applies to those categories that have an everyday language label and can be assumed to be part of the linguistic and cultural knowledge of speakers. Finally, the term *category of discourse*, which is used in the title of this chapter, arises out of the compilation practice of the LOB and the Brown

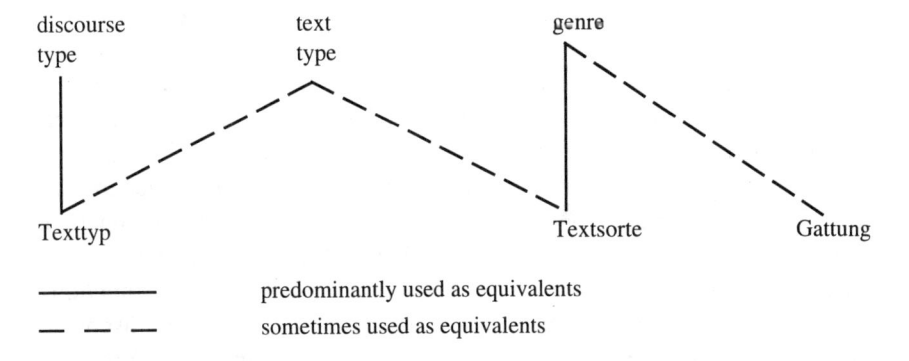

```
discourse              text                genre
type                   type
  |                    /\                   /\
  |                   /  \  ─ ─            /  \  ─ ─
  |                  /    \    ─ ─        /    \    ─ ─
  |                 /      \      ─ ─    /      \      ─ ─
  ↓                /        ↘         ↘ /        \         ↘
Texttyp                    Textsorte              Gattung
```

——————   predominantly used as equivalents
— — —   sometimes used as equivalents

Figure 4. *Terminology in English and German for categories of discourse*

corpus and is the more neutral label, given that these corpora are not structured according to any overlap-free categorisation.[11]

5.2.1.1 *Function and structure — basic discourse types*

This section cannot really seek to do justice to the abundant literature on discourse typologies. However, there are certain basic criteria which are used in almost every classification: Dimter (1985), for instance, demonstrates that the characteristics *communication situation, text function* and *text content* underlie the majority of everyday language text categories, while Diewald (1991) integrates these features into an hierarchical model. S*ituation* is the highest-ranking factor and consists of the features +/-dialogue, +/-face-to-face, and +/-oral. It determines what she calls *basic* text types ("Grundtextsorten") of a supposedly universal status. In the present study, all the text categories used belong to written monologue discourse, which is -dialogue, -face-to-face, and -oral, and which is thus furthest away from the canonical situation of utterance. Typologically relevant criteria within the domain of this basic text type must therefore come from other, lower-ranking, factors.[12]

Following Diewald's scheme, there are three further important components: the *function of discourse* ("Textfunktion"), *social factors* ("Handlungsbereich"), and the theme or *discourse topic* ("Redegegenstand"). Of those three, the latter two are negligible for the purpose of classifying discourse in the present context: social factors are quite stable in public, printed communication and would ultimately lead back to matters of style, while discourse topics as such are a much too open list to be constitutive for text types at this level of analysis. The basic function or intention that lies behind a certain text, however, is a crucial criterion for discourse classification: it constitutes the intersection of external and internal text-building factors. In one way or another, most taxonomies of textual functions depart from Bühler's (1934) "Organon-Modell", which distinguishes three basic functions of the linguistic sign ("Ausdruck", "Darstellung", "Appell") and thereby identifies *expression, representation,* and *"appeal"* as basic textual functions. Departing from Bühler's model, *expressive* discourse, *reference* discourse, and *persuasive* discourse are established as basic text types (e.g. Kinneavy 1971; Grosse 1976).[13] In a similar way, concepts from speech act theory have been introduced into text typologies, differentiating, for instance, *expressive, representative* and *directive* text types (cf. Brinker 1985) on the basis of the principal illocutionary types (Searle 1969).

There is a second paradigm that is widely used in text linguistics, which rests on a much older approach to classifying discourse: in principle with an origin in rhetorical theory, there are the four — again supposedly basic — text types *narration, description, exposition,* and *argumentation*. Faigley/Meyer (1983) put this classificational scheme down to the influence of the nineteenth-century rhetorician Bain (1866); in modern linguistics, one of the most frequently cited text typologies based on exactly the same categories[14] is Werlich (1976). As the closeness to rhetoric suggests, these basic discourse types relate to discourse *structure* rather than *function*, but, ultimately, both aspects are not independent of each other.[15] To make the interconnection clear, the three ubiquitous functions of language derived from the communication triangle are plausibly reduced to two: due to the inherently reciprocal nature of communication, the expressive or speaker-oriented function is in fact closely related to the hearer-oriented aspect, so that both can be subsumed under a more general *interpersonal* function.[16] This reduction to two basic functions of language closely corresponds to what Malinowski (1923) called the two ways of language use, namely "narrative speech" (representation) and "speech-in-action" (appeal) (p.312); the same is implied in Halliday's distinction of an *ideational* and an *interpersonal* meaning or function, introduced in 2.1.3.

Virtanen's (1992b) prototype-based approach to classifying discourse is, to my knowledge, the most elegant solution to such an interdependence of structure and function: she distinguishes the function or purpose of a discourse (her type *of discourse*) and the textual surface structure (her type *of text*); where both coincide, these are "direct" or "primary" uses (Virtanen 1992b:299). For instance, a text may have a narrative purpose and/or be realised in a narrative structure. What is particularly interesting about this approach is that the taxonomy of functions and the taxonomy of structures, which are roughly the same as the two outlined above, contain categories with differing flexibility to correlate with each other: in particular, Virtanen is able to show that a narrative type of text, i.e. a narrative textual surface structure, "seems to be able to realise any type of discourse" (1992b:303), i.e. any type of discourse purpose. An argumentative surface structure, by contrast, "seems to be more or less restricted to direct use, i.e., to the realisation of the argumentative discourse type [= function]" (Virtanen 1992b:303). Vice versa, narrative purposes essentially surface as narrative structures, while argumentative purposes can occur in a range of different surface forms.

Although Virtanen only deals with narration and argumentation at either end of a direct-indirect use continuum, the argument can probably be extended to the remaining discourse types, to description and exposition, as well: description would probably also be more prone to primary uses than argumentation. In fact, description is the natural equivalent of narration, depending on how reality is viewed: Kinneavy (1971), for example, distinguishes between *static* and *dynamic* modes of viewing so that description means looking at something at a particular time, and narration at how it changes across time.[17] Exposition, by contrast, much like argumentation, is a concept which rather evokes intention or purpose, because "from a pragmatic point of view, [it] means 'to explain' — [and] it is common to find explanations that rely on narrations, descriptions [...]" (Faigley/ Meyer 1983:308).[18]

One can thus attibute a more prototypical or more basic status to narration and description, which ultimately rest on the ideational aspect of Halliday's language functions. In both, language serves to express what the speaker as an *observer* views (cf. Halliday/Hasan 1976:27). Argumentation and exposition, by contrast, relate more directly to functions or intentions, thus to the interpersonal function of language, because the speaker as an *intruder* is explaining or evaluating what he is talking about, and thereby attempts to convince a hearer of his line of argument or explanation.[19] It is their ideationally determined nature that lies behind Virtanen's (1992b:305) characterisation of narrative — and one must add now description — as a "strong" type of discourse *in terms of structure*; there is a direct relation between prototypical functions and prototypical forms. Argumentation and exposition are more hearer-oriented and thus functionally defined; they are suitably described as types of discourse strong *in terms of function*.

It is thus the inherent co-presence of the ideational and the interpersonal aspect of language that underlies the apparent confusion between textual structures and textual functions in traditional text typologies. *Figure 5* summarises the differences as discussed so far: resting on the predominant language function on the one hand and on what the speaker is actually doing on the other, narration, description, exposition and argumentation are in this way turned into suitable labels for basic discourse types, which will be of use in the following.

5.2.1.2 *Convention — the status of genre*

In contrast to the limited number of text types, which are defined by textual functions and textual surface structures, there is no closed system of genres. As outlined above, these are textual categories that form part of the linguistic competence of speakers and that can best be discerned by the fact that everyday language labels are given to them. Genres arise out of *conventions* of linguistic usage, because "from day to day, comparable situations occur, prompting comparable responses. These responses become a tradition, which tend to function as a constraint in any new response in the form" (Miller 1984:152). Conventions and traditions thus link linguistic features to particular situational and functional conditions, whereby the whole concept represents a complex interplay of factors. Genres are also highly culture-specific and do not

```
        ideational function              interpersonal function
       (speaker as observer)             (speaker as intruder)
        ─────────┴─────────               ─────────┴─────────
   dynamic         static            explaining         evaluating
   viewing         viewing
      │               │                    │                │
   narration      description          exposition      argumentation
```

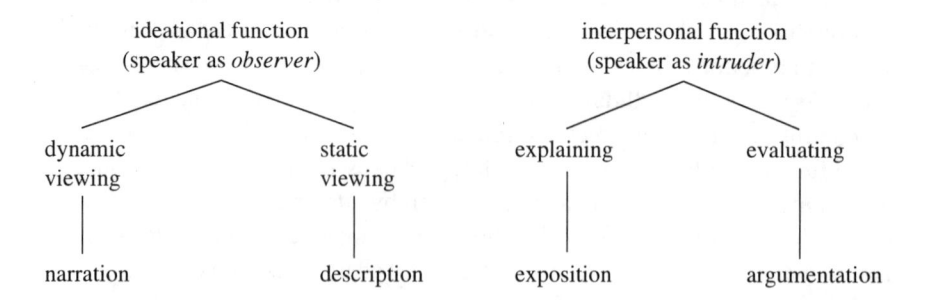

Figure 5. *Four basic text types and the functions of language*

normally meet the requirements of a homogeneous, overlap-free and exhaustive text typology.

Much effort has been spent in the text linguistic literature in describing the impact of genre-specific knowledge on text production and comprehension, a substantial part within work on special languages (e.g. Dudley-Evans 1989; Swales 1990). In particular, these efforts emphasise that what could be called the "genre competence" of speakers and hearers has an essential impact on their expectations, and consequently on their tolerance for the breaking of expectations, as regards the occurrence or non-occurrence of certain linguistic features. Genre conventions thus determine "what is common and what is rare in different functional varieties of language" (Enkvist 1984:58).[20] Vice versa, particular linguistic items or combinations of them can function as a typical marker of a certain genre so that their presence or absence will have an impact on text comprehension (cf. Nystrand 1986). In this sense, a genre is also "a way of elaborating not the text itself but rather the communicative event" (Nystrand 1986:75), i.e., it constitutes part of the basic instruction for cooperating with a text. In that respect, it has a strong top-down processing effect.

Nonetheless, genres are only "clusters of characteristics" (Virtanen 1992b:296), which is again a prototype-like view of the concept (cf. Rosch/Mervis 1975). If genres are understood as prototypes, they consist of a core and a periphery, allowing for variation and deviation. This becomes significant if the occurrence of an individual linguistic feature such as inversion is assumed to be a matter of convention, because "the relative frequency of an occurrence is often less decisive than the immediate likelihood of finding it in the specific context" (de Beaugrande/Dressler 1981:16). It is not necessarily the case that contexts which actually provide numerous occurrences of inversion also best illustrate its full discourse functional potential. Rather, it may be a relative unexpectedness, due to certain genre conventions, that creates an even stronger effect in discourse.

This was implied above (cf. 4.2.3) when describing the procedural use of FI as against its real topic change work. The visual impact reading created by FI correlates with only a limited class of genres, at most with passages of a certain kind in others, in which this effect is suitable and desirable. In texts like, for instance, guidebooks or layout descriptions, the visual impact effect is part of their genre conventions and inversions are a way to conform to them; at the same time, they are "a way for the text producer to maximise receiver-orientation" (Virtanen 1992b:297). On the other hand, only "a text full of surprises [...] carries a lot of information" (Virtanen 1992b:297), even if at the cost of additional interpretive effort. It is out of a breaking of expectations, rather than of the adherence to conventions, that a topic change function of inversion and its contribution to discourse structure can arise; as a result, in certain genres inversion may be less frequent overall, but may be nonetheless more "meaningful" and effective.

Genre conventions are thus not directly reflected by quantitative patterns, i.e. by relative frequencies of linguistics forms. The basis of comparison would always be only a "fiction of language-as-a-whole" (Enkvist 1991:10). This means that, even if inversion proves to be quite frequent in certain genres, it can nonetheless be more interesting to investigate it in detail in others. On the other hand, the contribution that the construction makes to discourse under conditions of displacement (cf. 5.3) is not necessarily measurable in quantitative terms at all.

Moreover, the categories which structure the LOB and the Brown corpus into fifteen sub-corpora do not always meet the requirement of constituting homogeneous, clear-cut genres, not even when following the loose practice whereby everyday language labels serve as main indication for the presence of a certain genre. Genres that form part of everyday knowledge are usually recognised as such by their readers on the basis of the context in which they are encountered; clarification of the "communicative event" (Nystrand 1986:75) is triggered beforehand on the basis of what are *pre-signals* for genres: titles and sub-titles, print, placement (of an article), the kind of newspaper, book, series etc., in which a text is published.

From further information provided in the corpora or within the texts themselves, some of the five text categories used (cf. *table ii* in the appendix) thus contain several genres as relevant sub-categorisations, which are the following:

text category in the corpus genre(s)
'Press: reportage'   reportage
'Press: editorial'   editorial
                                                letter to the editor

'Press: reviews'   review
'Belles-lettres, biography,   biography
  essays'   essay[21]
'Learned and scientific   scientific writing[21]
  writing'

5.2.2 Inversion in a corpus of written non-fictional discourse

5.2.2.1 Syntactic variation and a corpus-based approach

Corpus work on syntactic, as compared to morphological or lexical, features faces a number of problems. First, a relatively large corpus is required to obtain a sufficient number of occurrences (cf. de Haan 1992). In the case of inversion, this was to be particularly expected because previous studies had already shown that, depending on the kind of discourse samples chosen, inverted sentences may be virtually absent for considerably long stretches of text. For instance, using 64 text samples amounting to a total of 128,000 words from four text categories of the Brown corpus,[22] Ellegård (1978) found a share of approximately 5% of verb subject sequences (cf. p.57), including, however, and dominated by, inversion after *there* as well as interrogative sentences. In the same vein, in de Haan's (1992) analysis of two 20,000 word samples of fictional texts, inversion does not appear among the ten most frequent sentence patterns.

It must also be taken into account that corpus texts are running text and, as such, are frequently composed of various passages with characteristic sequences of syntactic phenomena. This has been brought forward in many corpus-based studies, for instance in de Haan (1993), where sentence length and sentence patterns are shown to be not randomly distributed, but to vary largely in consecutive stretches of individual texts. Presumably, the same holds for word order variation as well; thus, if one treats corpus texts as "randomised" samples (de Haan 1993:17), i.e. as collections of sentences which are in principle unrelated, one neglects that certain syntactic phenomena in fact occur in clusters and are not evenly distributed. With respect to this, individual text passages are discussed in 5.2.2.3, following the quantitative analysis in 5.2.2.2.

Finally, as has recently been argued by Jucker (1992), syntactic phenomena do not easily lend themselves to an analysis that rests on paradigmatic relations between linguistic variables, i.e., on a concept of choice such as presented above. Therefore, even though it has been useful to investigate the semantic differences between inversion and CWO by considering them as alternative constructions, the range of possible options is ultimately wider, including, for instance, *there*-constructions, indefinite subjects, passivisation, and maybe others, for some of the discourse functions attributed to inversion. This, however, leads to a complexity which can no longer be handled in quantitative terms, and which ultimately prohibits a real *corpus-based* approach in functional syntax, meaning adherence to "the fundamental 'total accountability' principle of corpus study" (Svartvik/Quirk 1980:9). In practice, *relative* frequencies of occurrence are therefore difficult to obtain, because the use of inversions, for instance, would then have to be related to the total number of clauses as well as to other presumably alternative constructions. Instead, if the occurrence of inversion is looked upon as a single phenomenon, it possibly expresses part of its discourse function and status by characteristic *mean squares* such as found for various text categories.

5.2.2.2 *Inversion in five text categories of the LOB and the Brown corpus*
The LOB and the Brown corpus are compiled according to various selection principles, but their textual categories constitute genres rather than text types, with some of them being composed of several genres. Nevertheless, these corpora provide a useful survey of the distribution of inversion over different kinds of texts and in particular allow for relating the patterns of usage to functional text characteristics. Biber (1988, 1989), in his computational analysis of the same corpora in terms of the distribution and frequency of 67 linguistic features, excluded inversion and other bare word order phenomena, which allows me to challenge — with regards to its comprehensiveness — his claim of having identified the "potentially important linguistic features — those that have been associated with particular communicative functions" (Biber 1988:72). I think that the semiotic process described in chapter 4 gives ample reason to assume a substantial communicative function for inversion, and therefore makes it worthwhile to consider its distribution in the corpora, as well.

For the five text categories under investigation, *table 3* presents the results for the patterns of occurrence of the different formal inversion types (cf. 3.1.2) in absolute frequencies. On the basis of the results discussed in 5.1.3, the distinction between British and American texts is no longer maintained.

In that the samples vary in number (see *table i* in the appendix) for the reasons given above, only the categories 'press: reportage', 'belles-lettres, biography, essays' and 'scientific writing' are directly comparable, while 'press: editorial' and 'press: reviews' contain considerably fewer text samples. Therefore, *table 4* shows the mean squares, in addition to absolute frequencies, of inversion occurrence in the different text categories, this time on the basis of the functions identified in chapter 4. In order to further condense the frequen-

Table 3. *Usage frequencies of formal inversion types in five written non-fictional text categories of the LOB and the Brown corpus*

	rep.	ed.	rev.	bbe.	sc.writ.	total
AdvP	12	8	10	15	10	**55**
PP	41	24	18	60	28	**171**
VP	14	4	7	9	7	**41**
AdjP	4	6	11	7	7	**35**
total FI	71	42	46	91	52	**302**
pro	5	19	9	20	15	**68**
corr	4	9	5	11	14	**43**
add	3	13	7	21	17	**61**
neg	3	20	9	11	17	**60**
total SAI	15	61	30	63	63	**232**
total inversion	**86**	**103**	**76**	**154**	**115**	**534**

Table 4. *Usage frequencies (absolute figures and mean squares) of functional inversion types in five written non-fictional text categories of the LOB and the Brown corpus*

	text category (no. of texts)	rep. (68)	ed. (54)	rev. (34)	bbe. (68)	sc.writ. (68)	**total texts (292)**
presentative/	absolute	71	42	46	91	52	**302**
predicative FI	mean	1.0	0.8	1.4	1.3	0.8	**1.0**
anaphoric/cataphoric	absolute	12	41	21	52	46	**172**
+ constituent-focussing SAI	mean	0.2	0.8	0.6	0.8	0.7	**0.6**
constituent-focussing	absolute	3	20	9	11	17	**60**
SAI	mean	0.04	0.4	0.3	0.2	0.3	**0.2**
	total absolute	86	103	76	154	115	**534**
total inversion	total mean	**1.3**	**1.9**	**2.2**	**2.3**	**1.7**	**1.8**

cies, and in view of the "squishy" transitions between the functional types discussed in 4.3, these are subsumed into three groups as follows:

(a) presentative/predicative FI:
 AdvP-inversion, PP-inversion, VP-inversion, AdjP-inversion

(b) anaphoric/cataphoric + constituent-focussing FI/SAI:
 pro-inversion, corr-inversion, add-inversion

(c) constituent-focussing SAI:
 neg-inversion

The way in which the different types of inversion dominate in the different text categories can be interpreted in the light of the discourse functions that they have so far been said to assume. In particular,

(a) presentative and predicative FI turns out to be most frequent in reviews, biographies and essays, least frequent in editorials and scientific writing, with reportages lying somewhere in between. This probably has to do with the two-fold function that these structures fulfil and that has above been set apart as *procedural* uses as opposed to real *topic change* uses: reviews as well as biographies and essays are probably most prone to both kinds of uses, containing clusters of FI where geographic localities, exhibitions and other places are depicted in detail, and otherwise using them as a topic change device which contributes to the structure of the discourse. Both uses are found in reportages as well; however, this category in principle contains a range of possible sub-genres,[23] in which the need for procedural uses differs and may also vary widely from one text to the next. This is one reason why a more detailed analysis of news reporting will be undertaken in 5.3.2. The lower values which editorials and scientific writing have for FI uses, by contrast, are in my view attributable to the fact that these deal with individual topics over longer stretches of text and thus have fewer topic change turns. Certainly, there is also less need for procedural uses when building up an argument on political or scientific matters.

(b) the anaphoric/cataphoric + constituent-focussing types, which constitute grammaticalised clause linkage and complex constructions, are quite evenly distributed in four out of the five text categories, with the notable exception of press reportage. Reportages are a strongly information-based genre (cf. Lüger 1983), or, vice versa, the least argumentative in kind. Thus, they have relatively little need for complex, cohesive syntactic structures, but predominantly follow principles of "increasing specification" (Lüger 1983:68) or, in case of longer reports and reportages, "chronological" (p.74) or "descriptive/local" structures (p.78). Editorials, reviews, biographies, essays and scientific writing, by contrast, have rather different kinds of discourse organisation; in particular, they rely much less on relations from the outside world but, instead, require more internal cohesive links, which the speaker "makes up" according to the necessities of his line of argument or explanation.

(c) constituent-focussing SAI is again quite similarly distributed over the five text categories, and for roughly similar reasons. It occurs to an almost negligible extent in press reportages, because these rarely, if at all, contain direct expressions of the presence of the speaker; thus, there is rarely the need for, or adequacy of, directly speaker-based prominence and, consequently, for emotive meaning. All other genres, by contrast, are more hospitable to this kind of meaning, with editorials, the explicit genre for comment, expectedly in the lead.

Overall, the distribution of inversion over the five text categories quite plausibly confirms the semantics and discourse functions as identified in chapter 4. The quantitative picture also confirms the characterisation of inversion as a device of emotivity and subjectivity (cf. 4.2.4); so that, following the total densities of occurrence, the categories would be ordered in the following way from most to least subjective kinds of discourse:

biography/essay > review > editorial > scientific writing > reportage

Interestingly, this ordering corresponds to an intuitive characterisation of the genres in question in terms of their subjectivity. That is, it is probably part of the "genre competence" (in the sense outlined above) of most English speakers that we consider biographies, essays, reviews and editorials as more subjective kinds of texts, and scientific writing and reportages as less subjective ones. The distribution of inversion over these genres, and with that the degree to which the construction is relatively more or less expected, confirms the existence of such genre conventions and at the same time justifies calling inversion a *marker of subjectivity*.

5.2.2.3 *Typical uses and characteristics of text categories*

I shall now proceed by discussing for each category individual passages that have provided typical uses of inverted constructions. The aim is to account for the affinities of the various functional types of inversion with the genres under discussion on the one hand, and with the text types as introduced in 5.2.1.1 on the other. Most of the genres are functionally determined and thereby also reflect affinities of inversion with text types in terms of a predominant *function*, while individual passages within the genres illustrate the particular relations to different *surface structure* characteristics.

(a) press reportage: Reportages are frequently characterised as the *information-based* portion of newspaper texts[24] (cf. Lüger 1983:66); from a functional viewpoint, they can be assigned to what is primarily a *reference* or *representative* type of discourse. Wikberg (1992) further describes the category 'press: reportage' contained in the LOB and the Brown corpus as *narrative* and claims that it differs from fiction mainly "in dealing with actual events" (p.248). In the same vein, in Biber (1989), who establishes a typology of English texts on the basis of clusters of linguistic co-occurrence along five parameters of variation, 73% of the category 'press: reportage' from the LOB corpus occur in the text type "general narrative exposition" (p.21). Their distinctive characteristics are found to be "marked informational focus" and "moderate narrative concern" (Biber 1989:31).

These characterisations are not without problems; however, they fit into the text typology introduced in *figure 5* above, in which narration was said to be a discourse type by virtue of being a surface structure relating to the ideational function of language. A narrative character of press reportages is thus in line with its being information-based or representative discourse as well. Much more often, however, than constituting *dynamic* viewing in the form of narration, reportages in fact contain *static* viewing in the form of description. On the one hand, a descriptive passage can serve real procedural ends, i.e. primarily create a visual impact reading, or it can function as a real focus management device within the discourse organisation. Examples of each case are discussed in the following.

(15) WASHINGTON Thousands of bleacher-type seats are being erected along Pennsylvania Avenue between the Capitol and the White House for the big inaugural parade on Jan. 20. [...] Pennsylvania Avenue, named for one of the original 13 states, perhaps is not the most impressive street in the District of Columbia from a commercial standpoint. But from a historic viewpoint none can approach it.

MANY BUILDINGS <u>Within view of the avenue are some of the United States government's tremendous buildings</u>, plus shrines and monuments. Of course, 1600 Pennsylvania, the White House, is the most famous address of the free world. <u>Within an easy walk from Capitol Hill where Pennsylvania Avenue comes together with Constitution Avenue, begins a series of great federal buildings</u>, some a block long and all about seven-stories high. [...]

SEATS ON SQUARE <u>Along this avenue which saw marching soldiers from the War between the States returning in 1865 is the National Archives building</u> where hundreds of thousands of this country's most valuable records are kept. [...] Many spectators will be occupying seats and vantage point bordering Lafayette Square, opposite the White House. <u>In this historic square are several statues</u>, but the one that stands out is that of Gen. Andrew Jackson, hero of the Battle of New Orleans. (BRW, rep., text 8)

(15) is a passage from a longer reportage of the Brown corpus and contains several FI occurrences, used to create a visual impact reading. At the same time, they all introduce topic entities which are further treated in the following discourse; thus, the locative relations expressed in the fronted constituents are also constitutive for the structure of the entire passage. The result is what Lüger (1983:78) calls "descriptive" or "local structuring" and is typical of an "eyewitness" perspective of a text; it is thus not surprising that FIs are used, whereby the speaker adopts a viewpoint from within the scene expressed. Such eyewitness types of reportages thus mainly supply FI constructions which are clear procedural uses and generally further FI occurrence in clusters.

However, this is not typical of all kinds of reporting; otherwise, the FI value for this genre would have been substantially higher. The other main principle, according to which especially shorter news and reports are structured, is the principle of "increasing specification" (Lüger 1983:68), which is often justified by the fact that news texts are rarely read to the end: the most crucial information thus has to appear at the beginning of the text, or at least at the beginning of each paragraph. The result is the kind of structure exemplified in (16), where each FI supports the transition from a more general topic (*artists, others assisting, persons chosen as something*) to the concrete persons introduced into that frame:

(16) A preview party for sponsors of the event and for the artists is set for April 8. The event will be open to the public the following day. Proceeds will be used by the section to further its program in

science, education and social action on local, national and international levels.
NOTED ARTISTS Mrs. Monte Tyson, chairman, says the work of 100 artists well-known in the Delaware Valley area will be included in the exhibition and sale. Among them will be Marc Shoettle, Ben Shaen, Nicolas Marsinaco, Alfred van Loen and Milton Avery, [...].
OTHERS ASSISTING Mrs. Jerome Blum and Mrs. Meyer Schultz are co-chairmen this year. Assisting as chairmen of various committees are Mrs. Alvin Blum, Mrs. Leonard Malmud, Mrs. Edward Fernberger, [...].
When the Achaeans entertained last Wednesday at their annual Carnival masquerade ball, Miss Margaret Pierson was chosen to rule over the festivities, presented at the Municipal Auditorium and chosen as her ladies in waiting were Misses Clayton Nairne, Eleanor Eustis, Lynn Chapman, [...]. (BRW, rep., text 18)

(16) illustrates topic change uses of FI, whereby sub-topics are derived from more comprehensive topics. Alternatively, an FI may also introduce a higher-level topic, which has a strong expectation-creating effect. An example of this is (17), in which the FI occurs at the beginning of a reportage from the LOB corpus; following the main news and preceding a more detailed account, two more general discourse topics are announced by this modified version of the idiom, which puts the whole story into a light of special newsworthiness:

(17) A SIXPENNY BARGAIN AT THE STOCK EXCHANGE
An unchanged dividend of 300 per cent is being paid on the ordinary shares of Neville Develoments. And thereby hangs a tale and a great deal of money.
Neville Developments is a Birmingham company run by shrewd chartered accountants. (LOB, rep., text 16)

This has not meant to be an exhaustive account of the various uses of inversion in the category 'reportage', but it has been sufficient to illustrate that one finds procedural as well as topic change work. It is probably a consequence of this diversity of uses that there is a very uneven distribution of occurrences over the individual samples; there is strong reason to assume that the overall values would have been much lower, had there not been several "real" (= eyewitness) reportages in the sample. By contrast, as will be shown in 5.3.2, a big share of news and reporting texts in fact contain virtually no inversions at all.

(b) editorial: As the category 'editorial', or comment, suggests, there should be no doubt about the nature of this genre: it is duly characterised as primarily *argumentative* (cf. Wikberg 1992:248), and, within taxonomies of journalistic writing, it is found among the "persuasive" (Lüger 1983:82) types of discourse. Interestingly, within Biber's (1989) typology, an even higher percentage of editorials than of reportages appear in the category "general narrative exposition", namely 86%; while no editorials, and only a small part of the genre 'letter to the editor' (11%), occur in his type "involved persuasion". Without wishing to question here Biber's method of identifying text types or the adequacy of the labels he uses, this strongly supports the claim made in 5.2.1.1, namely, that argumentation is a discourse type which is defined in terms of its function, rather than by necessary surface structure characteristics.

Thus, an argumentative function can presumably be realised by a broad range of textual surface structures. For example, descriptive passages are easily incorporated into an argument, so that one finds occurrences of FI in editorials which are in fact similar to those from reportages and other genres. However, commenting on a topic generally implies sticking to it for a longer stretch of the text, maybe even for the whole of it; thus, in editorials, there are overall fewer FIs and fewer potential topic changes as compared with other genres. Also, the number of procedural uses is relatively lower: first, since argumentation is a matter of facts and conclusions (cf. Toulmin 1958) and a visual impact reading thereby least likely to be adequate and, second, since comments presuppose a certain level of previous knowledge and only selectively contain informative (narrative or descriptive) passages themselves (cf. Lüger 1983:84). In case of temporarily informative purposes, these give rise to "indirect" (cf. Virtanen 1992b) uses of narration and description, which are then put into the service of the function of argumentation.

Nonetheless, some patterns of inversion usage quite typically reflect the persuasive intention behind an editorial. There are lower, though not negligible, frequencies of presentative/predicative FI, higher shares of grammaticalised complex structures and sentence linkage, and more freqeunt occurrences of constituent-focussing SAI. Especially the latter two characteristics directly relate to argumentation as a discourse type in terms of function:

transitions from descriptions to evaluations or conclusions, for instance, give rise to more complex syntactic structures. By contrast, FI constructions and their topic change potential are used in argumentative discourse, occurring not — as in other genres — at minor turns of the focus of attention within the course of an argument, but rather at major turns: for instance, at the beginning of a new paragraph or in concluding passages, i.e. at the end of an argument or the entire text. An example for this is (18), where the topic *national complacency* has been dealt with over a certain passage and is treated, in a sort of conclusion, by relating it to a competing topic of equal relevance, *lack of any real sense of national unity*:

(18)   This complacency is a poor basis for policy; and a poor substitute for that sense of moral purpose for which the Prime Minister and the Chancellor have appealed.
[...] The British system has never taken kindly to government by coalition, which is certainly not the answer now; but <u>almost as disturbing as the national complacency is the lack of any real sense of national unity</u>. (LOB, ed., text 12)

In (18), the *AdjP-inversion* is an instrument of evaluation, which is symptomatically accompanied by two other devices of "author comments" (cf. Jones 1983:87ff.), *certainly* and *apparent*. In addition, as shown in 4.2.3, the fronted AdjP itself gains evaluative meaning by virtue of being implicitly anchored to the speaker (= *disturbing to me*).

A similar device for author comments are focussed constituents followed by SAI, whereby, for instance, negative items not only mark a negated predication, but attach speaker-based, hence subjective, prominence to them. An example is given in (19), where particular concern with the negative semantics is expressed and spread into a paragraph full of facts. This is meant to give support to the initial, explicit comments marked by *it is shameful* and *worse still*:

(19)   CHILDREN [...] It is shameful that such a levy should be collected by a Minister of Health. Worse still. There is the tax on childhood. Pregnancy, like death, is democratic. The last war forced the state to protect the health of children through the Maternity Clinic. With the help of the National Health Service it has become a possession beyond price. All mothers go there. The solicitor's wife, the schoolmaster's wife, the clerk's wife, the plumber's wife, and the

wife of the chap who is doing a stretch in gaol. Never has the health of children been better. Never has mortality been so low. (LOB, ed., text 14)

Finally, the relative density of pronominal and correlative FI and SAI structures in editorials has already been noted. As discussed in 4.2.3, the anaphoric and cataphoric items involved in them constitute cohesive links which are always of an internal, speaker-based, kind. They do not express relations from within the scene; thus, the expression of such relations has to be taken as explicit intervention on the part of the speaker, as his shaping of the events or relations from the outside world into a form which fits the intended reasoning. Passages such as (20), which link discourse entities by pronominal constructions, are therefore typical ways of mentioning facts in persuasive discourse, as are uses such as (21), where a new topic entity takes the place of the former one:

(20) Purchase tax, at four rates varying from five to 50 per cent, spreads its net so wide that it is almost simpler to list some of the items not affected. Food and sweets, fuel and light are not taxed; nor are books, magazines, children's clothes, some kitchen equipment, sheets and towels.
  No services bear any kind of tax. On the other hand, a wide range of consumer durables is affected; so are most household goods and appliances; and so, too, are cosmetics, radios, records, jewellery, toys, cameras, carpets, wallpaper, most clothes, hats, gloves and furniture. (LOB, ed., text 7)

(21) It is not only Mr. Butler, the deserving candidate for Downing Street, who is in trouble. So are many other prominent contenders for the Premiership in the radical sector of the party. (LOB, ed., text 8)

The usage of inversion in persuasive discourse is thus a more direct expression of the interpersonal function of language, as fits the purpose of the underlying discourse type as a whole. By contrast, in the subjectivity scale presented above editorials stand only in the middle. This is probably attributable to the fact that the persuasive intention requires to a much lesser extent the effect of FI that the speaker shifts his viewpoint within the displaced scene expressed by the text. Such changes in perspective are only needed at major turns in the argument, whereby they are less frequent overall, but, where occurring, nonetheless perform substantial discourse work.

(c) reviews: Reviews, at first sight, have a lot in common with editorials: they have equally been characterised as primarily *argumentative* (cf. Wikberg 1992:48), or as a "persuasive" kind of journalistic discourse (Lüger 1983:87). Nonetheless, there are linguistic peculiarities to both of them that arise out of differences in terms of discourse topic on the one hand — typically, reviews deal with art, music, films, books, TV and radio programs — and of an argumentative purpose of a slightly different kind on the other. In particular, reviews have a stronger representative sub-component: a typical review consists of both a representative and a persuasive part (cf. Lüger 1983:88). This dual nature is also reflected in Biber's (1989) language typology, where reviews occur with equal shares (47% each) under "general narrative exposition" and "learned exposition"; the difference is that the latter is "markedly non-narrative [...] and explicit in reference" (p.27), while both are non-persuasive and strongly informational.

As "non-narrative" suggests, the representative component of this genre is mainly realised by descriptive passages. This explains the high frequency patterns of FIs, many of which are clear procedural uses. They create a visual impact reading, whereby the object to be reviewed is virtually put "before the mind's eye" of the reader. It is indeed plausible that discussing and evaluating, for instance, an object of art is preceded by the creation of a mental image of it. Typical uses of inversion are thus one as in (22), where a whole scene is evoked in a descriptive passage, or, even more typically, those in (23) and (24), where the concrete visual impact obtained after directional and deictic adverbs furthers an effect of displaced immediacy (cf. 5.3.1), of being in the middle of the scene itself. In all three examples, this is underlined by a symptomatic use of the present tense:

(22) THE NEW BOOKS
BEHAN BESTOWS AN ACCOLADE ON DELANEY
She's the flower in a cultural desert, he says.
   It is mid-morning on a Dublin Sunday. The streets are tranquilly sunny and still, for the town is at Mass. Most of it. In the front room of a house in Anglesey Road is a congregation who never actually go to church, but who are gathered with devotion around Brendan Behan and a brandy bottle.

Where the boys are. In the hallway are the empties; through the door hearts are full, hopes are high. There are still a few amber inches in the bottle.

Present are some hard-core Friends of Brendan. They listen with many an obliging guffaw to the brandy owner's solo swish on his anecdotal roller-coaster, with occasional stops for an old I.R.A. or a Connemara tear-jerker.

PLUCKILY <u>Also present is a London journalist</u> who arrived [...]. (LOB, rev., text 6)

(23) Within two days Mr. Lisbon had a record contract. And they hauled his thumb-tacked joanna the thirteen miles to London for his first session.

<u>Now along comes his solo disc</u>, featuring two of his own compositions, "Deerstalker" and "Almost Grown Up". (LOB, rev., text 4)

(24) Mr. Richardson has left his stamp so clearly on the rest of this film that some credit must be given to him; but <u>here is undeniably a performance of surprising range and deep emotion</u>, [...]. (LOB, rev., text 3)

Despite the overall persuasive purpose of these texts, these are uses of FI which would be less expected in other kinds of persuasive discourse — certainly not in political editorials — and which arise out of the peculiarity of this genre that it is mainly defined by its limited range of discourse topics. For reviews are texts which deal with concrete objects and events, rather than with abstract argumentation. Nonetheless, (24) contains an instance of FI which marks a passage as an author comment, indicated by *undeniably*, and which corresponds to the other, above-mentioned, usage in persuasive discourse. Most typically, it is present in *AdjP-inversion*, as in (25):

(25) This director is at last being re-evaluated and given his proper place in the history of the German film. <u>Most charming was his tongue-in-cheek "Unheimliche Geschichten" (1920)</u>, five ghost stories with a light touch, [...]. (LOB, rev., text 2)

AdjP-inversions such as the one in this example dominate most distinctly in reviews, and, to a lesser extent, in editorials (cf. *table 3* above). Reviews are less distinctly marked in terms of the usage of other inversion types. However, they are almost in the lead in the overall frequency of inversion usage and are justifiably considered a rather subjective kind of genre.

(d) biography and essays: This category represents the most heterogeneous grouping of genres and, in particular, contains many samples from longer works or monographs. Contributions to the overall structure of the texts are therefore made out less easily and can only be justified for individual passages. This is why only a very brief discussion of this category follows.

Wikberg (1992) characterises it as *"expository*, in part *argumentative"* discourse (p.248; my emphasis), which is a first indication of the fact that once again this is a discourse type defined in terms of function rather than structure. In Biber (1989), only text samples from biographies are used, which dominate in "general narrative exposition" (57%); the remaining 43% are spread apart over "scientific exposition", "learned exposition" and "imaginative narrative". In a range of other studies (Biber/Finegan 1988, 1989, 1992), essays are, by contrast, found to be ",literate' from a situational perspective" and having "an informational (or argumentative) purpose" (Biber/Finegan 1992:693). Moreover, from a diachronic perspective, they are said to have "drifted" "towards more 'oral' characterisations [... and to] have tended to become more involved, more situated and less abstract in style" (Biber/Finegan 1992:695).

Even though the corpus analysis carried out here could not make the distinction between occurrences in biographies and occurrences in essays, the overall frequencies of inversion usage allow a characterisation of the entire category as rather subjective, which would also support the "drift" hypothesis. However, apart from being a matter of convention, which a drift in style or genre pattern suggests, these genres are also prone to inversion from a functional viewpoint, i.e. for reasons of the underlying discourse type. One reason is that they favour descriptive passages; to illustrate this, I repeat as (26) the example of a procedural use discussed in 4.2.3:

(26) I was very much aware of this as I stood, a few weeks ago, in the "Ring", the Market Place of the Old City.
The temptation to find "sermons in stones" was almost irresistible. There, in the centre of the "Ring", stands a magnificent statue of Jan Hus, the Bohemian reformer and martyr who, in 1406, went to the stake rather than renounce what the Council of Constance had judged to be his heresies. On his left is the Tyn Church, austerely

Gothic, and a symbol of the Hussite reform movement of which it was the spiritual centre in the fifteenth century. <u>On the other side of the "Ring"</u>, stands one of the many Baroque Churches, which in Prague bear witness to the Catholic revival of the seventeenth century.
But that is not all. <u>Linking the "Ring" with the south bank of the Ultava river is a splendid modern thoroughfare</u> cut towards the end of the nineteenth century through the heart of what was formerly the Prague Ghetto. And <u>at the far end, high on the north bank of the river, stands a colossal figure of Joseph Stalin</u>, forever looking down towards the Market Place [...]. (LOB, bbe., text 66)

This passage could just as well have been taken from a guidebook or from a personal travel report. It supports the claim that biographies and essays, which are a very personal kind of treatise, in general favour visual impact readings. For the same reason, there is also a stronger tendency to use FI after directional adverbs and PPs, i.e. to express real dynamic presentative processes, as in (27):

(27)   So at 3 p.m. the car drove up to the Hall, and <u>out of it stepped our Bishop with the Archbishop of Canterbury</u>! (LOB, bbe., text 3)

At the same time, biographies and essays, much like editorials and reviews, also favour author comments; as in (28), these are regularly fitted into the complex explanatory or argumentative structure:

(28)   This is of no little importance: even Lytton Strachey was, in the end, no match for the character of Queen Victoria, and this may well be the reason why [...]. <u>Of no less importance is the fact</u> that the present Queen is likely to reign. (LOB, bbe., text 57)

Thus, in this category, there are uses of inversion such as have been stated for all the other genres; besides, these are the highest frequencies overall. To account for this, it is important to note that biographies and essays, in contrast to newspaper genres, are not necessarily published within the context of an institution such as a newspaper. Instead, they are usually directly published under the name of the author, be it of an entire book or of an individual essay published somewhere else. It is therefore not astonishing that the crucial property of these genres is their more personal style, particularly since it has recently been found that they tend to drift towards a conventionally more oral style (cf. Biber/Finegan 1992). Significantly, in the case of inversion, this more oral characterisation is performed by typical written language means.

(e) scientific writing: Finally, scientific writing has also been characterised as an *"expository,* in part *argumentative"* (Wikberg 1992:248; my emphasis) type of discourse, but nonetheless it displays some quite different biases. Biber (1989) assigns the scientific texts he uses to "scientific exposition" (44%) and "learned exposition" (31%), two clusters which "represent types of informational exposition" (p.27). They differ from each other mainly for topical reasons (natural science, engineering, technology, medicine vs. humanities, social sciences, education, law).

No further differentiation within this category has been taken into account, which, for the category as a whole, results in rather medium values for inversion usage. This has above been attributed to the fact that, in science, dealing with a certain topic usually requires its discussion in some detail. As a result, fewer topic changes, and thus fewer FIs, are to be found. Also, visual impact readings are generally less suitable in a scientific treatise because the nature of the argument is often highly abstract; for this reason, FIs, where they occur in scientific discourse, are most likely meant as an author comment, rather than as a mental evocation of a scene. This finds its expression in PPs, VPs and AdjPs followed by FI, which express abstract textual links rather than locative relations. The changes in focus induced by FI therefore mainly concern ideas which are part of the argument, rather than concrete objects from a scene. In addition, an FI can create an adversative link: in passages (29) and (30), one could potentially add *however* to each FI, the meaning of contrast being underlined by the fronted predicates *doubtful, out of the question, hidden behind,* and *distinguishable*:

(29) A nation such as Switzerland could be neutralized by agreement and could be relied upon to protect its neutrality; more doubtful, but possible, (with an assist from the North) was the neutralization of the Latin American countries; out of the question was the neutralization of Asia and Africa. (BRW, sc.writ., text 42)

(30) National identification was reflected juriprudentially in law theories which incorporated this Hegelian abstraction and saw law, domestic and international, simply as its formal reflection. [...] Hidden behind Hegelian abstractions were more practical reasons for a changing jurisprudence. Related to, but distinguishable from,

nationalism was the growth of democracy in one form or another. (BRW, sc.writ., text 42)

Apart from these peculiarities in FI usage, scientific writing is mainly determined by its predominant function of explaining and, sometimes, evaluating and is thereby again a discourse type defined by function rather than structure. For this reason, much like editorials, scientific writing is further characterised by a relatively high density of complex structures and also by a considerable share of constituent-focussing SAI. These uses are more direct functions of argumentation and exposition, or, in more general terms, intervention of the speaker (as intruder; cf. 5.2.1.1) into the discourse. Two final examples are (31) and (32), again in the vicinity with markers of author comments such as *of course*, adversative *but*, *merely*, and *unfortunately*, as well as the metaphors *laissez-faire* and *credo*:

(31) Of course it had always been of European origin in fact, but it had maintained a universal outlook under the natural law theory. Now, with virtually every writer, not only was the European origin of public law acknowledged as a historical phenomenon, but the rules thus established by the advanced civilizations of Europe were to be imposed on others. (BRW, sc.writ., text 42)

(32) The theory did not require, though it unfortunately might acquire, a Hegelian mystique. It was merely a rationalization and ordering of new institutions of popular government; it was not opposed to either justice or morality; it merely wished to minimize subjective views of officials who wielded public authority.
Particularly was this true as laissez-faire capitalism became the dominant credo of Western society. (BRW, sc.writ., text 42)

Passages (29) – (32) come from one single text of the Brown corpus, while there are considerable parts of this category of discourse where inversions were very infrequent. This strengthens the impression that, in scientific writing, the usage patterns of inversion are quite divergent, and probably differ along dimensions which are not taken into account in the structure of my corpus. Apart from matters of discourse topic, where social sciences are probably more hospitable to inversion than, for instance, natural sciences and technical subjects, a notable difference between scientific articles and scientific monographs, at least for American English, was mentioned above. There are certainly also other factors at work, which could help to establish scientific sub-genres.[25] That, overall, scientific writing occurs rather at the lower end of the subjectivity scale presented above is intuitively plausible, given its predominant discourse function to convince by way of scientific reasoning. As such, in diachronic terms, it has undergone the least drift towards more involved, less abstract and more situation-dependent styles (as shown in Biber/ Finegan 1992). Matters of convention have not yet outruled matters of function here.

5.3 Inversion and discourse under conditions of displacement

The discussion in chapter 4 has emphasised the relevance of *displaced speech* for the usage of inversion in discourse. These are conditions under which discourse deals with events that are not part of, hence *displaced from*, the immediate environment of both speaker and hearer. Furthermore, in 5.1.1, it has been argued that it is written discourse in particular which has a strong inclination to deal with displaced events. They relate to, and thereby build up, a universe of discourse of their own. Under such conditions, the context of communication, which is "experience that is immediate" (Chafe 1992:231) is not, or is only marginally, the focus of attention; instead, the consciousness of language producers and receivers focusses on "experience that is displaced from the immediate environment in which the possessor of the mind is located" (Chafe 1992:231).

The relationship between deictic and lexical presentative FI has shown that full inversion is a device which, especially in written discourse, makes the presence of a discrepancy between the displaced matters with which the text deals and the immediate consciousness of the speaker himself less openly felt. Though SAIs, by contrast, are more direct expressions of the stance of the speaker himself, they have also become characteristic of writing, in particular of literary styles that allow for emotionality and subjectivity. In principle, SAI is thus also related to discourse prone to conditions of displacement.

Nonetheless, the fact is that certain kinds of written discourse, such as short news or very technical and juridical writings, almost never use inversions of the types discussed here; nor is their occurrence in others, where they seem to be in principle suitable, predictable in any sense. This is what I want to consider in the following: I shall have a closer look at those types of discourse or parts of a discourse which, in a study of a limited range of newspaper texts, I have found more prone to inversion usage. After presenting general affinities of inverted word order with conditions of displacement in non-fictional discourse in 5.3.1, I shall, in 5.3.2, discuss the results from a study of news reporting, i.e. of texts that deal with political — and as such displaced — events. My aim is to illustrate that the most relevant factor for the use of FI is an effect of displaced immediacy, while both FI and SAI mark different ways in which a speaker can be subjectively present in a text.

5.3.1 *Basic affinities in non-fictional discourse*

Chafe (1992, 1994) discusses the different ways in which displacement is handled in language, i.e., how displaced matters can be reproduced by a choice of linguistic devices. Though Chafe's work mainly focusses on the distinction between fiction and non-fiction, his approach is applied here to differences among non-fictional texts, whereby I follow up on the discussion of genres from 5.2.2.3. Using news reporting as an example, I return to the discussion of the variety of forms that reportages appear to have and which was assumed above to underlie a quite uneven distribution of inversion usage over the individual samples within this category (cf. 5.2.2.2).

Displacement is a general property of human language and has been defined as the capacity of language, more precisely of the consciousness of language producers and receivers, to "alternate its focus between experience that is immediate and experience that is displaced" (Chafe 1992:231). The author of a discourse is first of all the *proximal* consciousness of speech and operates in the immediacy of the speech situation, while a person who has experienced certain events at another location or time has a *displaced* consciousness of his own. These former kinds of — originally immediate — *experience* can, later or elsewhere, be reproduced via language and then obtain the status of *events*. If an author focusses, not only on displaced matters, but also on another, displaced, consciousness, he presents events in a way similar to immediate experience, the effect of which is called *displaced immediacy*. This interrelation is illustrated in *Figure 6*. (See next page).

It is one of the characteristics of non-fictional discourse that the proximal consciousness of speech is a real person. In news reporting, however, the predominant task is to inform about political events; thus, journalists mainly focus on displaced matters and rarely on the immediacy of their own situation. As a result, political facts are typically treated as events, and not as displaced experience. It is rarely the journalist's own experience that he has to report; information which finds its way into a newspaper normally reaches the paper by way of press agencies, eyewitness reports, statements by official organs, or so-called "informed sources". In other words, what has originally been immediate experience is usually sifted through a number of intermediaries. Depending on the extent to which the journalist processes the material obtained into a discourse organisation of his own, his role as speaker varies in kind. These speaker roles, introduced in the following, are one feature according to which various sub-genres of news reporting can be distinguished.

(a) <u>speaker as reporter:</u> Political facts that come from external sources are most efficiently presented as "hard news" (cf. Lüger 1983:66), which deviate in all respects from what Chafe (1994:201ff.) discusses as *qualitative* properties of immediate experience. First, in terms of *continuity*, events in hard news are presented as "experiential islands" (Chafe 1994:202), i.e. chunks of experience that are shaped according to the needs of the addressees. This is, for instance, represented by the principle of increasing specification, a typical discourse organisation of hard news (cf. 5.2.2.3), which is diametrically opposed to the continuous nature of an experience. Second, instead of the "fine-grained *detail*" (Chafe 1994:203; my emphasis) available in the immediacy of an experience, an event is usually strongly reduced and very selectively treated. Finally, *deictic* elements "that locate an experience in space and time, and also with respect to a self" (Chafe 1994:205) are normally absent.

Figure 6. *Immediacy and displacement reproduced into language*

As a result of these features, hard news treats political matters as clearly displaced events, but the speaker is not displaced in his consciousness. He therefore lets his language flow from a location in space and time that is recognisably different from the events being talked about. In other words, the journalist as a *reporter* uses *immediate speech dealing with displaced events*. It is the kind of news reporting which, I have found, is marked by a virtual absence of inverted constructions. An example for such a short news text is given in (33):

(33) MP not to face charges
Bribery charges against Harry Greenway, Conservative MP for Ealing North, are to be dropped, the Queen Prosecution Service said yesterday. Mr. Greenway was accused of accepting gifts, including foreign holidays, in return for using parliamentary influence on behalf of Plasser Railway Machinery in connection with British Rail contracts. The decision, by Barbara Mills, the director of public prosecutions, follows the acquittal of all defendants in another trial involving Plasser Railway. (Times, 15 Dec.92, p.2)

(b) speaker as experiencer: There are forms of news reporting in which the proximal consciousness of the speaker turns out to be in a displaced mode and focusses on another, distal consciousness (cf. Chafe 1994:198ff.). In journalistic writing this is, for instance, the case when a report is written by a correspondent who has had access to the immediate experience of political events, or at least pretends to have had such. Sub-genres of reports thereby arise, sometimes explicitly marked as an "eyewitness report" or, alternatively, by mentioning of the name and location of the correspondent. This is usually enough to prepare the reader for a more personal mode of reporting. It is in these kinds of contexts that one finds that the author not only focusses on events, but also on the experience or quasi-experience itself. A symptom of this is that the presentation of political news maintains more characteristics of immediate experience in terms of temporal continuity, richness of detail and the use of deictic expressions. The effect is one of *displaced immediacy*, achieved by one or several qualities of immediacy being added to a displaced experience (cf. Chafe 1994:226ff.). Assuming the position of a displaced consciousness, the journalist shifts his ground back in time, from the reporter to a previous — or pretended — position as an *experiencer*.

Langacker's (1990) approach to subjectivity, applied earlier (cf. 4.2.3), distinguishes objective from subjective construal of the speaker's ground:

depending on whether the speaker is objectively put "onstage" or remains, subjectively, off the scene expressed via language. There are thus in principle two alternative ways in which a speaker can relate back to his own experience, of which the latter was said above to create the typical context of FI usage. This claim can now be substantiated by observations from news reports: notably, by the fact that there are mainly occurrences of FI in the absence of an objective mention of the speaker in the text. To illustrate this, consider (34), which contains several markers of an objective construal of the speaker's ground, while in (35) the nature of immediate experience is expressed subjectively:

(34) WELCOME to Travnik — Have a Nice Stay, read the sign as <u>our</u> Warrior sped into the town. <u>We</u> travelled along the main street, past broken windows, buildings riddled with bullet-holes, destroyed by shells.

People waved their appreciation. [...]

<u>We</u> pass the most shelled building in the town — the hospital — and on to the frontline village of Turbe — [...].

<u>I</u> am with the Colonel Bob Stewart, commanding officer [...]. It is one of the best organised, most professional British operations <u>I</u> have ever seen — and one <u>we</u> can be proud of.

<u>My journey from Split on Sunday to Sarajevo</u> brought home to me the sheer scale of the operation [...]. (Times, 15 Dec.92, p.1)

The passage in (34) displays *spatiotemporal* displacement (cf. Chafe 1994:200) in that the correspondent focusses on his own displaced experience. It does, however, not involve displacement of *self*, because the ground is construed objectively by first person pronouns. Nonetheless, there is already an effect of displaced immediacy, which is due to the maintenance of relative continuity, a richness of details rather unusual for ordinary news reporting, and, most explicitly, to the switch to immediate deixis in form of the present tense in the middle of the report. This is a kind of context where, compared to hard news, inversion is more likely to occur, because its viewpoint meaning would add a further component of displaced immediacy. It is, however, done without here, since it is objective reference to the previous experience that is chosen instead. The effect of displaced immediacy gets lost once the speaker sets in to reflect upon this experience (*my journey from*), which flows again from a consciousness recognisably different from the location of the events reported.

By contrast, (35) displays displaced immediacy that arises out of a subjectively construed ground:

(35) Yesterday they muzzled their guns for the first time, but the atmosphere was tense.
One Serb sharpshooter, the barrel of his AK-47 automatic rifle poking out of a second-floor window, glared at UN troops as they scrambled into position on both sides of the bridge.
Spotting him, a French soldier flopped down with his arms curled around a sniper rifle with long sights, and aimed at the building. [...]
Two bursts of gunfire rang out. Journalists and some UN officers ducked in alarm.
French soldiers herded the journalists back to the boulevard and behind the wreckage of two rusted trucks dragged across the intersection to shield civilians. [...]
<u>On one side of the street leading to the bridge was a burnt-out restaurant. On the other stood the shell of a newspaper kiosk.</u>(Guard, 11 Feb.94, p.6)

In this passage, an impression of immediate experience gets created for a number of reasons. First, by means of a narrative structure, there is a relative temporal continuity, i.e., the order of presentation in the text is identical to the order of occurrence of the represented events. Second, the passage contains a number of details which would certainly be irrelevant in hard news (*second-floor window*, *arms curled around*, *rusted trucks*); these support the eyewitness nature of the text, which was also explicitly marked as such. Last but not least, there are two instances of FI, whereby the speaker assumes a viewpoint within the universe of discourse. Instead of appearing objectively "onstage", which could be done by first person pronouns (*On one side of the street* [...], *we see* [...]), he chooses to remain "offstage" and only subjectively assumes his role as an experiencer. In addition to spatio-temporal displacement, this attitude now also involves displacement of *self*: the speaker focusses on "events and states that originated in the consciousness of someone else" (Chafe 1994:200). Following Chafe, it is empathy with the discourse world established that facilitates displacement of self (cf. 1994:249); thus, the occurrence of FI in news reporting indicates at least a reduction in objectivity within this genre.

(c) speaker as architect (of discourse organisation): Not every full inversion in news reporting is meant as an instruction for the reader to focus on the displaced consciousness of the reporter as an experiencer. Many news texts, especially those not explicitly marked as eyewitness reports, have a purpose beyond that of reproducing an experience of a scene, location or event; the more a report aims at providing an analysis of the news, the more apparent this becomes. Certainly, this intention underlies editorials and comments. It is due to this analytical intent that these texts can also be found to sometimes make use of fully inverted constructions.

FI constructions that occur in articles aiming at an analysis of their news generally follow constituents that give a more abstract local or temporal orientation, or one that is an entirely nonlocative property ascribed to the subject. These are kinds of lexical information that, if expressed in the preposed constituent, obviously do not stem from an immediate experience of the speaker, so that the reader will have to look for another kind of ground he is invited to share. The "experience" in question alternatively consists in the speaker's own reasoning, in the textual relations among topics which he builds up when organising his discourse. Instead of a physically existent, displaced, situation, the reader may thereby be invited into the mind of the speaker, into how he sees, relates and evaluates the facts which are presented in the text. In this way, FIs no longer produce displaced immediacy by virtue of a "stop-look-see strategy" (Enkvist 1991:9), but fulfil topic change and structure-building functions: they invite the reader into *the immediacy of the speaker's organisation of discourse*. No longer reflecting relations within a world previously experienced by the speaker and possibly reproduced with an effect of immediacy, FIs can also relate to the text event itself; they construe relations among discourse entities, such as they are "made up" by the speaker in his mind.

Strictly speaking, those uses of inversion are not a device of news reporting, but are typical of evaluation, analysis, and comment. As such, they most commonly occur in genres with a more interpersonal function, i.e. in expository and argumentative discourse. Ultimately, they mark a speaker or *author comment*, "an author [...] speaking more directly to his reader" (Jones 1983:77). Thereby, the perspective expressed by FI becomes one from the speaker's own explanation or argumentation. His role, however, is not one of an overt commentator within the text, but one which could be labeled *architect* of the discourse organisation. Like the architect of a house, the speaker does not show up objectively in his own reasoning. In texts with a predominant informational function, such as news reports, this function is usually added to individual passages only.

There are also, of course, objective alternatives of commenting on and structuring a discourse. Full inversions as expressions of the speaker as architect of textual and evaluative relations may therefore not occur as long as the speaker does not avoid coming on stage. By contrast, they are particularly well suited if the speaker does not wish to enter the scene objectively, but chooses to present the relations that hold between discourse entities as a mental world, without explicitly entering it himself. It is nonetheless symptomatic that FIs that fulfil a function of this kind typically co-occur with other "markers" of author comments (cf. Jones 1983:87ff.). This holds, for instance, for the passages given in (36) and (37), in which, significantly, both inversions occur in the final paragraph of the reports. They are justifiably considered a means of concluding analysis and evaluation:

(36) Sri Lanka's human exports have brought some profit to the country. Last year, for example, [...].

Against that, however, must be measured the cost of having lost the talent, industry and enterprise of so many Sri Lankan citizens who prefer to live almost anywhere but in their homeland. (Econ, 3 Apr.93, p.62)

(37) The newspaper complained that Roger Altman, the deputy treasury secretary, is currently also interim chief of the Resolution Trust Corporation, another nominally independent agency which is examining aspects of Whitewater.

The Journal also attacked the appointment of Mr Clinton's Oxford and Yale classmate [...].

Mr Ludwig, another Renaissance weekend regular, is in charge of regulating national banks, including those in Arkansas linked to Whitewater.

Behind these complaints lies the tacit suggestion that some Clinton officials are intent on side-tracking or emasculating Mr. Fiske's Whitewater investigation while the democrats in Congress look the other way. (Guard, 11 Feb.94, p.4)

Both (36) and (37) contain further symptoms of the presence of the speaker, such as demonstratives in extended use (cf. Jones 1983:90). In addition, (36) displays a change in modality (*must*), which reflects a "shift in deictic standpoint" (Jones 1983:88), a metaphor (*cost*) and an adversative adverb (*however*). In (37), the evaluation is further supported by lexical means (*tacit suggestion*).

(d) <u>speaker as commentator:</u> In discourse under conditions of displacement, author comments represent "a *temporary departure from the main train of thought in a text*" (Jones 1983:77; his emphasis); as such they are the most immediate kind of speech in written discourse. Due to the fact that a "proximal consciousness alternates easily between the immediate and displaced modes" (Chafe 1992:235), the speaker can temporarily address the reader more directly. In this way, author comments become *immediate speech dealing with immediate matters*. As concerns the usage of inversion, it is constituent-focussing SAI that correlates with author comments of this immediate kind: since SAIs express how the speaker is affected by the fronted constituent, how he attaches relative prominence to them, they occur when the speaker assumes a direct role as *commentator* within the text.

As markers of this kind, most SAI constructions in newspaper language in fact occur in the commenting section, as did (38). The meaning of the two SAIs in this passage is roughly equivalent to the use of a sentential adverb, which is another typical marker of an author comment (cf. Jones 1983:96f.); it could be replaced, for instance, by *significantly*. Also, in this passage, the SAIs occur in sections which are shifted to the future tense, the inherent tense of analysis and prognosis:

(38) But the present electoral rules, based on a too-pure version of proportional representation, still have to be changed. <u>Only then will voters be able to wrest from party bosses the power to choose their government.</u>
 The voters get their chance to bring in new majority voting rules in a referendum on the upper house later this month. They will give the reforms a resounding Yes. Under pressure from public opinion, the lower house will probably follow suit. <u>Then and only then — some time in the autumn — will the country be able to elect a parliament so different from the present one</u> that it has the moral authority to broach the question of an amnesty. (Econ, 3 Apr.93, p.16)

SAI occurrence in news reporting is not excluded either, but marks individual passages as containing analysis, evaluation or comment. This is the context of (39):

(39) In any case, democracy was not — as Vizcaino Casas craftily insinuates — implanted after 1975. It was restored, having been brutally overthrown 39 years earlier, by none other than Francisco Franco himself.
<u>Nor was it necessary for Spain to endure a dictatorship in order to become prosperous.</u> Franco's initial impact on Spain, from which the country has arguably never recovered, was to ruin its economy. <u>Not until 1951 did GDP per head recover its pre-civil war level.</u> It would be an irony indeed if the Caudillo were to end up getting the credit for the "creation" of what he actually destroyed. (Guardw, 3 Jan.93, p.6)

There are again other markers of the presence of the speaker in the text that accompany the two occurrences of SAI in this passage: sentence adverbs (*arguably, indeed*), changes in modality (*was to, would be*), extraposition (*it was necessary*) and metaphors (*to be irony, getting the credit*).

To summarise, there are thus four different attitudes which a speaker can adopt when dealing with displaced matters in journalistic discourse; these have been illustrated for the context of political news reporting. Out of these roles, which are repeated in *figure 7*, the lower three (in the box) have an affinity with

immediacy and displacement in language	role of the speaker
immediate speech dealing with displaced events ⟶	reporter
displaced immediacy ⟶	experiencer
immediacy of speaker's organisation of discourse ⟶	architect
immediate speech dealing with immediate matters ⟶	commentator

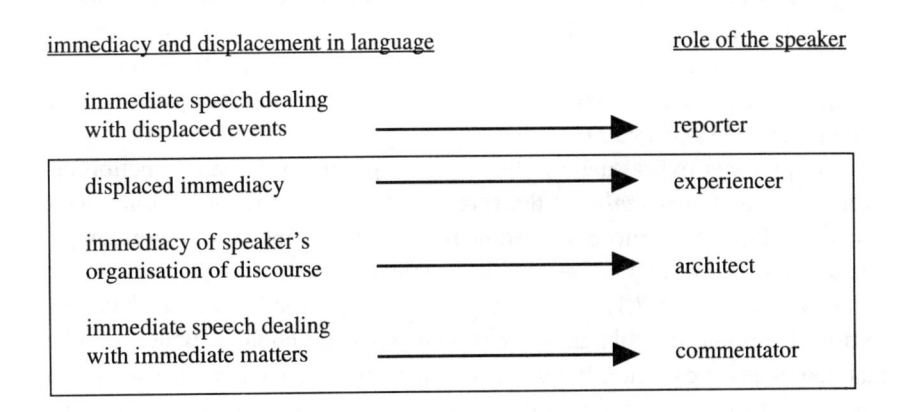

Figure 7. *Immediacy and displacement and role of the speaker*

the use of inversions of various kinds. Though inversion is not necessarily predictable in these contexts, these can be considered the conditions under which it potentially occurs and in fact makes its contribution to the marking of these speaker roles.

5.3.2 Displaced immediacy, organisation of discourse and comment in political news reporting

To complete the picture of the affinities of inversion with conditions of displacement on the one hand, and with categories of discourse on the other, the results from a second, non-quantitative, corpus study will now be discussed. The aim is to show in more detail how and when inversions actually occur in different newspaper genres, and to test the hypotheses formulated so far about the compatibility of inversion with the various speaker roles in journalistic discourse. Since these, however, do not form part of any everyday categorisation of newspaper texts, I have used the political sections of a limited number of issues of various newspapers and magazines, subsuming them as political news reporting in general.[26] The genres that this corpus provides comprise everyday language categories such as hard news, soft news, report, reportage, political comment and news analysis, though, depending on the peculiarities of the individual papers, the assignment of a clear-cut genre category is not always easy. What all texts have in common is that they deal with political news, but this does not necessarily imply mere information: in the genres with the least dominant ideational function (comment, news analysis), information is often only a subordinate purpose, while, even in the so-considered information-based genres (hard and soft news, report, reportage), it is rather the rule than the exception that these also have other objectives, such as comment and analysis.

Despite this hybrid nature of many newspaper texts, the distinction between *news* and *comment* is at the core of most classifications of journalistic discourse. It must therefore have some relevance in terms of a "genre-competence" of speakers and hearers with an effect on both text production and comprehension (cf. 5.2.1.2). Above, such genre-specific knowledge has been said to determine the tolerance for certain linguistic choices, which implies that genre-specific — non-linguistic and linguistic — devices must somehow contribute to the signalling of the presence of a certain genre. Particularly important in journalistic discourse are of course those kinds of information which indicate that the journalist leaves his "neutral" position as a mediator of information and more directly intervenes in the presentation of the textual material.

It is, first of all, by means of *pre-signals* that readers of a newspaper are instructed about the nature of the genre which they encounter. Pre-signals can have the form of extra-sections or columns, sometimes explicitly titled, the titles and sub-titles of the article itself, or special conventions in format or print. On the basis of such signals, it is in general possible for the reader to discern the predominantly informative part of a newspaper, concerned with *ideational* content, from the more specialised, and more *interpersonal*, sections (cf. 5.2.1.1). Most newspapers use explicit signals as soon as they depart from what is considered the basic function of the press: to inform their readers. "Comment is free, facts are sacred" — pre-signals therefore have to indicate when the "sacred" role of the journalist, the *observer*, is abandoned, and a "freer" role as *intruder* adopted instead (cf. 5.2.1.1). On the basis of the previous analysis, it is to be expected that these are also the kind of signals that prepare the ground for inversion usage.

As pre-signals for more informative, as opposed to more comment-like, genres, the following are used in the newspapers and magazines from which I have drawn my sample of texts:

(a) Absence of any of the signals presented under (b) and (c) can be interpreted as presence of *news* (discourse type: (mostly) *description*). News in this sense can take the form of hard news,[27] report or reportage; however, especially the quality papers and weekly magazines do not care to consistently mark any such further distinction explicitly most of the time.

(b) *Comment* as discourse with a primary function to *evaluate* (discourse type: *argumentation*) is typically pre-signalled by either explicit naming of genre such as "comment" (*The Guardian, The Guardian Weekly*), "commentary" (*The Guardian*), "editorial" (*The Washington Post* as included in *The Guardian Weekly*) or "political sketch" (*The Times*), and/or the naming of individual sections or pages as "the leader page" (*The Guardian*), "leaders" (*The Economist*) or "opinion" (*Newsweek, Daily Express*). It may also just be indicated by a placement on a special page or in a framed box, often headed by the newspaper's logo (*The Times, The Daily Telegraph, The Guardian Weekly*).

(c) *News analysis* or discourse with a primary function to *explain* (discourse type: *exposition*) is pre-signalled in more diverse ways. It is sometimes explicitly announced as "analysis" (*The Guardian*); alternatively, some papers have set up special rubrics, such as, for instance, "The week in Britain" and "The USA this week" in *The Guardian Weekly* and "Public Lives" in *Newsweek*. As indicated above, however, a component of analysis is usually integrated into longer reports and reportages. In particular, this sometimes suggests itself because of the kind of titles or sub-titles chosen: if the title contains, for instance, a rhetorical question, a thesis, or an explicit announcement of some kind of analysis, the reader will expect an analytical reasoning, rather than mere information, to follow. (40) is an example of a rhetorical question in the sub-title, which suggests the presence of news analysis, while (41) illustrates how a thesis together with the naming of a correspondent implies that an analysis is following at least on top of a report:

(40) THE NEW ROMAN CONQUEST
Catholic and Anglican leaders are playing down the defections — but does the RC mafia have a different agenda? (Guard, 25 Febr.94, p.2)

(41) ROMANIA RETURNS GAZE TO NAZI PAST
Julian Borger sees the myth of a second world war dictator working to comfort a traumatised state. (Guard, 25 Febr.94, p.5)

These are thus the kinds of pre-signals that are probably used by readers (and that can be used by a discourse analyst) to identify articles from political newspaper sections as news, comment, or news analysis.[28] Affinities of inversion with the three genres are discussed under (a) – (c) below. However, the overall picture in news reporting also substantiates the claim made above that FI as well as SAI are markers of subjectivity in discourse (cf. 5.2.2.2). Since subjectivity by definition requires the distinction between the immediacy of the speaker's ground and the displacement of the events reported to become blurred, inversions are generally not expected as long as the speaker functions as mere reporter, i.e. uses immediate speech dealing with displaced events. This is what was claimed as a basic affinity in the previous section (cf. *figure 7*). But there also seems to be a correlation between the degree of subjectivity in news reporting, such as provided for by press-, newspaper- and genre-specific conventions, and the occurrence of inversion, such as it can be noted for this register on the basis of the texts investigated. Evidence for this is:

- a relatively rare use of inverted constructions in most — especially the daily — newspapers, at least as concerns the political sections. The issues of *The Times*, *The Daily Telegraph* and *The Daily Express* contained exactly one FI each and no SAI construction.

- a somewhat greater proneness to inversion usage of the weekly magazines and papers, such as found in one issue each of *The Economist* (6 FIs, 15 SAIs), *Newsweek* (8 FIs, 3 SAIs) and *The Guardian Weekly* (6 FIs, 7 SAIs).

- a remaining relevance of matters of convention, which apparently allow for more or less subjectivity within an individual newspaper's style. Two issues of *The Guardian* supplied considerably more inversions (one issue contained 9 FIs and 4 SAIs, another 4 FIs and 2 SAIs), and spread over news as well as comment and analysis, than did the other daily newspapers.

Also, relatively modest absolute figures, though on the basis of a considerable amount of newspaper language, confirm the quantitative results from my corpus study, in particular the nature of the category reportage as the least subjective kind of discourse. In addition, the divergence in numbers suggests what has already been argued above: namely, that it is plausible to assume that, when inversions are less frequent overall, the effect which they produce can be even stronger and more "meaningful" (cf. 5.2.1.2). Therefore, the remainder of this section focusses on individual occurrences of inversion in the three genres news, comment, and news analysis, accounting for their usage in terms of the roles of the speaker introduced above.

(a) news: This genre is most directly affected by the incompatibility of inversion with the bare role of a reporter: it is to be expected that the construction is virtually absent here, and even more so, the briefer the text is. Sections such as "News in brief" (*The Times*, *The Guardian*), "The week" (*The Guardian Weekly*), "In brief" (*The Daily Telegraph*, *The Economist*), "The world this week" (*The Economist*) or "Periscope" (*Newsweek*), as well as pages titled "News'", which contain a range of short articles (*Daily Express*), have indeed been found not to supply any occurrence of inversion whatsoever.

By contrast, the longer the news texts are, the greater becomes at least the potentiality of encountering an inversion. Basically, this is due to two different kinds of contexts: those, on the one hand, where the author assumes a role as experiencer and produces an effect of displaced immediacy. On the other hand, even in news, the speaker often subjects the material to his own discourse organisation or temporarily assumes the role of commentator within the text.

The attitude of an experiencer is typical of news and reports written in a more personal style, often by a correspondent given by name, and it is even more typical of longer reportages. Foreign news is also more prone to FI occurrence, probably because their scenery is more relevant to the reader than is the familiar setting of home news. Usually, in those more personal kinds of news texts, the use of FI producing displaced immediacy is accompanied by corresponding linguistic devices, such as can be made out in the following two sample passages:

> (42) The 53-year-old businessman brandished his yellow membership card. He tossed it over. "There is no point in me holding on to it now," he said.
>
> The burnt-out Dream City cinema club is adjacent to Smithfield and to the City. [...]
>
> Through a red door, a set of rickety stairs led to the first floor and reception. The stairways and bannisters were wooden, and fire was bound to spread quickly. [...]
>
> Cinema One had a 21-inch television screen in a stand, and bench seats. <u>At the back was a set of stairs leading to a tiny balcony</u>, where sexual activity took place.
>
> Another stairway led to Cinema Two, where there was an open space for customers to liaise. (Guard, 28 Febr.94, p.7)

(42) is a descriptive passage, which forms part of an article reporting on a fire. It therefore makes sense that there is a special interest to inform the reader about the concrete location involved. This eyewitness perspective is supported by the introduction and quoting of individual persons; the whole purpose is to invite the reader to feel "on the spot", where the aftermaths of the events are still being felt. In this kind of context, the FI does not mark an interpersonal function of the text, but rather a special direct manner of information, namely by means of displaced immediacy.

(43) also produces an eyewitness perspective, again pre-signalled by a strongly descriptive textual beginning:

> (43) Yigal Chazan in Crkvine reports on UN troops trying to keep the peace

SERBS STICK TO THEIR GUNS IN GAME OF HIDE AND SEEK
Gleaming in the winter sunshine, Bosnian Serb guns strung out along this ramshackle hilltop village point menacingly towards Sarajevo's western suburbs, three days after the expiry of NATO's ultimatum for heavy weaponry to be withdrawn or put under United Nations Control.
[...]
<u>Beside the Warriors lie piles of razor wire that should by now have enclosed the cannons and mortars.</u> UN patrols trudge along the sludgy Crkvine escarpment, as the Serbs clean and oil their guns.
The impasse is perhaps the most glaring example of the Serb's half-hearted compliance with Nato's demands. (Guard, 25 Febr.94, p.5)

Here, the FI creates displaced immediacy, and at the same time it structures the text into a descriptive sub-part and an analysing section which is to follow. A clear indication of that is the overt comment *is perhaps the most glaring example*. Thus, it is not that the speaker's role as an experiencer needs to be present in the whole of a report in which an inversion occurs; the construction can also support the organisation of the article: in (43), it is the perspective of the speaker expressed by the inversion that provides the transition between the two paragraphs and that forms the starting-point for a more personal evaluation. In both cases, however, some kind of speaker presence prepares the ground for the usage of inversion.

There may also be a transition within a news text from the main informative body to background information, or to more directly speaker-based comments, initiated by means of an inversion. When an FI performs a topic change function, such as discussed in 4.2.3, it usually provides a new discourse topic and thereby symptomatically occurs paragraph-initially. In that case, it reflects the role of the speaker as architect of the organisation of his article. In terms of the structure of otherwise mostly decriptive news texts, the initiation of a change in focus represents a *digression* from the expected progression. The usual functions of digressions in informative texts are to yield "informative background" or an "evaluation" (cf. Giora 1990:305), which perfectly correponds to the nature of predicative FIs: they start out from locative PPs, which constitute static locative properties, or from directly evaluative predicates, expressed by AdjPs and abstract PPs. In both cases, a presentative mechanism provides a new discourse topic as background to the main line of the text. FIs of this kind thereby become *digression markers* in informative texts, reflecting the role of the author as architect of discourse structure. Following Giora's terminology, a digression alternatively provides *informative background* or *evaluative material*.

In the news texts investigated, FIs as digression markers symptomatically co-occur with other linguistic devices that mark the intervention of the speaker into the way he presents his news material. Ultimately, these news reports have a strong component of analysis or evaluation as well. Digressions in the form of informative background are exemplified by the following two passages:

(44) GAMES WITHOUT FRONTIERS ON COMMUNISM'S BORDER WITH CAPITALISM
Kevin Rafferty experiences the unreal cold of Panmunjom, where the cold war's unfinished business is taken seriously.
The air is still and quiet, eerily so. A flock of geese flies past in the mantlepiece formation. [...]
It is a minor miracle [...].
In the end, according to the computer simulation, the South Koreans backed by strengthened US forces would win, but it would take a bloody six months of struggle. Seoul, only a howitzer's throw from the border, would be devastated.
<u>On top of this comes the nuclear threat.</u> North Korea signed the Nuclear Non-Proliferation Treaty in 1985, [...]. (Guard, 25 Febr.94, p.11)

(44) is the beginning of the article, which very much starts out as an eyewitness report, but soon leads over to passages containing comments of the speaker. For instance, this is marked by the extraposition *It is a minor miracle*, by modality, as well as by the use of *bloody* in the paragraph preceding the inversion. The demonstrative pronoun in the front-shifted constituent is in extended use and is thereby another marker of a speaker comment (cf. Jones 1983:90f.): it summarises what has so far been dealt with and, with the change in perspective inherent in FI, leads over to the next discourse topic. The FI at the beginning of the new paragraph initiates an informative sub-part of the article and, as an informative digression within the main line of the article, introduces a new topic. *The nuclear threat* is a higher-level topic, which serves

as some kind of heading for the entire report to follow. In (45), by contrast, two sub-topics are anchored to a summary of what has been preceding:

(45) [...] and follows accusations by Tory MPs that police officers passed on the information and that some may have been paid for doing so.
Mr. Condon said: [...]
A Yard statement said that [...]
The statement added that [...]
<u>Leading the Tory expressions of outrage were Nigel Waterson, MP for Eastbourne and a friend of Mr Milligan, and Sir Jerry Wiggin, MP for Weston-super-Mare.</u>
They and other MPs were considering moving an amendment [...]. (DailTel, 11 Febr.94, p.2)

FIs as digression markers for evaluative material are illustrated by (46) and (47). (46) occurs paragraph-initially and provides an evaluative background for the next chunk of information, while (47) terminates the introductory presentation of facts in the first paragraph of the news report and represents the conclusion on the part of the speaker. The inversion placed at the end of the paragraph serves as the topical sentence for the entire report:

(46) But he knows his party's anti-immigration stand during the elections helped it reduce the electoral threat from rightist Jean-Marie Le Pen, whose extremist National Front won no seats in the Assembly.
<u>More tricky is the unemployment issue</u>, which helped the Socialists in last month's elections. On Balladur's first day at work, the number of French jobless topped 3 million for the first time. (NW, 12 Apr.93, p.14)

(47) Europe remains disunited, mired in recession, threatened by massive emigration from the south and east. <u>Over Europe's thinkers and leaders hangs a pall of gloom reminiscent of the deep "Europessimism" of the early 1980s.</u> (NW, 12 Apr.93, p.10)

To summarise, in news with its primarily informative function, inversions have a clear function of structuring the discourse into separate sub-parts. They therefore occur only in longer news texts. Either the inversion adds a temporary perspective of immediacy to the information about a scene or event from the outside world; or, alternatively, it can mark a digression from the mainly descriptive progression of news, providing informative background or an evaluation. These functions hold for the occurrence of FI in this genre, while SAI is virtually absent.

(b) comment: Commenting articles seldom have a speaker as an experiencer, i.e., they seldom make use of the effect of displaced immediacy, added to the reproduction of an actual scene or event. The role of the speaker as architect of textual relations is not very frequent either, less frequent in any case than in news and news analysis. On the one hand, this has to do with the mere length of the texts: comments, at least in the daily newspapers, tend to be rather brief and do not really contain many major topic turns. The other factor is probably that comment is "free": the speaker need not avoid coming out into the open. In comments, speakers thus often prefer the use of personal pronouns instead of FIs, objectively anchoring a new discourse topic to their own ground and thereby producing explicit comments.

By contrast, what is quite frequent in commenting articles are pronominal constructions containing SAI, which anchor new topics to anaphoric reference. Also, not surprisingly, comments easily make use of constituent-focussing SAI, in which the speaker is objectively present as the commentator. The few FIs that one finds in comments nonetheless serve to introduce topics, i.e. arise out of a role of the speaker as architect of the discourse organisation. In them, the perspective expressed is usually directly related to the immediacy of the argument. This is particularly well reflected by the occurrence of deictic presentative FIs, which, as in (48), introduce topics by anchoring them to the immediacy of the text itself. As indicated by the past tense in this example, reference is nonetheless made to the discourse world established, so that the immediacy is shifted here into the displacement of *the departing old year*:

(48) BACK TO PIT ONE

The departing old year, with a steel-tipped boot, set old wounds bleeding again. Blood and irony. Here were the coal unions — the NUM, Nacods, and UDM — patrolling to the High Court claiming that the Coal Board and Government had acted illegally when they tried to close 31 pits at a stroke. And here was the Court agreeing with them. No strikes; no threats. (Guardw, 27 Dec.92, p.10)

In view of the richness of metaphors, there is sufficient evidence in this passage for the symptomatic co-presence of other markers of a speaker comment. The overall role of the speaker is clearly one of a commentator; this is not evaluative material *added to* information, but evaluation in its own right. In the terms introduced above, we have here immediate speech dealing with immediate matters. The deictic FIs are textual metaphors of the originally situational presentative construction (cf. 4.1.2.1); they make reference to the speech event shared by both the speaker and the hearer, which stresses the interpersonal nature of them. They do not primarily express ideational meaning, but directly (deictically) refer to the immediacy of the comment itself.

Longer comments also make use of more abstract lexical FIs, which do topic change work similar to the effect in news illustrated above. Again, the fronted constituents usually express relations within the argument of the speaker, rather than being directly taken from the experiential content of the outside world. In comments, however, it is not that inversions mark digressions from a descriptive type of discourse; instead, they are constitutive *parts of the argumentation*, contributing to an argumentative discourse type. Therefore, symptomatically, FIs in comments are often accompanied by adversative markers, which corresponds to the dialectic character of argumentation. (49) and (50) illustrate the difference:

(49) How has it happened? Of course it is a complicated story, but <u>through it runs a simple truth</u> that does not need a PhD in planning to comprehend. You cannot slash the housing budget in half and cut new council homes from 110,000 a year to fewer than 10,000 and expect there will be no problems. (Guardw, 20 Dec.92, p.12)

(50) China is Asia's least satisfied power. For most of the 1980s Deng Xiaoping kept defence fourth of his four modernisations, after agriculture, industry and science. Since 1990 defence spending has doubled. As China's economy prospered, it was bound to want a modern army. But <u>along with fancier tanks, ships and aircraft has come another worrying change</u>: China's ambition to project power far beyond its borders. (Econ, 3 Apr.93, p.15)

The inversions in these passages belong to the main line of the text itself: a change in focus initiates a counter-argument in (49) and leads over from the recall of facts to the core of the problem treated in (50).

Another case in which an FI in a comment supports the argumentation is when it expresses some kind of evaluation and thereby initiates an evaluative sub-part; most typically this is the conclusion drawn from prior reasoning. For instance, this was the case in (36), discussed above and repeated here as (51). It comes from the end of an article, which is also its conclusion:

(51) Sri Lanka's human exports have brought some profit to the country. Last year, for example, [...].
 Against that, however, must be measured the cost of having lost the talent, industry and enterprise of so many Sri Lankan citizens who prefer to live almost anywhere but in their homeland. (Econ, 3 Apr.93, p.62)

In this example, the inversion functions as a marker of *evaluation*, and not of an evaluative digression, as noted above about news.

In sum, it is the anchoring of the more abstract fronted lexical constituents to what is the speaker's own argument and evaluation, as well as the direct stance expressed by constituent-focussing SAI, that underlie a natural affinity of inversion with editorials (cf. 5.2.2.2), and with the role of commentator in general (cf. 5.3.1). This affinity, however, does not necessarily find its expression in quantitative predominance, which would cause only an "inflation" of its effect. Instead, it is the placement of the inversion within the article that often causes a substantial discourse function. In terms of the speaker roles, inversion in comments reflects the speaker as the architect of discourse structure and, more commonly, as the commentator on the events involved: the construction is a marker of (parts of) the argumentation and of evaluation in this genre.

(c) news analysis: News analysis is still another kind of genre that primarily has an interpersonal function. Instead of exploiting inversion as a marker in its own right, however, it displays a synthesis of the various functions that inversion has in news and comment. First, an effect of displaced immediacy is not excluded in this genre, because analysis, to a greater extent than comment, requires prior and explicit information about the news event itself. Second, for analysing the context and the background of news, the organisation of discourse has greater priority, so that what was said to be an analytical sub-component — possible, but not inherent — in news has its proper justification in news analysis: relations among discourse topics, putting entities "onstage" by means of the subjective presentative mechanism of FI, typically arise out of the speaker's own analysis. Finally, comment is in principle permitted in news analysis, whereby constituent-focussing SAI is rarely, but possibly, found.

Most occurrences of FI in this genre again help to structure the usually longer texts into relevant sub-parts. In particular, these parts derive from the topical structure of the analysis. The speaker is almost necessarily the architect of his own analysis; in that, the occurrences are similar in kind to the instances quoted above from longer news texts (cf. (44) – (47)). (52) illustrates how sub-topics are derived from prior topics by means of two FIs in news analysis, while, in (53), a summarising, higher-level topic follows previous, anchoring, information:

(52) Though he was referring to a historical phenomenon that had been supplanted by improved interchurch relations, his comments were seized by those intent, in the wake of the vote on women priests, on talking up the destruction of the Established Church through mass defections to papal ranks.

<u>Leading the media proselytisers is a small cabal of Catholic writers of conservative mind</u> commanding a disproportionate amount of column inches to preach their gospel. The Guy Fawkes of this conspiracy to turn England Catholic is historian and left-to-right political convert Paul Johnson.

<u>Aspiring to the role of Titus Oates are William Oddie</u> who, proving the old adage about over-zealous converts, has been slagging off his erstwhile spiritual home at every turn with misplaced enthusiasm of the Spanish Inqisition, <u>and Lord Rees-Mogg</u>, who has turned his column in the Times over to an assault on every vestige of Anglicism. (Guard, 25 Feb.94, p.2)

What the two *VP-inversions* in this passage show is that, in news analysis, it is more typically the case that one finds predicative, instead of purely locative, constituents fronted. Again, these do not have the function of primarily expressing ideational content. In addition, as in (53), the higher-level topics introduced often have an evaluative meaning (*glorious*), so that the FI is again often accompanied by further markers of author comments, such as a metaphor (*horizon*):

(53) South Koreans seem curiously unable to make a clear judgement of their kinfolk across the border, and Seoul is the worst place to go for intelligent (or intelligence) assessment of the North.
   On the horizon of a reunited, or at least reconciled, Korean peninsula lies a yet more glorious prospect. It was set out last May in a speech by Kim Deogryong, a key confidant of the President. (Guard, 25 Feb.94, p.8)

The discourse contributions of FI to news analysis are thus not of a basically different kind, compared to the ones noted for news and comment. In news, however, the reader in the first place expects being informed; inversion usually delimits the informational body from an inserted or concluding analytical sub-part. By contrast, in texts pre-signalled as analysis, the analytical, speaker-based attitude is expected and dominates. Analysis as a whole is immediate speech dealing with immediate matters, since it is the immediate concern of the text to analyse and to explain the events and facts under discussion. Thus, while news is often structured according to varying roles of the speaker, out of which the architect and the commentator constitute more or less distinct digressions, news analysis is more directly structured by the course of the analysis itself. For establishing an expository discourse type, the relations among discourse topics are an important device. In this sense, FI in news analysis, marking *sub-parts of an exposition* or analysis, functions similarly to the way it marks parts of the argumentation in comment.

Since the explanatory purpose of news analysis does not preclude direct commenting either, one encounters constituent-focussing SAI in this genre as well. However, especially when pre-signalled jointly with comments, as in the section "comment and analysis" of *The Guardian*, the genre can in fact no longer be clearly separated from the texts intended to be read as comments. Example (54) comes from this section and could be news analysis, due to the rhetorical question in the title. It could, however, be just as well that the article was intended as a comment by the paper:

(54) A NOOSE THAT COULD CHOKE THE LIBERAL VOICE
   Is democracy in danger when MPs vote for reforms much of the electorate won't back?
   [...] What gives this revived populism power is the fact that the liberals have an Achilles' heel: a long tradition of bypassing popular consent that is echoed by this week's votes. Nowhere has this

been more evident than in the US, where for 30 years reformers used the Supreme Court rather than Congress to define and enforce rights for blacks and women. (Guard, 25 Febr.94, p.2)

To conclude, one should not oversimplify the correlation between genres, speaker roles and the occurrence of inversion. It would go too far to suggest that a very neat, in the sense of a predictable, picture of inversion occurrence is produced by the roles which a speaker in journalistic discourse assumes and by the claimed affinities. On the one hand, the everyday genre categories that a newspaper cares to signal do not consistently involve one attitude; a proximal consciousness alternates easily between the immediate and the displaced mode, so that the roles of the speaker can change within the course of a text. On the other hand, the affinities that inversion has with these roles do not imply that word order is the only way in which these can be marked; on the contrary, a range of alternative devices, usually of a more objective kind, exists. Some of them have been discussed here as well and could be shown to mark contexts of potential inversion occurrence.

With these limitations in mind, the conditions of immediacy and displacement underlying the different speaker roles can now be applied to the three genres distinguished within news reporting; the outcome is *figure 7a*, a modification of *figure 7*. Again, the lower three conditions (in the box) are those that have an affinity with inversion usage.

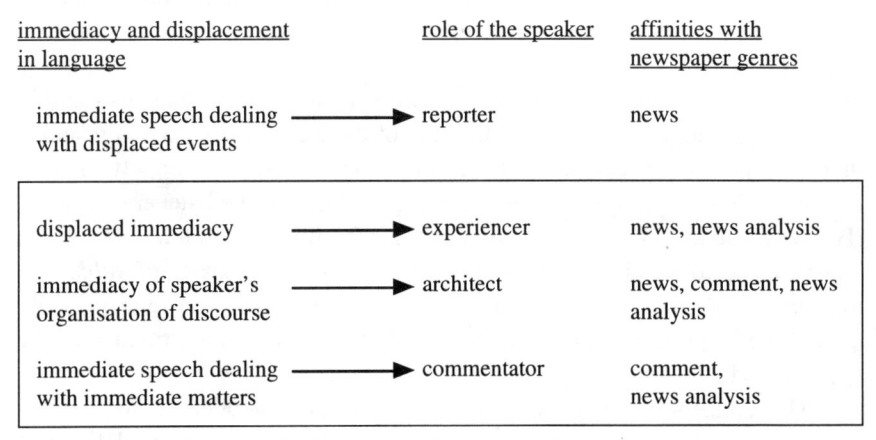

immediacy and displacement in language	role of the speaker	affinities with newspaper genres
immediate speech dealing with displaced events	⟶ reporter	news
displaced immediacy	⟶ experiencer	news, news analysis
immediacy of speaker's organisation of discourse	⟶ architect	news, comment, news analysis
immediate speech dealing with immediate matters	⟶ commentator	comment, news analysis

Figure 7a. *Immediacy and displacement, role of the speaker and newspaper genres*

5.4 Summary: inversion as a discourse marker

There is a common core in what has been said in this and the preceding chapter on the usage and function of inversion in actual discourse: both added subjectivity as well as contributions to discourse structure are concerned with *interpersonal* meaning. Thereby, the meaning of an inverted sentence such as defined by the linguistic system, in terms of its ideational content as well as its being word order deviant from the norm, additionally carries, like discourse markers in conversational discourse, a communicative force "due to the definition of the discourse slot in which it is used" (Schiffrin 1987:317). Three different kinds of communicative force have been distinguished, corresponding to different *speaker attitudes*: the use of an inversion reflects roles of the speaker as experiencer, architect (of discourse structure), and commentator. Their effect in discourse has been described as reproducing displaced immediacy, building up organisational parts, or commenting on the content expressed. Interpersonal meaning also has a corresponding effect on the hearer-side, which is overall one of *hearer-involvement*.

Word order choices of this kind are thus expressions of the speech or communicative event itself, which is an effect that clearly goes beyond their ideational meaning. As shown in chapter 4, the ideational content of an inversion is roughly equivalent in truth-conditions to that of the "normal" or canonical word order counterpart, so that the level of meaning of the clause as a representation of experience is not affected. By contrast, previous studies had already shown that inverted word order changes the meaning of the clause as a message, reflecting — sometimes just encoding — its thematic or information structure. My analysis of inversion has not questioned the justification of these claims. What this study has shown, however, is that inversion also — and in my view primarily — affects the meaning of the clause as an *exchange* and is therefore justifiably called a *marker of interpersonal meaning*. It directly derives from the speaker or writer "doing something to the listener or reader" (Halliday 1985:53; for complete quote cf. 2.1.3). It is only in this sense that it makes sense to speak of a syntactic construction as a carrier of *subjective* meaning: a formal device, word order, which has ideational and possibly textual meaning, in addition becomes a direct outflow of the presence of the speaker in the text and of speaker-hearer-relations.

The concept of "discourse marker" is usually applied to markers in spoken, basically conversational, language, for which it has been defined as "sequentially dependent elements which bracket units of talk" (Schiffrin 1987:31). In that "sequential dependence" indicates "that markers are devices that work on the discourse level" (Schiffrin 1987:37), this kind of function also holds for the analysis of many inversions as suggested here: their "bracketing" — or structuring — contribution to discourse arises out of the functional potential of re-ordering within the English word order system. Inversion attaches a particular perspective or prominence to a predication, or to an individual item within it, and is thereby apt to structure the discourse into separate units of one viewpoint at a time. These are not, however, units "of talk" determined by conversational turn-taking; the focus management task of FI as well as the speaker's stance expressed by SAI are typical of the "desituated" (Chafe 1994:45) context of writing and of an — in principle — irrelevant identity of both speaker and hearer. Instead of an objective construal of the communicative ground, by which in spoken discourse "a speaker's involvement with his or her audience is manifested [...] in a speaker's more frequent reference to him- or herself" (Chafe 1982:46), inversions only subjectively involve the speaker and hearer in the communicative event itself. They let the focus remain on the displacement of the matters concerned and structure the text by directing the focus of attention within the displaced ground of its own universe of discourse.

Although, in the corpus study, matters of *convention*, for instance writing conventions in British and American English, or genre conventions underlying the text categories of the LOB and the Brown corpus, have turned out to play a part in determining the usage of inversion in discourse, the core of the account has been a functional one. As such, the role of a discourse marker has more direct affinities with basic *types of discourse* than with conventions underlying various *genres*. By way of convention, most genres or their component parts represent different discourse types as well, defined by basic functions and structures as outlined in 5.2.1.1. That is how one can account for the kind of evidence, discussed in the previous section, that genres are prone to the usage of inversions to varying degrees. First and foremost, however, the status of inverted word order depends on the type of discourse in which it occurs: it reflects a speaker-based choice in English which exploits the cognitive processes underlying linearisation and thus brings an interpersonal component into any expression of ideational content; this is more or less counter to expectations in discourse with a primarily ideational function and gives rise to its role as a *digression* marker in informative texts; while in discourse with a primarily interpersonal purpose, it is a *constitutive* marker of discourse structure, of argumentation and exposition, both of which it structures by performing topic change or by leading over to direct comment and evaluation.

Apart from the interpersonal component, the contributions of FI and SAI to a discourse are nonetheless quite distinct: The various SAI types express that (and how) the speaker is affected by the item fronted or how he relates predications to each other; hence, SAI adds subjectivity or intervention on the part of the speaker in the way he presents his material to any predication in which it occurs. In that, it can mark structural parts of a discourse, such as evaluation or comment, where an evaluating or commenting attitude is not established beforehand or would not be expected overall. In discourse with a primarily ideational function, it thereby inserts *speaker comments*, while in discourse with an evaluative purpose, it is better characterised as a reflection of an overall *subjective attitude* or *style*. FI, by contrast, always involves some kind of localisation, upon which the presentative mechanism rests, and functions like a *discourse marker* closer to the understanding of Schiffrin (1987), because it is the nature of the "discourse slot" (cf. quote above) in which it is used that determines what it actually marks at a given point of a discourse. The conditions for its positioning furthermore depend on whether it occurs in a discourse type "strong" (cf. Virtanen 1992b:305) in terms of structure (narration and description) or in one more directly defined by an interpersonal function (argumentation and exposition).

The inherent potential of FI as a discourse marker derives from the basic deictic prototype underlying all of its forms. Deictic presentative FI starts out from what was said above to be an endophoric, or internal, use of deictic adverbs. This is in fact a process similar to the use of temporal adverbs as discourse markers in conversational discourse: *now* and *then*, if used as markers and not as adverbs, relate to "discourse time" rather than "event time", in any case they do not mark (deictic) "reference time" (Schiffrin 1987:228ff.):

> *now* marks a speaker's progression through discourse by displaying upcoming attention to a new idea unit, speaker orientation and/or participation framework. *Then* indicates temporal succession between prior and upcoming talk. (p.261)

This is parallel to my analysis of the relationship between deictic and lexical presentative inversion presented in chapter 4. There it was claimed that the internal, i.e. discourse marker, use, instead of an external, i.e. adverb, use of deictic adverbs starting an inversion comes about as the result of a textual, metaphorical usage, which they undergo in presentative constructions. The presentative meaning is the same in lexical presentative and lexical predicative FI, but related to a reference situation established by the text. The parallelism between a deictic and a lexical presentative mechanism is thus due to what Schiffrin (1987) calls an *anaphoric property*, for instance of *then*: in that "*then* refers to prior discourse time to establish succession between events", it can also mark "succession between other units of talks such as ideas, topics, and actions" (p.250). The fronted constituents in lexical FI constructions also establish an anaphoric link to prior discourse, which gives the anchoring of the new to the old ground; besides expressing relations between events, states or discourse entities — their ideational content — they thus link units of discourse and gain an interpersonal, discourse marker meaning.

Due to their temporal meaning, *now* and *then* have a natural potential to mark progression in discourse, but most FIs arise out of predications which contain locative, and mainly static, properties assigned to the subject. Dynamic presentative processes, by contrast, i.e. temporal or directional adverbs or PPs followed by a dynamic lexical verb, are more restricted in use, mainly to fiction or to relatively vivid accounts of an event, which justify an invitation for *dynamic viewing* (cf. 5.2.1.1). They create expectations and tension that go beyond a mere focus management task performed by FI. The majority of forms of FI, by contrast, rest on *static viewing*; they therefore represent discourse markers typical of a descriptive kind of progression within a text. But ordering in discourse necessarily means linearisation, which is why only narration has, in the actual chronology of events, one ordering where the conceptualisation of events corresponds to their actual unfolding in time (cf. Carroll/von Stutterheim 1993). In description, however,

> unlike narratives, [...] there is no prototypical sequence inherent to the content to be expressed that can serve as a basis for defining the order in which information can be selected for mention and linearized in the text. (p.1014)

While *now* and *then* thus only *select* one possible relation (succession) from an underlying ideational discourse structure by making it explicit (cf. Schiffrin 1987:320), the majority of static FI types in fact virtually *create* how the states of affairs and entities under description are to be viewed. It is due to this freedom of order in which discourse entities are presented that FIs offer themselves particularly well as discourse markers building up more abstract kinds of a discourse structure. They do not require an experiential counterpart, but can structure a discourse more freely along relations between discourse entities. These relations must still have ideational plausibility, but, being created by the speaker, mainly have textual and interpersonal significance.

The majority of FI are in this sense inherently descriptive and virtually *build up* a descriptive discourse type in terms of *structure*. When a text deals with an actual description of states from the outside world, inversions also fulfil a descriptive *function* and then produce an effect of displaced immediacy: a descriptive structure reproduces relations from an actual scene being evoked, which will be taken as an instruction *to "view" the scene mentally*. In the case of non-descriptive textual functions, however, FIs build up more abstract descriptive structures, organising discourse along relations between discourse entities. In that case, discourse organisation can be said to follow a principle of "similarity", which Giora (1990:303) claims to be the categorical structure of all non-narrative texts. In any case, in the absence of a concrete descriptive purpose, FI serves as a discourse marker which instructs the reader *to perform a change in his focus within the discourse organisation*. Given other ideational (descriptive, but not about locations, or narrative) functions, these changes will be taken as *informative or evaluative background*, while, in the more interpersonal (argumentative, explanatory) discourse types, they initiate *constitutive sub-parts* of argumentation and exposition.

Chapter 6

Summary and conclusion

This study has focussed on the various forms of subject-verb inversion in Modern English with the aim of providing a semantic and discourse-functional analysis of them. With the exception of some more specialised types and of grammaticalised inversion in interrogative sentences, the entire range of constructions that allow for reversal of subject and verb have been treated. A considerable share of word order variation such as possible in Modern English has thereby been covered.

The approach has been a strictly synchronic one and has sought to handle a complex interplay of factors. The theoretical foundations for this have been laid in chapter 2. First, there are the structural prerequisites of Modern English, in which word order is first and foremost determined by syntactic function. When variation takes place, other levels of sentential meaning, but not the semantic and grammatical role structures, are affected (2.1). On the one hand, as a result of this rigidity of the English word order system, word order variation gives rise to constructions which represent deviations from the norm (2.2). On the other hand, linearisation phenomena in a language also underlie natural or cognitive principles. The sentence-initial position, in particular, is one of natural salience and therefore in general used for "urgent tasks" (Givón 1985:199), typically for providing a (re-)orientation or a grounding. In addition, reordering in a rigid word order language bears a newsworthiness of its own (2.3). My semantic analysis has suggested that it is out of the interplay of these factors that an extra-meaning of inversion arises. This meaning, in turn, defines the function of inversion in discourse and underlies its affinities with textual structures and functions that make up four basic discourse types. Finally, there are also conventions at work that determine the usage of inversion in various genres. Particularly relevant are those that deal with the expression of subjectivity in discourse and with necessities and patterns of focus management. On the basis of two text corpora, evidence has been provided that there is a substantial correspondence between genre-specific conventions and the occurrence of inversion as a marker of subjectivity and a discourse marker.

As main parts of the study, the analysis of the semantics of the various inversion types (chapter 4) and the findings about the usage and distribution of them in actual discourse (chapter 5), classified according to various textual relations, have been set apart. Prior to this core of the argument, a comprehensive formal taxonomy of inversion has been established (3.1). In this taxonomy, due to the diversity of the phenomenon, no single syntactic or semantic criterion could be applied consistently. Separate systems had to be used for defining the various types of FI and SAI respectively. It was this lack of a unified system that suggested the later transition from the formal to a functional classification (illustrated in 4.3, *figure 3*): this process has confirmed the usefulness of the formal categories used, while nonetheless emphasising the need for a functional classification that was to allow for more gradual transitions among the individual types.

One impetus from previous studies that prepared the ground for the complex interplay of form and function concerned the history of English inversion and the process of word order grammaticalisation (3.2): the semantics of the different constructions could ultimately only be made out with reference to their degree of grammaticalisation and to the remaining choice for exploiting the function of ordering and reordering in English. Ultimately, only the history of inversion as an "optional rule" (Stockwell 1984:577), with consequent "limiting" (p.584) of the obligatory, fully grammaticalised types on the one hand, and remaining "optional" (p.585) types on the other, could account for what are today the different forms of inverted constructions. In Modern English, the various inversion types now differ from each other in that they constitute either obligatory (most SAI types), grammaticalised presentative (FI after deictic adverbs), remaining optional (most FI types after locative constituents), or innovated obligatory (after nonlocative constituents) constructions. The diachronic factors have thus provided an important background for an understanding of the formal heterogeneity of Modern English inversion.

A range of prior synchronic studies had also touched upon aspects of the inversion phenomenon which proved relevant for the present analysis. Within formal approaches (3.3), there was the ongoing discussion of the structure-preserving constraint that has given an impetus to consider inversion as a symptom of speaker subjectivity and, in particular, to regard FI as a device for expressing the speaker's point of view in discourse. This analysis has shed a new light on the fact that inversion is, if not strictly excluded from embedded clauses, a predominantly main clause phenomenon. Another relevant formal issue was the adequate syntactic analysis of FI. Within a Lexical Functional Grammar formalism, for instance, an FI had been said to reflect a mismatch of the categorial structure with the grammatical functions of the clause. Even without detailed syntactic testing, the idea of a mismatch between various levels of sentence structure is equally implied in the difference between ideational and interpersonal meaning suggested here.

Previous functional accounts of inversion (3.4) had been concerned with FI constructions almost exclusively. The majority of them have centred around claims for a focus-marking and a basically presentative function of FI, while the information-packaging approach to it is more recent. I have spelled out from the beginning why I found these functional accounts unsatisfactory in at least one respect: focus-marking, presentative function, and information-packaging do not say anything about the reasons why inversion is so — apparently — unpredictable in occurrence, absent in many texts, but "clustering" in others. Also, the functions previously claimed for FI are shared by a range of other constructions in English, so that the discourse conditions giving rise to inversion had so far not been sufficiently defined. There was also need for both a more comprehensive and a more differentiated treatment of inversion: on the one hand, taken that all forms of inversion in Modern English involve reordering of subject and verb as a speaker-based choice, an account of FI ultimately had to relate to SAI as well. On the other hand, there was need for a more detailed analysis of the various FI types, due to substantial differences among some of them, especially among *AdvP-*, *PP-* and *AdjP-inversion*.

Finally, the discussion of related phenomena (3.5) has shown that, although other word order phenomena had often been treated jointly with inversion, because they share with it the status of a non-canonical sentence, none of them has exactly the same discourse meaning. While *there*-insertion is a more freely available — and grammaticalised — presentative construction than FI, preposing is much more local in its effect. Left-dislocation is, like FI, concerned with reference and the negotiation of topic entities in discourse, but it is basically a conversational phenomenon. The discourse meaning of most inversions, by contrast, is tied to discourse under particular conditions, especially to written language and to conditions of displacement.

The semantic analysis developed in chapter 4 has, as a first step, compared the various formal types of Modern English inversion with their canonical word order counterparts (4.1). As the presentative prototype of full inversion, the construction after deictic adverbs has been identified, from which the mechanism of inversion following fully specified lexical constituents is functionally derived. Lexical inversion, however, is typically operating under conditions of displacement. SAI constructions, by contrast, carry a meaning that either involves an instruction to link sentences anaphorically or cataphorically — the majority of them with almost obligatory SAI — and/or attach particular prominence to the constituents initially placed. In the latter case, the constituents are either "inherently" prominent and are therefore today automatically followed by SAI, or they are, by means of AuxSV order, signalled to be so. These various meanings of the different inversion types as well as their interrelatedness have been worked into a functional classification of English inversion in 4.3.

An additional semantic component of inversion concerns the viewpoint of the speaker, expressed by FI, and the degree of subjectivity carried by both FI and SAI (4.2). This aspect has been able to shed some light on the restrictions at work in embeddings, because an inversion becomes acceptable in a subordinated statement if this statement is plausibly made from the speaker's point of view. Thus, the meaning of FI is to produce a perspective in discourse, which creates an effect of focus management in discourse. Various uses of the focus management task have been discerned: a basic procedural use, and more sophisticated topic change and structure-building contributions. It has also been shown that topic change and topic construal can be realised objectively, by explicitly providing a ground from the universe of discourse, or subjectively. In that case, it is an additional effect of the FI construction that it creates its own point of reference. By reflecting the viewpoint of a discourse entity, which is either from the text or created as a reference point, FI becomes a device for expressing speaker subjectivity and the presence of the speaker within the respective universe of discourse. In addition, given that all inversions are marked — and as such more unexpected — in Modern English than are respective canonical word order versions, both FI and SAI are syntactic patterns that carry additional subjective and emotive meaning.

Summary and Conclusion

The outcome of the semantic analysis has been applied to the reality of discourse in chapter 5. It has been the aim of the corpus work to investigate in relative detail the conditions that determine the usage of inversion, its frequency and placement, in naturally-occurring text. For this, reference has been made both to the quantitative results as well as to extensive discussions of individual occurrences in context. The assumption was that, if a syntactic variant carries an extra-meaning, its usage and function in discourse should in fact depend more on functional text characteristics, and less on matters of mere convention or style.

In that respect, it has also been possible to explain previous evidence from other studies in the light of the functional factors identified here. On the one hand, as concerns spoken and written mode, it is the desituatedness of writing which lies at the heart of an affinity of inversion with the written language and with more subtle expressions of subjectivity. In terms of colloquial and literary style, on the other, it was noted that inversion types seem to be the more linked to real ("positively") literary styles, the more they differ from the underlying prototypes: presentative FI and SAI following items that have "inherent" prominence. It is only the deictic, perception-based type of FI as well as some of the SAI types most advanced in grammaticalisation that are relatively common in spoken mode and oral style.

Significantly, the only interspeaker varieties considered, namely British and American English, have not revealed substantial differences in inversion usage. In the corpus, the usage patterns found over various genres have turned out to be more divergent than those noted for British and American English in their own right. This suggests a priority of functional as opposed to conventional factors at work. Only within the limits of how various genres make use of the discourse function of inversion, smaller discrepancies have been found: suggesting higher relevance of writing prescriptions in British English, which sometimes seem to cause reluctance to use FI as a rather "condensed" way of writing, while most SAI types appear to be part of a stylistic ideal of "good" writing.

The core of the corpus work about the usage of inversion (5.2) was based on an analysis of extracts from the LOB and the Brown corpus, of an overall size of 584,000 words. The categorisation from these corpora has been maintained, using sample texts from five out of the fifteen discourse categories. Problems with this categorisation gave rise to a prior discussion of discourse typologies, not only to discuss the inconsistencies I had to face: all corpus studies ultimately face the problem of classifying discourse, if they seek to avoid the fallacy of resting on a "fiction of language-as-a-whole" (Enkvist 1991:10). It was one of my major objectives to solve this problem adequately, so that I have singled out from the abundant text linguistic literature those classificatory tools that are most appropriate for handling it.

As a first step, it has been mandatory to distinguish discourse types on the one hand, following basic functions and structures of a text, and genres as conventions of usage on the other, defined by the linguistic — as part of the cultural — competence of speakers. Both notions in principle suggest the assumption of a prototype-based perspective, in order to come to an appropriate taxonomy; discourse types, however, also form a close system. Four prototypes have been defined: on the basis of the ideational and the interpersonal functions of language, description and narration follow the structure of ideational content, while argumentation and exposition reflect more directly interpersonal aspects of a text (cf. *figure 5*). This classification makes it possible to hold apart matters of (surface) structure and matters of underlying function: narration and description are "strong" in terms of structure and therefore able to realise different kinds of discourse function, while argumentation and exposition are "strong" in terms of function, but can occur in a range of different surface forms. It was this distinction that has been able to account for an asymmetry between, for instance, the frequency and the function of FI in various kinds of contexts: FIs, basically descriptive in kind, are more frequent in descriptions in terms of a structure, but their effect is more complex in discourse types defined by other functions.

Distinguishing surface form and purpose of a discourse has also been the starting-point for the interpretation of my corpus results. That means that text types and genre-conventions have not been taken as if they were reflected by simple frequencies of linguistic surface characteristics. On the contrary, for all the results, it has been necessary to argue that, assuming that extra-meaning arises out of the breaking of expectations, quantitative results have only limited significance. It is thus not always requisite to search for those sources that yield the highest quantitative results;[1] nor are these necessarily the most interesting contexts when studying a discourse function.

The corpus analysis has nonetheless yielded a clear outcome as concerns the overall degree of subjectivity such as reflected by the occurrence of inversion in the texts: the picture corresponds to a characterisation, via genre conventions, of the various text categories as more or less subjective. Biographics and essays appear to be the most subjective kinds of discourse, which can be attributed to a higher relevance of the identity of the speaker. In addition, the samples in this category come from longer texts, probably calling for a more complex kind of focus management. Following in the subjectivity scale are reviews and editorials, which can be accounted for in the light of their dominant persuasive discourse function. Finally, scientific writing and reportages are least prone to the usage of inversion, which could be expected in view of their primarily informative purpose. On the basis of this evidence, it is probably justified to call inversion a marker of subjectivity.

In the last step of the analysis (5.3), basic affinities of inversion in discourse under conditions of displacement have been spelled out and could be attributed to different kinds of speaker attitudes. These have been described for political news reporting in journalistic discourse. First, there is an affinity with contexts in which an FI focusses on "real" displaced events and produces an effect of displaced immediacy. This makes an event look more like an experience; accordingly, the position of the journalist changes from mere reporter to experiencer. It is not the case, however, that the majority of contexts in which an inversion is likely to occur are concerned with the reproduction of actual scenes described. Usually, inversions reflect a more directly interpersonal intention, even in so-considered objective news reporting. On the one hand, this is the case when an FI, due to its focus management effect, contributes to the author's own discourse organisation; the speaker becomes an architect of relations among discourse entities. On the other hand, both FI and SAI sometimes constitute direct comments or evaluations made by the speaker as a commentator. It could be observed that all three speaker roles have a symptomatic co-presence with other markers of author comments, which has been interpreted as further evidence for the status of inversion as a marker of subjectivity and of speaker-presence.

These affinities of inversion have been illustrated by individual cases of occurrence, and of remarkable absence, in different genres of political news reporting, in the light of their text-typological characteristics and other conventions. While inversion is virtually absent in brief news that require a mere reporter, its occurrence is more frequent, the longer the news texts are. In longer reports and reportages, FI occurs in descriptive passages and produces an experiencer's perspective; in that, it often marks a digression from the main informative body of a text. It also introduces evaluative material, in which case it contributes to the structuring of a report into separate functional sub-parts. Finally, in comments and news analysis, FI is more prominent, if not in frequency, at least in placement and effect: it is usually more directly related to the speaker's own reasoning, to constitutive parts of argumentation or exposition, or it marks direct comments within the text. The latter is the function that it shares with SAI, which almost exclusively occurs in texts with purposes other than reporting. In principle, inversion is thus evidently more likely to occur in texts with a primarily interpersonal function, even though it is sometimes selectively more frequent in individual descriptive texts.

The conclusions drawn from the corpus analysis have been summarised in 5.4. Both FI and SAI have a strong component of interpersonal meaning: SAI inserts speaker comments into discourse with a less interpersonal function, while it reflects an overall subjective attitude or style in discourse with a direct evaluative or explanatory purpose. FI creates displaced immediacy in descriptive discourse, but, in other types of discourse, functions like a discourse marker that induces a change in focus within the discourse organisation or provides informative and evaluative background. Word order variation thus clearly affects the meaning of the clause as an exchange: it is overall a discourse marker reflecting speaker-presence and hearer-involvement.

Appendix
Corpus texts and other sources of occurrences

Table i. Corpus texts from the LOB and the Brown corpus - sources and distribution

text category	LOB samples	LOB words	BROWN samples	BROWN words	total samples	total words
rep.	34	68,000	34	68,000	**68**	**136,000**
ed.	27	54,000	27	54,000	**54**	**108,000**
rev.	17	34,000	17	34,000	**34**	**68,000**
bbe.	34	68,000	34	68,000	**68**	**136,000**
sc.writ.	34	68,000	34	68,000	**68**	**136,000**
total	**146**	**292,000**	**146**	**292,000**	**292**	**584,000**

Table ii. Composition of corpora extracted from the LOB and the Brown corpus

A. Press: reportage
01 - 19   National daily
20 - 26   National Sunday
27 - 30   Provincial daily
41 - 44   Provincial weekly

B. Press: editorial
01 - 11   National daily
12 - 16   National Sunday
17 - 24   Provincial daily
25 - 27   Provincial weekly

C. Press: reviews
01 - 06   National daily
07 - 11   National Sunday
12 - 14   National weekly
15 - 16   Provincial daily
17   Provincial weekly

G. Belles-lettres, biography, essays
01 - 06   Biography, memoirs
36 - 41   Literary essays and criticism
42 - 47   Arts
51 - 66   General essays

J. Learned and scientific writing
01   Natural sciences
36   Education
40 - 47   Politics and Economics
51 - 54   Philosophy
55 - 59   History
60 - 63   Literary criticism
64 - 67   Art
68   Music
69 - 74   Technology and engineering

Table iii. Issues of newspapers and magazines (as used in 5.3.2)

The Times	December	15, 1992
The Guardian	February	11, 1994
	February	25, 1994
	February	28, 1994
The Daily Telegraph	February	11, 1994
The Daily Express	February	11, 1994
The Guardian Weekly	December	20, 1992
[including articles from	December	27, 1992
The Washington Post]	January	3, 1993
The Economist	April	3, 1993
Newsweek	April	12, 1993

Table iv. Other primary sources

International Herald Tribune	January	13, 1992
	January	20, 1992
The Economist	January	4, 1992
	January	11, 1992
Newsweek	January	13, 1992
	January	20, 1992
Time	January	20, 1992

Ehrlich, Susan. 1990. *Point of View: a Linguistic Analysis of Literary Style*. London: Routledge.
Rouse, W.H.D. 1973."The crocodile and the monkey". In: *The Giant Crab And Other Tales from Old India*, London: Minerva Press.
Rouse, W.H.D. 1973. "The giant crab". In: *The Giant Crab And Other Tales from Old India*, London: Minerva Press.
Waller, Robert James. 1992. *The Bridges of Madison County*. New York: Warner.

Notes

Chapter 1
1. In the very beginning of my research, other scholars who had been previously working on the topic pointed this out to me as a further explanandum. In particular, I owe this and some other ideas to my personal communication with Georgia Green and Betty Birner, which I gratefully acknowledge, at the occasion of the 1993 LSA Linguistic Institute.
2. The appendix contains a list of the corpus texts chosen, the issues of newspapers and magazines used, as well other primary sources, which have provided some further, more randomly collected, instances.

Chapter 2
1. Topic and theme are not always used interchangeably. The discussion here deals with topic only, while theme is reserved for the particular approach developed by Halliday (1985) and discussed in 2.1.3 below.
2. That the given->new, or more discourse-familiar->less discourse-familiar, pattern also underlies one of the most recent accounts of inversion (Birner 1992, 1994) will be discussed below (3.4.2).

Chapter 3
1. The case is different for what is termed *VP-inversion* here, which consists of a special type of fronted predicative constituent, displaying adjectival properties, and of *be* operating as copula rather than auxiliary.
2. This definition does not refer, as, e.g., Birner's (1992: 16) definition of inversion, to the logical subject following the verb; instead, subject is understood in the traditional way as the grammatical subject. In English, subject in this sense can be identified unambiguously by grammatical concord of person and number. Arguments in favour of a different syntactic status of the subject in inversions will be briefly discussed in 3.3.2 below.
3. In that respect, my analysis differs from Birner's (1992) classificatory system, for whom *AdvP-inversion* consists of non-locative anaphoric adverbs, while inversion after preposed locative and temporal adverbs is classified as *PP-inversion* (cf. p. 48). The reasons why I do not follow this practice will become clear in the course of chapter 4.
4. This category does not include sentences which have an initial PP subject. In a case like (i), following a "semantic extension" (Langacker 1993: 15), the PP behaves grammatically like a noun and serves as subject; (i) is therefore no instance of an inversion:

(i) Near the fire is warmer. [= Langacker 1993: (8b)]

5. In strictly grammatical terms, *VP-inversion* would also fall into this category. However, a *be*+participle construction is also very similar to a predicative copular construction. It is therefore part of the FI group.

6. There are numerous ways of classifying SAI in the literature. My impression is that none of them achieves an overlap-free distinction of types. While, e.g., Jacobsson (1951) follows a basically semantic approach, in that he draws the main line between "negative or restrictive introductory members" and "non-negative introductory members", closest to my classification is Schmidt's (1980), who uses a mixture of semantic ("after negative, restrictive or affective adverbs" (p. 11), "after other openers" (p. 13), "after *so, nor, neither*, and *no more*" (p. 14)) and constructional ("in complex sentences with special heads" (p. 11), "correlative clauses" (p. 12), "in comparative *than* and *as* clauses" (p. 14)) criteria.

7. Note also that it is the SAI option which is typical of "formal (especially literary) style" (Quirk et al. 1985: 1144).

8. As Denison (1993: 28) has to admit, V-3 is "a somewhat unhappy choice of label for a situation in which the verb follows the subject regardless of whether or not there is any pre-subject element".

9. Stockwell (1984) always speaks of "grammaticization" and "grammaticized" forms. Apart from direct quotes, I stick to the terms *grammaticalisation* and *grammaticalised*, since they are more widely used in the literature on this topic (cf. Hopper/Traugott 1993).

10. In one respect, I consistently disagree with Schmidt's (1980) claims, in that she refers to the overall function of inversion as to assign "stress" (cf., e.g., p. 298). Although she takes care not to confuse "rhythm" (i.e. prosodic factors), "emphasis" (seemingly understood as highlighting or additional prominence) and "balance" or "functional weight" (i.e. information status) (cf. p. 20) and concludes that "most of the inversions [...] can be explained in more concrete terms than rhythm" (p. 23), in the course of her argument, she identifies any kind of highlighting achieved through word order variation with stress; for instance, she claims that "inversion, by moving the subject out of its unmarked position in the clause, produces stress on the subject" (p. 25).

Her conclusions, although based on a profound analysis of the discourse conditions of inversion in earlier stages of English, are therefore not directly transferable to the kind of functional statements envisaged here. It is in my view much safer to restrict stress as referring to prosodic (i.e. intonational) prominence, which is an epiphenomenon of —and an alternative spoken-language device for — the meanings encoded by word order. But stress does not denote a sentence- or discourse-level function, especially not when dealing with written discourse.

11. Stein (1990) finds that it is an "intensity semantics" of *do* that is at the heart of its evolution from Middle to Modern English and that focusses on the whole proposition, rather than on a constituent (cf. p. 278ff.).

12. My impression is that this possibility is today increasingly exploited in American English, especially in American newspaper language. An occurrence such as (i) may therefore exemplify something like a "re-rise" process, a reversal of previous limiting:
(i) Thus does Mr Karadzic provide a timely reminder of why he is high on U.S. Secretary

of State Lawrence Eagleburger's newly announced list of war criminals. (WashP, 27 Dec.92, p.15)

The occurrence will also be discussed in more detail in 4.1.2.4.

13. In the same chapter, Hopper/Traugott (1993: 88) emphasise that a word order shift "rarely, perhaps never, occurs independently of other word order factors". In that respect, the shift from OV to VO order is certainly a related issue, which must nonetheless be neglected here, given "the complexities of the history of English word order" (p. 91).

14. For Stockwell (1984), interrogatives are the third major type that has shown limiting of V-2, but, for the above-given reasons, they need not be discussed here.

15. The subclass of locative adverbs which triggered obligatory inversion in Old English have remained an exception. They are still more or less obligatory in many contexts, either because the canonical word order is infelicitous (as in (i) as opposed to (ii)), or because the two constructions do not possess the same truth-conditions: if (iii) occurs in an email message, *here* refers to the message itself. (iv), by contrast, is true if the paper is located where the writer is:

(i) The economy, Berlin, the Common Market - here are three issues whose gravity has during the past few days led to regretful sighings over the impracticability of a National Government. (LOB, ed.)

(ii) ?The economy, Berlin, the Common Market - three issues are here whose gravity has during the past few days led to regretful sighings over the impracticability of a National Government.

(iii) Here is the paper I promised you last week.

(iv) The paper I promised you last week is here.

I do not want to answer the question whether FI after these (basically deictic) adverbs is a simple continuation of OE obligatory inversion. FI must here also be considered grammaticalised, since (iii) does not have the same propositional meaning as (iv), but rather "means" a presentative process. More on this will be said in 4.1.1 below.

16. Among the embedded inversions that I have found were 4 FI and 3 SAI constructions. It is important to note that the FI occurrences come from relative clauses exclusively, since a similar observation has already been formulated by Aissen/Hankamer (1972). They conclude that it would be worthwhile to look for a distinction "different from the root/nonroot distinction, which will account for the fact that relative clauses allow SVI [= FI] and other embedded Ss [= sentences] do not" (p. 502).

17. It is hard to delimit locative and nonlocative constituents on syntactic grounds. On the one hand, certain prepositional phrases are strictly restricted to copular *be* (cf. (i)), while participles, followed by *be* as an auxiliary, may in fact occur with a lexical verb (as in (ii)), especially when conjoined with a prepositional phrase (as in (iii)):

(i) Of greater concern to many proliferation experts is the political braindrain [...]. (NW, 13 Jan.92, p. 12)

(ii) Counting to five sat Little Johnny Jones. [= Birner 1992: (61a), p. 63]

(iii) Crashing through the woods came a wild boar. [= Bresnan 1994: (5a)] In principle, however, Bresnan (1994: 75) is right in that "English also has inversions of nonlocative phrases [...], which are restricted to *be*".

18. Theme in LFG is defined "as the argument of which the location, change of location, or direction expressed by the locative argument is predicated" (Bresnan 1994: 80). This definition is given for clarification here, but is not used in the rest of my study.

19. An exception is Green (1982), who treats the "colloquial and literary uses" of both FI and SAI. Her results concern the stylistic dimension of inversion and are summarised in 5.1.2.

20. This definition is very similar to Prince's (1981a) notion of "open proposition". An open proposition is obtained if, by replacing one constituent by a variable, the rest of the sentence is already known in the discourse, i.e., represents salient shared knowledge (cf. Prince 1981a: 256).

21. These conditions have also been referred to as the *evocation of a presuppositional set*, whereby "selecting one member out of a presuppositional set amounts to contrasting this set member with the other members of the same presuppositional set" (Enkvist 1980: 137).

22. However, I do not share Drubig's claim that "SVI [= FI] sentences [...] have two foci specifying 'new' information which the speaker does not expect to be in the addressee's consciousness at the time of the utterance" (Drubig 1988: 85). More on this will be said in later chapters.

23. Instead, Bolinger (1977: 91) ascribes to it the meaning of "generalised location". There is no real consensus in the literature about whether *there* in *there*-inserted constructions has lost part of or all of its locative meaning (for a discussion see, e.g., Erdmann 1990), but I use the arguments here that speak in favour of holding both constructions apart.

24. For reasons of identifiability in written discourse, I have only considered those instances of there, where, as in (89) and (90), it is followed by another locative constituent.

25. For preposing, especially for *NP-preposing*, *topicalisation* is also widely used. However, I prefer to use *preposing*, since topicalisation in a functional sense (cf. 2.1.1) would in principle apply to certain inversion types (and to left-dislocation) as well.

26. The assumption that shared fronting correlates with shared function and that inversion serves an additional function related to the reversal of the subject and verb is not discussed in detail here. Ward/Birner (1994) convincingly argue that the function of preposing does not necessarily apply to inversion, and that inversion is therefore not simply the sum of preposing and subsequent inversion. For the whole of the argument, I refer to their discussion; see also Birner (1992: 22ff.).

27. This statement does not concern so-called "yiddish-movement" (cf. Prince 1981a; Ward 1988) and "ironic preposing" (Ward 1988), which are not taken into consideration here.

28. Following Quirk et al. (1985), disjuncts and conjuncts appear canonically in sentence-initial position, while it is less clear whether adjuncts fall under the definition of preposing given above: possibly, only "predication adjuncts in front position" (p. 1379) are non-canonical, particularly when they have complement-near status. Adjuncts like that can also be followed by FI, as in (i) vs. (ii):

(i) Into the stifling smoke we plunged. [= Quirk et al. 1985:p. 1379]

(ii) Into the stifling smoke plunged the desparate mother. [= p. 1379]

Whether (i) should be considered a preposing remains in principle unresolved, while, in the case of entire adverbial clauses or those initiating major shifts (as in (103)), it is certainly not plausible to speak of either placement as leftward (or rightward) movement.

29. Geluykens also includes PPs as an optional variant to left-dislocated NPs, as in (i) and (ii):

(i) As for Steve, he likes beans. [= Geluykens 1992: (29), p. 20]

(ii) With regard to Steve, he likes beans. [= (33), p. 20]

Such instances display the typical function of initial adverbials as dealt with above. Left-dislocation as defined here could be the result of the "syntactisation" or "grammaticalisation" of these discourse functions (cf. Geluykens 1992: 157).

30. For the purpose of discussion here, it suffices to consider only those cases where there is strict coreferentiality between the left-dislocated NP and the pronominal element. Cases which Geluykens (1992) calls "Quasi-LDs", characterised by a "partitive relationship" (p. 22) such as in (i) and (ii), can be neglected, especially since they do not sound quite acceptable with a bare NP, as in (iii):

(i) As for London, Trafalgar Square is nice. [= Geluykens 1992: (36), p. 21]

(ii) As for linguistics textbooks, the library has plenty of books. [= (43), p. 22]

(iii)?London, Trafalgar Square is nice. [= (44), p. 22]

31. The prosodic notation is left out here.

Chapter 4

1. Ward/Birner (1992: 577) apply a similar argument to a subtype of FI, to *VP-inversion*.

2. This is in line with Halliday/Hasan's (1976) claim that "there is a logical continuity from naming (referring to a thing independently of the context of situation), through situational reference (referring to a thing as identified in the context of situation) to textual reference (referring to a thing as identified in the surrounding text); [...]" (p. 32).

3. Significantly, the reading of an existential scale sentence has also been labelled "presentation scale".

4. The same basic difference underlies Longacre's (1983) doubts "whether existence is a predicate in the sense that the other predicates are. [...] Is not existence rather a condition of predication?" (p. 235).

5. This is in fact a precondition for inversion serving as a device for re-focussing *known* discourse entities (cf. Stein 1995: 136).

6. Birner (1992: 220f.) identifies a few cases in which the preposed constituent in an inversion is deaccentable. However, she has to conclude that "prior evocation in the discourse is a necessary, but not sufficient, criterion for the deaccentability of the connecting element in the preposed constituent" (p. 226); in other words, even evoked information

is rather often likely to be accented. As I shall show in 4.2.3, this reflects the need to ensure that the location serving as anchoring point is unambiguously identified and suggests a high probability for inversion ending up bi-focal.

7. In the same vein, Birner (1992: 180f.) states a strong, but incomplete, correlation of full verbs with semantically locative constituents.

8. This is also implied in Drubig's (1988: 83) decision to concentrate primarily on inversion with "real" locative and directional phrases.

9. Sundby (1970: 47) explicitly argues for prepositional properties of the ing-participle.

10. In the same vein, Schmidt (1980: 294) remarks on the use of full verbs that, for instance, *With him ran his faithful jogging partner* is semantically equivalent to *With him was his faithful jogging partner*.

11. Birner (1992: 186) treats this type of "non-PP non-locative NBI [= non-*be* inversion]" as adverb inversion.

12. Cases where an auxiliary is used as a pro-form for the verb (as in (i)) have to be considered SAI (but are grouped *anaphoric/cataphoric* in function; cf. 4.3.), even though the subject is still the focus of the construction:

    (i) The State Department keeps approving of "meaningful negotiations" and so even does President de Gaulle [...]. (LOB, ed.)

13. This is of course why there is the same restriction as for other FIs that "when the subject is a pronoun no inversion is possible" (Quirk et al. 1985: 881).

14. This distinction is also made, in particular, by Schmidt (1980) and Stein (1995). Both accounts have been discussed already in section 3.2.

15. Algeo (1988), by contrast, finds instances of *and nor* such as (i) in his corpus and considers them "peculiarities of British usage" (p. 15):

    (i) But doctors prescribing the pills were not told of the maker's doubts, and nor was the Government's drug watchdog, the Committee on Safety of Medicine. [= Algeo 1988: 15]

16. With phenomena of this kind, judgements of acceptability are always delicate. For the examples taken from other authors, their marking as unacceptable (*) or questionable (?) is taken over from the authors quoted. Some of these judgements may in fact remain doubtful, depending on the context that comes to one's mind, but this is a part of the phenomenon under discussion.

17. Work on free indirect discourse also takes the occurrence of inversion as one of its linguistic markers: it is interpreted as a typical device whereby is signalled that "the subjectivity of the non-speaker is reported by a speaker, who identifies or empathises with the non-speaker" (Brinton 1995: 188). For instance, (i) and (ii) are from passages of free indirect discourse analysed by Brinton and contain several inversions:

    (i) Here are two men; three women; there is a cat in a basket; myself with my elbow on the windowsill - this is here and now. [= Brinton 1995: (13a)]

    (ii) Never had she imagined she could look like that. Is mother right? she thought. [...]. [= (23)]

18. It is the notion of *assertion* itself that lies at the heart of the problem. The same is put forward in Green (1976), who formulates doubts about a "non-circular definition of assertion" (p. 390) in Hooper/Thompson (1973). I do not provide a watertight definition of assertion either; instead, the discussion here serves to illustrate that point of view represents a more general property of discourse, be it part of, independent of, or overlapping with, whatever notion of assertion.

19. Part of this account has already been brought forward by Green (1976), especially the relevance of first as opposed to third person factives (cf. p. 388) and of tense (cf. p. 395).

20. Contexts which make such a shift more unlikely provide the clearest counter-evidence to Emonds' structure-preserving constraint. It is therefore not surprising that the largest proportion of counterexamples brought forward in the root-transformation controversy contain a first person pronoun or an epistemic matrix clause.

21. Apparently, one needs at least a relative clause here. As will be shown further down, this is probably due to the fact that the whole procedure is rather costly and therefore requires some further treatment of the topic introduced to justify the effort.

22. Since *there*-constructions have been excluded for various reasons, I only consider inversion after *here*. Drubig (1988) also notes that in procedural descriptions, where *there*-insertion can compete with inversion, "*there*-sentences are typically (if not exclusively) used for summarising statements, or when there is no need to turn around and look" (p. 87).

23. Banfield's (1982) formalism is not my concern here, but it grasps much of the meaning carried by syntax as outlined here.

24. In *Figure 2*, instead of establishing further categories, the alternative combinations of grounding mechanisms and frames of reference are illustrated by way of examples.

25. This is in line with the remarks made above on the relative non-prominence of verb semantics in a scene-setting process.

26. As explicated in 4.1.2.4, pronominal adverbs followed by an auxiliary pro-verb are SAI in strictly formal terms. However, they also place the (informational) focus on the subject so that, functionally, they behave like anaphoric/cataphoric FIs. For this reason, there is also an anaphoric/cataphoric function on the FI side of the figure.

Chapter 5

1. In this context, it is possible to use the terms *text* and *discourse* interchangeably.

2. The *interactive/content-focussed* distinction is also close to Chafe's (1982) well-known *detachment/involvement* dichotomy.

3. The majority of corpus-based studies of inversion from the outset restrict their analysis to written texts (Hartvigson/Jakobsen 1974; Erdmann 1979, 1990).

4. For a term paper at the University of Düsseldorf, 50 pages of the printed version of the London-Lund Corpus were analysed, with a finding of one single inversion after here and one after pronominal *so* (*there* excluded).

5. Though, for methodological reasons, Birner (1992: 248) justifiedly stresses that her preponderance of written tokens does not necessarily reflect a higher percentage of written

vs. spoken inversions in general, this proportion nonetheless contributes to the general impression of inversion having a written language affinity.

6. The notion of *situatedness* is closely related to Nystrand's (1986) "doctrine of autonomous texts", whereby written text is characterised as "autonomous and context-independent and spoken utterance as concrete and context-bound" (p. 84); the same is reflected in the notion of detachment, feature 2 above.

7. See Jucker (1992) for a comprehensive discussion of different approaches to style. It is also justifiably emphasised there that styles are usually treated as conglomerates of linguistic features, reasonably identifiable only on the basis of comparison against an explicit or implicit norm (cf. Jucker 1992: 11).

8. For the size of the corpora extracted from each text category, see *table i* in the appendix; for their more detailed structure *table ii* in the appendix. The reason why the extracted corpora for the different text categories are of different size is that the LOB and the Brown corpus offer different numbers of samples for different categories, ranging from 17 'press: reviews' to 77 and 80 in the categories 'belles-lettres, biography, essays' and 'scientific writing', which are the largest of the categories I have used. Where available, I have stopped my analysis after 34 samples (68,000 words); otherwise, I have used all the samples in the respective categories.

9. A good methodological overview of the multi-feature/multi-dimensional analysis of textual variation is given in Biber (1988: 63ff.).

10. This is the result of a pilot study, presented in an M.A. thesis at the University of Düsseldorf, on the occurrence of inversion in British and American linguistic writing. The more substantial differences were in fact found, not between the two varieties, but between American articles as opposed to American monographs.

11. A more detailed discussion of the structure of the LOB and the Brown corpus is found in Wikberg (1992).

12. It is interesting to note that the presence of a particular basic text type is always and directly reflected by certain linguistic features, in particular by the system of deictic expressions (cf. Diewald 1991: 304). For lower-ranking typological criteria, which are more relevant here, there is in most cases no such necessary correlation and thus more room for matters of real choice and convention.

13. Kinneavy (1971) distinguishes *literary* discourse as a fourth discourse type, but, since literary texts are neglected here for the reasons given above, I shall not discuss the problems that arise with expanding the taxonomy in this way.

14. Werlich's (1976) has a fifth category *instruction*, which can obviously be neglected here.

15. This is exactly the kind of criticism that Faigley/Meyer (1983: 306) have about Werlich (1976), namely, that he mixes up textual function and textual surface characteristics.

16. In fact, the linguistic sign in the sense of Bühler's "Ausdruck" is only very loosely connected with a respective third function in most text typologies. Most authors reformulate this aspect of the triangle, either implicitly, as e.g. Gülich/Raible (1975: 154), who identify the expressive function with the overall intention of communication, or explicitly, as Diewald (1991: 318), who replaces expression by function of contact ("Kontaktfunktion").

17. The same distinction is expressed in Longacre's (1983) parameter "+/- contingent temporal succession", whereby he also defines the difference between narrative and expository discourse.

18. Many authors make similar distinctions, e.g., between "aim of discourse" and "mode of discourse" (Kinneavy 1971), "notional type" and "surface structure" type (Longacre 1983), or "text type" and "text form (variant)" (Werlich 1976). I shall, for reasons of simplicity, stick to *function* and *structure*.

19. That the outcome is coherent text is the reflection of the third, the textual, function, which is always at work independently, regardless of a particular function or structure.

20. In that respect, genres are closely related to styles. For instance, Enkvist (1984: 57) claims that "the discussion of the connection between a certain genre or text type, [...], and sentence structure leads into stylistics, in that different styles can be said to offer different degrees of resistance to the use of different types of devices that regulate textual fit". However, genre (and text type) are more comprehensive concepts, in particular since there is a tradition which deals with text types and genres in terms of superstructures (van Dijk 1980), thereby strongly emphasising, not only the occurrence of linguistic features, but the role of the form of the text as a whole (p. 128). And inversions, as analysed in 4.2.3, have already been shown to contribute to the structure of a discourse, rather than to merely signal the choice of a certain stylistic level.

21. Within these categories, the LOB and the Brown corpus further subcategorise the texts according to discourse topic. Since, as mentioned above, discourse topics are in principle open lists, or at best constitute sub-genres of different kinds, I have not followed this practice.

22. Three of the text categories investigated by Ellegard (1978) have also been used here, namely 'press: reportage', 'belles lettres/biography/essays' and 'learned and scientific writing'. In addition to that, Ellegard uses 'fiction: adventure and western' and calls this category "popular fiction".

23. One useful taxonomy of information-based newspaper texts is found, for instance, in Lüger (1983), to whom I shall repeatedly refer in the following.

24. I neglect more specialised newspaper genres such as weather reports or TV programs. The difference, or rather the fuzzy borderline, between different modes of reporting, such as contained in Lüger's (1983) taxonomy, comprising real (hard and soft) news, short news, report and reportage will be neglected here, because in the LOB and the Brown corpus this distinction is not made. The issue of different kinds of reporting will be taken up again in 5.3.2.

25. This problem is explicitly mentioned in the manual accompanying the LOB corpus (Johansson 1978). In particular, it is noted there that "there was a problem of overlap between the subject categories G [belles-lettres, biography, essays] and J [scientific writing] 'Literary Criticism and Arts'. The solution has been to place the more discursive criticism in Category G, and the more closely text-based in Category J" (p.18). It is obvious that the result of this "discursive" vs. "text-based" criterion can only be a very loose borderline between the two.

26. Table iii in the appendix lists the issues of the newspapers and magazines which have been scanned for inversion usage in this part of my study.

27 I do not include the category *soft news* here. Its share in the political section of especially the quality papers is rather negligible.

28. The genre categories continue to be based on Lüger (1983). In terms of an ideational vs. an interpersonal function, his category *news analysis* is characterised by an expository text structure (cf. Lüger 1983:78) and has a primarily interpersonal purpose. This is in line with the discourse types identified in 5.2.1.1, where exposition was assigned the interpersonal function of explaining, and also follows the practice of some newspapers, which have a separate page "News and analysis" (e.g., *The Guardian*).

Chapter 6

1. In retrospect, this also justifies my selection of texts, i.e. the restriction to non-fictional discourse and the focus on newspaper language. Literary discourse — certainly, guide-books or other descriptive texts — might have yielded a more substantial database, but, paradoxically, with probably less interesting results.

References

Aissen, Judith and Hankamer, Jorge. 1972."Shifty subjects: a conspiracy in syntax?". *Linguistic Inquiry*: 501-504.
Algeo, John. 1988."British and American Grammatical Differences". *International Journal of Lexicography* 1(1): 1-31.
Ariel, Mira. 1988."Referring and accessibility". *Journal of Linguistics* 24: 65-87.
Ariel, Mira. 1990. *Accessing Noun-Phrase Antecedents*. London: Routledge.
Bain, Alexander. 1866. *English Composition and Rhetoric*. New York: Appleton.
Banfield, Ann. 1982. *Unspeakable Sentences: Narration and Representation in the Language of Fiction*. London: Routledge.
Beaugrande, Robert-Alain de and Dressler, Wolfgang U. 1981. *Introduction to Text Linguistics*. London: Longman.
Bell, Allan. 1984."Language style as audience design". *Language in Society* 13: 145-203.
Biber, Douglas. 1987."A textual comparison of British and American writing". *American Speech* 62: 99-119.
Biber, Douglas. 1988. *Variation across Speech and Writing*. Cambridge: Cambridge University Press.
Biber, Douglas. 1989."A typology of English texts". *Linguistics* 27(1): 3-43.
Biber, Douglas and Finegan, Edward. 1988."Drift in three English genres". In: Merja Kytö et al. (eds.), *Corpus Linguistics, Hard and Soft*, Amsterdam: Rodopi, 83-102.
Biber, Douglas and Finegan, Edward. 1989."Drift and the evolution of English style: a history of three genres". *Language* 65(3): 487-517.
Biber, Douglas and Finegan, Edward. 1992."The linguistic evolution of five written and speech-based English genres from the 17th to the 20th centuries". In: Matti Rissanen et al. (eds.), *History of Englishes: New Methods and Interpretations in Historical Linguistics*, Berlin: Mouton, 688-704.
Birner, Betty J. 1992. *The Discourse Function of Inversion in English*. (Unpublished Ph.D. Dissertation, Northwestern University.)
Birner, Betty J. 1994."Information status and word order: an analysis of English inversion". *Language* 70(2): 233-259.
Bolinger, Dwight. 1977. *Meaning and Form*. London: Longman.
Bolinger, Dwight. 1989. *Intonation and its Uses*. Stanford: Stanford University Press.
Bresnan, Joan. 1994."Locative inversion and the architecture of universal grammar". *Language* 70(1): 72-137.
Bresnan, Joan and Kanerva, Joni M. 1992."Locative inversion in Chichewa: a case study of factorization in grammar". In: Tim Stowell and Eric Wehrli (eds.), *Syntax and Semantics. Vol. 26: Syntax and the Lexicon*, New York: Academic Press, 53-101.

REFERENCES

Brinker, Klaus. 1985. *Linguistische Textanalyse: Eine Einführung in Grundbegriffe und Methoden*. Berlin: Schmidt.
Brinton, Laurel J. 1995."Non-anaphoric reflexives in free indirect style: expressing the subjectivity of the non-speaker". In: Dieter Stein and Susan Wright (eds.), *Subjectivity and Subjectivisation*, Cambridge: Cambridge University Press, 173-194.
Brown, Gillian and Yule, George. 1983. *Discourse Analysis*. Cambridge: Cambridge University Press.
Bühler, Karl (1934) 1982. *Sprachtheorie: Die Darstellungsfunktion der Sprache*. Stuttgart: Fischer.
Carroll, Mary and von Stutterheim, Christiane. 1993."The representation of spatial configurations in English and German and the grammatical structure of locative and anaphoric expressions". *Linguistics* 31: 1011-1041.
Chafe, Wallace L. 1976."Givenness, contrastiveness, definiteness, subjects, topics and point of view". In: Charles N. Li (ed.), *Subject and Topic*, New York: Academic Press, 27-55.
Chafe, Wallace L. 1982."Integration and involvement in speaking, writing, and oral literature". In: Deborah Tannen (ed.), *Spoken and Written Language: Exploring Orality and Literacy*, Norwood NJ: Ablex, 35-54.
Chafe, Wallace L. 1985."Linguistic differences produced by differences between speaking and writing". In: David R. Olson *et al.* (eds.), *Literacy, Language, and Learning: the Nature and Consequences of Reading and Writing*, Cambridge: Cambridge University Press, 105-23.
Chafe, Wallace L. 1992."Immediacy and displacement in consciousness and language". In: Dieter Stein (ed.), *Cooperating with Written Texts: The Pragmatics and Comprehension of Written Texts*, Berlin: Mouton, 231-255.
Chafe, Wallace L. 1994. *Discourse, Consciousness, and Time*. Chicago: The University of Chicago Press.
Chomsky, Noam. 1971."Deep structure, surface structure, and semantic interpretation". In: Danny D. Steinberg and Leon A. Jakobovits (eds.), *Semantics: An Interdisciplinary Reader in Philosophy, Linguistics and Psychology*, Cambridge: Cambridge University Press, 183-216.
Coopmans, Peter. 1989."Where stylistic and syntactic processes meet: locative inversions in English". *Language* 65(4): 728-751.
Creider, Chet A. 1979."On the explanation of transformations". In: Talmy Givón (ed.), *Syntax and Semantics. Vol. 12: Discourse and Syntax*, New York: Academic Press, 3-21.
Declerck, Renaat. 1984."The pragmatics of *it*-clefts and *wh*-clefts". *Lingua* 64: 251-289.
Denison, David. 1993. *English Historical Syntax*. New York: Longman.
Diewald, Gabriele Maria. 1991. *Deixis und Textsorten im Deutschen*. Tübingen: Niemeyer.
Dijk, Teun A. van. 1980. *Textwissenschaft*. München: Deutscher Taschenbuch Verlag.
Dijk, Teun A. van and Kintsch, Walter. 1983. *Strategies of Discourse Comprehension*. New York: Academic Press.
Dik, Simon. 1981. *Functional Grammar*. Dordrecht: Foris.
Dik, Simon *et al.* 1983."On the typology of focus phenomena". In: Teun Hoekstra *et al.* (eds.), *Perspectives on Functional Grammar*, Dordrecht: Foris, 41-74.

Dimter, Mattias. 1985."On text classification". In: Teun A. van Dijk (ed.), *Discourse and Literature*. Amsterdam & Philadelphia: John Benjamins, 215-230.
Downing, Pamela A. 1995."Word order in discourse: by way of introduction". In: Pamela Downing and Michael Noonan (eds.), *Word Order in Discourse*, Amsterdam & Philadelphia: John Benjamins, 1-27.
Downing, Pamela and Noonan, Michael (eds.). 1995. *Word Order in Discourse*. Amsterdam & Philadelphia: John Benjamins.
Drubig, Hans Bernhard. 1988."On the discourse function of subject verb inversion". In: Josef Klegraf Dietrich Nehls (eds.), *Essays on the English Language and Applied Linguistics on the Occasion of Gerhard Nickel's 60th Birthday*, Heidelberg: Julius Groos Verlag, 83-95.
Dryer, Matthew S. 1994."Focus, pragmatic presupposition and activated propositions". (Unpublished manuscript, SUNY Buffalo.)
Dudley-Evans, Tony. 1989."An outline of the value of genre analysis in LSP work". In: Christer Lauren and Marianne Nordmann (eds.), *Special Language: from Human Thinking to Thinking Machines*, Philadelphia: Claredon, 72-79.
Ehrlich, Susan. 1990. *Point of View: a Linguistic Analysis of Literary Style*. London: Routledge.
Ellegard, Alvar. 1978. *The Syntactic Structure of English Texts*, Göteborg: Acta Universitatis Gothoburgensis.
Emonds, Joseph E. 1969."A structure-preserving constraint on NP Movement transformations". *Papers from the 5th Regional Meeting of the Chicago Linguistic Society*, 60-65.
Emonds, Joseph E. 1976. *A Transformational Approach to English Syntax: Root, Structure-preserving, and Local Transformations*. New York: Academic Press.
Enkvist, Nils Erik. 1980."Marked focus: function and constraints". In: Sidney Greenbaum et al. (eds.), *Studies in English Linguistics for Randolph Quirk*. London: Longman, 134-52.
Enkvist, Nils Erik. 1984."Contrastive linguistics and text linguistics". In: Jacek Fisiak (ed.), *Contrastive Linguistics: Prospects and Problems*, Berlin: Mouton, 45-67.
Enkvist, Nils Erik. 1987."A note towards the definition of text strategy". *Zeitschrift für Phonetik, Sprachwissenschaft und Kommunikationsforschung* 40(1): 19-27.
Enkvist, Nils Erik. 1991."Discourse strategies and discourse types". In Eija Ventola (ed.), *Functional and Systemic Linguistics - Approaches and Uses*, Berlin: Mouton, 3-22.
Erdmann, Peter. 1979. *Inversion im heutigen Englisch*. Heidelberg: Carl Winter.
Erdmann, Peter. 1988."(Non-) inverting negatives in clause-initial position in English". In: Josef Klegraf and Dietrich Nehls (eds.), *Essays on the English Language and Applied Linguistics on the Occasion of Gerhard Nickel's 60th Birthday*, Heidelberg: Julius Groos Verlag, 66-82.
Erdmann, Peter. 1990. *Discourse and Grammar: Focussing and Defocussing in English*. Tübingen: Niemeyer.
Faigley, Lester and Meyer, Paul. 1983."Rhetorical theory and readers' classifications of text types". *Text* 3(4): 305-325.
Fillmore, Charles J. 1981."Pragmatics and the Description of Discourse". In: Peter Cole (ed.), *Radical Pragmatics*, New York: Academic Press, 143-166.
Finegan, Edward and Besnier, Niko. 1989. *Language: Its Structure and Use*. San Diego CA: Harcourt Brace Jovanovich.

REFERENCES

Firbas, Jan. 1979."A functional view of *ordo naturalis*". *Brno Studies in English* 13: 29-59.
Firbas, Jan. 1986."On the dynamics of functional sentence perspective". In: Charles R. Cooper and Sidney Greenbaum (eds.), *Studying Writing: Linguistic Approaches. Vol. I*, Beverly Hills CA: Sage, 40-71.
Firbas, Jan. 1992. *Functional Sentence Perspective in Written and Spoken Communication*. Cambridge: Cambridge University Press.
Ford, Cecilia. 1993. *Grammar in Interaction*. Cambridge: Cambridge University Press.
Fox, Barbara A. 1985."Word-order inversion and discourse continuity in Tagalog". In: Talmy Givón (ed.) *Quantified Studies in Discourse. Special Issue of Text* 5(1/2): 39-54.
Fox, Barbara A."Morpho-syntactic markedness and discourse structure". *Journal of Pragmatics* 11: 359-373.
García, Erica C. 1979."Discourse without syntax". In: Talmy Givón (ed.), *Syntax and Semantics. Vol. 12: Discourse and Syntax*, New York: Academic Press, 23-49.
García, Erica C. 1994."Reversing the Status of Markedness". *Folia Linguistica* XXVIII(3-4): 329-361.
Gazdar, Gerald et al. 1985. *Generalized Phrase Structure Grammar*. Cambridge MA: Harvard University Press.
Geluykens, Ronald. 1992. *From Discourse Process to Grammatical Construction: on Left-Dislocation in English*. Amsterdam & Philadelphia: John Benjamins.
Giora, Rachel. 1990."On the so-called evaluative material in informative text". *Text* 10: 299-319.
Givón, Talmy. 1979. *On Understanding Grammar*. New York: Academic Press.
Givón, Talmy. 1984. *Syntax: a Functional-Typological introduction. Vol. I*, Amsterdam & Philadelphia: John Benjamins.
Givón, Talmy. 1985."Iconicity, isomorphism and non-arbitrary coding in syntax". In: John Haiman (ed.), *Iconicity in Syntax*, Amsterdam & Philadelphia: John Benjamins, 187-219.
Givón, Talmy. 1987."Beyond foreground and background". In: Russell S. Tomlin (ed.), *Coherence and Grounding in Discourse*, Amsterdam & Philadelphia: John Benjamins, 175-188.
Givón, Talmy. 1988."The pragmatics of word-order: predictability, importance and attention". In: Michael T. Hammond et al. (eds.), *Studies in Syntactic Typology*, Amsterdam & Philadelphia: John Benjamins, 243-84.
Givón, Talmy. 1990. *Syntax: A Functional-Typological Introduction. Vol. II*, Amsterdam & Philadelphia: John Benjamins.
Givón, Talmy. 1993. *English Grammar: A Function-based Introduction*, Vol.I. Amsterdam & Philadelphia: John Benjamins.
Givón, Talmy (ed.). 1983. *Topic Continuity in Discourse*. Amsterdam & Philadelphia: John Benjamins.
Givón, Talmy (ed.). 1985. *Quantified Studies in Discourse. Special Issue of Text* 5(1/2). Berlin: Mouton.
Green, Georgia. 1976."Main clause phenomena in subordinate clauses". *Language* 52(2): 382-97.
Green, Georgia. 1980."Some wherefores of English inversions". *Language* 56(3): 582-601.
Green, Georgia. 1982."Colloquial and literary uses of inversions". In: Deborah Tannen

(ed.), *Spoken and Written Language: Exploring Orality and Literacy*, Norwood NJ: Ablex, 119-154.

Green, Georgia. 1985."The description of inversions in Generalized Phrase Structure Grammar". In: Mary Niepokuj *et al.* (eds.), *Proceedings of the 11th Annual Meeting of the Berkeley Linguistics Society*, 117-146.

Greenberg, Joseph H. 1966."Some universals of grammar with particular reference to the order of meaningful elements". In: Joseph H. Greenberg (ed.), *Universals of Language*. 2nd Edition, Cambridge MA: The MIT Press, 73-113.

Grice, H. Paul. 1975."Logic and conversation". In: Peter Cole and Jerry L. Morgan (eds.), *Syntax and Semantics. Vol. 3: Speech Acts*, New York: Academic Press, 41-58.

Große, Ernst-Ulrich. 1976. *Texttypen: Linguistik nicht-literarischer Kommunikation*. (Unpublished Ph.D. Dissertation, Universität Freiburg.)

Gülich, Elisabeth and Raible, Wolfgang. 1975."Textsorten-Probleme". *Linguistische Probleme der Textanalyse: Jahrbuch 1973*. (Sprache der Gegenwart: Schriften des Instituts für deutsche Sprache Mannheim 35.) Düsseldorf: Schwann, 144-197.

Gundel, Jeanette K., Hedberg, Nancy and Zacharski, Ron. 1993."Cognitive status and the form of referring expressions in discourse". *Language* 69(2): 274-307.

Haan, Pieter de. 1992."The optimum corpus sample size". In: Gerhard Leitner (ed.), *New Directions in English Language Corpora - Methodology, Results, Software Developments*, Berlin: Mouton, 3-19.

Haan, Pieter de. 1993."Sentence length in running text". In: Clive Souter and Eric Atwell (eds.), *Corpus-based Computational Linguistics*, Amsterdam: Rodopi, 147-161.

Haegeman, Liliane. 1991. *An Introduction to Government and Binding Theory*. Oxford: Blackwell.

Halliday, Michael A.K. 1970."Language structure and language function". In: John Lyons (ed.), *New Horizons in Linguistics*, Harmondsworth: Penguin, 140-165.

Halliday, Michael A.K. 1985. *Functional Grammar*. London: Edward Arnold.

Halliday, Michael A.K. and Hasan, Ruqaiya. 1976. *Cohesion in English*. London: Longman.

Hammond, Michael T. (ed.). 1988. *Studies in Syntactic Typology*. Amsterdam & Philadelphia: John Benjamins.

Hartvigson Hans H. and Jakobsen, Leif K. 1974. *Inversion in Present-Day English*. Odense: Odense University Press.

Hawkins, John A. 1983. *Word Order Universals*. New York: Academic Press.

Hooper, Joan B. and Thompson, Sandra A. 1973."On the applicability of root transformations". *Linguistic Inquiry* 4(4): 465-97.

Hopper, Paul. 1979."Aspect and foregrounding in discourse". In: Talmy Givón (ed.), *Syntax and Semantics. Vol. 12: Discourse and Syntax*, New York: Academic Press, 213-41.

Hopper, Paul J. and Traugott, Elizabeth C. 1993. *Grammaticalization*. Cambridge: Cambridge University Press.

Horová, Eva. 1976."On position and function of English local and temporal adverbials". *Brno Studies in English* 12: 93-123.

Isenberg, Horst. 1978."Probleme der Texttypologie: Variation und Determination von Texttypen". *Wissenschaftliche Zeitschrift der Karl-Marx-Universität Leipzig* 27: 565-579.

Jackendoff, Ray S. 1972. *Semantic Interpretation in Generative Grammar*. Cambridge MA: The MIT Press.
Jacobsson, Bengt. 1951. *Inversion in English with Special Reference to the Early Modern English Period*. Uppsala: Almquist Wiksell.
Johansson, Stig. 1978. *Manual of Information to Accompany the Lancaster-Oslo/Bergen Corpus of British English, for Use with Digital Computers*. Oslo: University of Oslo Department of English.
Jones, Larry B. 1983. *Pragmatic Aspects of English Text Structure*. A Publication of The Summer Institute of Linguistics and The University of Texas at Arlington, Publication Number 67.
Jucker, Andreas H. 1992. *Social Stylistics: Syntactic Variation in British Newspapers*. Berlin: Mouton.
Kaplan, Jeffrey P. 1989. *English Grammar: Principles and Facts*. Englewood Cliffs NJ: Prentice Hall.
Kathol, Andreas and Levine, Robert D. 1992."Inversion as a linearization effect". *Proceedings of the North East Linguistic Society* 23, Vol. 1: 207-221.
Kemmer, Suzanne. 1995."Emphatic and reflexive *-self*: expectations, viewpoint and subjectivity". In: Dieter Stein and Susan Wright (eds.), *Subjectivity and Subjectivisation*, Cambridge: Cambridge University Press, 55-82.
Kinneavy, James L. 1971. *A Theory of Discourse: The Aims of Discourse*. Englewood Cliffs NJ: Prentice Hall.
Kjellmer, Göran. 1979."On clause-introductory 'nor' and 'neither'". *English Studies* 60: 280-95.
König, Ekkehard. 1988."Subject-operator inversion after negative expressions in English: semantic aspects of a notorious syntactic problem". In: Joseph Klegraf and Dietrich Nehls (eds.), *Essays on the English Language and Applied Linguistics on the Occasion of Gerhard Nickel's 60th Birthday*, Heidelberg: Julius Groos Verlag, 55-65.
Kuno, Susumu. 1987. *Functional Syntax: Anaphora, Discourse and Empathy*. Chicago: Chicago University Press.
Lambrecht, Knud. *Information Structure and Sentence Form: Topic, Focus and the Mental Representation of Discourse Referents*. Cambridge: Cambridge University Press.
Langacker, Ronald W. 1990."Subjectification". *Cognitive Linguistics* 1(1): 5-38.
Langacker, Ronald W. 1993."Reference-point constructions". *Cognitive Linguistics* 4(1): 1-38.
Lehmann, Christian. 1992."Word order change by grammaticalization". In: Dieter Stein and Marinel Gerritsen (eds.), *Internal and External Factors in Syntactic Change*, Berlin: Mouton, 395-417.
Levine, Robert D. 1989."On focus inversion: syntactic valence and the role of SUBCAT list". *Linguistics* 27(6): 1013-1055.
Li, Charles N. and Thomson, Sandra A. 1976."Subject and topic: a new typology of language". In: Charles N. Li (ed.), *Subject and Topic*, New York: Academic Press, 457-489.
Linde, Charlotte and Labov, William. 1975."Spatial networks as a site for the study of language and thought". *Language* 51(4): 924-939.
Longacre, Robert E. 1983. *The Grammar of Discourse*. New York: Plenum Press.

Lowe, Ivan. 1987."Sentence initial elements in English and their discourse function". *Occasional Papers in Systemic Linguistics II*, Nottingham, 5-33.
Lüger, Heinz-Helmut. 1983. *Pressesprache*. Tübingen: Niemeyer.
Lux, Friedemann. 1981. *Text, Situation, Textsorte*. Tübingen: Narr.
Malinowski, Bronislaw. (1923) 1949."The problem of meaning in primitive languages". In: Charles K. Ogden and Ivor A. Richards (eds.), *The Meaning of Meaning*, London: Routledge, 296-336.
Miller, Charles. 1984."Genre as social action". *Quarterly Journal of Speech* 70: 151-167.
Mithun, Marianne. 1987."Is basic word order universal?". In: Russell S. Tomlin (ed.), *Coherence and Grounding in Discourse*, Amsterdam & Philadelphia: John Benjamins, 281-328.
Mithun, Marianne. 1995."Morphological and prosodic forces shaping word order". In: Pamela Downing and Michael Noonan (eds.), *Word Order in Discourse*, Amsterdam & Philadelphia: John Benjamins, 387-423.
Morris, Charles W. 1938."Foundations of the theory of signs". In: Otto Neurath *et al.* (eds.), *International Encyclopedia of Unified Science*, Chicago: University of Chicago Press, 77-138.
Nystrand, Martin. 1986. *The Structure of Written Communication: Studies in Reciprocity between Writers and Readers*. New York: Academic Press.
Olson, David R.. 1981."Writing: The divorce of the author from the text". In: B. Kroll and R. Vann (eds.), *Exploring Speaking-Writing Relationships: Connections and Contrasts*, Urbana IL: National Council of Teachers of English, 275-289.
Olson, Gary M. *et al.* 1981."Cognitive Aspects of Genre". *Poetics* 10: 283-315.
Oosten, Jeanne van. 1986. *The Nature of Subjects, Topics and Agents: a Cognitive Explanation*. Bloomington IN: Indiana University Linguistics Club.
Osgood, Charles and Bock, Kathryn J. 1977."Saliency and sentencing: some production principles". In: Sheldon Rosenberg (ed.), *Sentence Production: Development in Research and Theory*, Hillsdale NJ: Erlbaum, 89-140.
Partee, Barbara H. 1986."Ambiguous pseudoclefts with unambiguous be". *NELS* 16: 354-366.
Payne, Doris L. 1990. *The Pragmatics of Word Order: Typological Dimensions of Verb Initial Languages*. Berlin: Mouton.
Penhallurick, John. 1984."Full-verb inversion in English". *Australian Journal of Linguistics* 4: 33-56.
Pratt, Mary L. 1977. *Toward a Speech Act Theory of Literary Discourse*. Bloomington IN: Indiana University Press.
Prince, Ellen F. 1978." A comparison of *wh*-clefts and *it*-clefts in discourse". *Language* 54: 883-906.
Prince, Ellen F. 1981a."Topicalization, focus-Movement, and Yiddish-Movement: A pragmatic differentiation". In: Danny K. Alford *et al.* (eds.), *Proceedings of the 7th Annual Meeting of the Berkeley Linguistics Society*, 249-64.
Prince, Ellen F. 1981b."Toward a taxonomy of given-new information". In: Peter Cole (ed.), *Radical Pragmatics*, New York: Academic Press, 223-55.
Prince, Ellen F. 1985."Fancy syntax and 'shared knowledge'". *Journal of Pragmatics* 9: 65-81.

Prince, Ellen F. 1992."The ZPG Letter: subjects, definiteness, and information-status". In: William C. Mann and Sandra A. Thompson (eds.), *Discourse Description: Diverse Linguistic Analyses of a Fund-raising Text*, Amsterdam & Philadelphia: John Benjamins, 294-325.
Pu, Ming-Ming and Prideaux, Gary D. 1994."Coding episode boundaries with marked structures: A cross-linguistic study". *Canadian Journal of Linguistics* 39(4): 283-296.
Quirk, Randolph *et al.* 1985. *A Comprehensive Grammar of the English Language*. London: Longman.
Ramsey, Violeta. 1987."The functional distribution of preposed and postposed 'if' and 'when' clauses in written discourse". In: Russell Tomlin (ed.), *Coherence and Grounding in Discourse*, Amsterdam & Philadelphia: John Benjamins, 383-408.
Rapoport, T. R. 1987. *Copular, Nominal, and Small Clauses: A Study of Israeli Hebrew*. (Unpublished Ph.D. Dissertation, MIT).
Reape, Mike. Forthcoming."Getting things in order". To appear in: Sijtsma Wietske and Arthur van Horck (eds.), *Discontinuous Constituency*, Berlin: Mouton.
Reinhart, Tanya. 1983. *Anaphora and Semantic Interpretation*. London: Croom Helm.
Rochemont, Michael S. 1986. *Focus in Generative Grammar*. Amsterdam & Philadelphia: John Benjamins.
Rochemont, Michael S. and Culicover, Peter W. 1990. *English Focus Constructions and the Theory of Grammar*. Cambridge: Cambridge University Press.
Rosch, Eleanor and Mervis, Carolyn. 1975."Family resemblances: studies in the internal structure of categories". *Cognitive Psychology* 7: 573-605.
Rudanko, Juhani. 1982."Towards a description of negatively conditioned subject operator inversion in English". *English Studies* 63: 349-59.
Safir, Kenneth J. 1985. *Syntactic chains*. Cambridge: Cambridge University Press.
Schachter, Paul. 1992."Comments on Bresnan and Kanerva's 'Locative inversion in Chichewa: a case study of factorization in grammar'". In: Tim Stowell and Eric Wehrli (eds.), *Syntax and Semantics. Vol. 26: Syntax and the Lexicon*, New York: Academic Press, 103-110.
Schiffrin, Deborah. 1987. *Discourse Markers*. Cambridge: Cambridge University Press.
Schmidt, Deborah Ann. 1980. *A History of Inversions in English*. (Unpublished Ph.D. Dissertation, The Ohio State University.)
Searle, John. 1969. *Speech Acts*. London: Cambridge.
Siewierska, Anna. 1988. *Word Order Rules*. London: Croom Helm.
Stein, Dieter. 1990. *The Semantics of Syntactic Change: Aspects of the Evolution of ‚do' in English*. Berlin/New York: Mouton.
Stein, Dieter. 1995."Subjective meanings and the history of inversions in English". In: Dieter Stein and Susan Wright (eds.), *Subjectivity and Subjectivisation*, Cambridge: Cambridge University Press, 129-150.
Stockwell, Robert. 1984."On the history of the verb-second rule in English". In: Jacek Fisiak (ed.), *Historical Syntax*, Berlin: Mouton, 575-592.
Sundby, Bertil. 1970. *Front-shifted 'ing' and 'ed' Groups in Present Day English*. Lund: CWK Gleerup.
Svartivk, Jan. 1966. *On Voice in the English Verb*. The Hague: Mouton.

Svartvik, Jan and Quirk, Randolph (eds.). 1980. *A Corpus of English Conversation*. Lund: Liber/Gleerups.
Swales, John M. 1990. *Genre Analysis: English in Academic and Research Settings*. Cambridge: Cambridge University Press.
Tannen, Deborah. 1982."Oral and literate strategies in spoken and written narratives". *Language* 58(1): 1-21.
Thompson, Sandra A. 1978."Modern English from a typological point of view: some implications of the function of word order". *Linguistische Berichte* 54: 19-35.
Thompson, Sandra A. 1985."Grammar and written discourse: Initial vs. final purpose clauses in English". In: Talmy Givón (ed.), *Quantified Studies in Discourse. Special Issue of Text* 5(1/2): 55-84.
Tomlin, Russell S. 1983."On the interaction of syntactic subject, thematic information, and agent in English". *Journal of Pragmatics* 7: 432-441.
Toulmin, Stephen. 1958. *The Uses of Argument*. Cambridge: Cambridge University Press.
Traugott, Elizabeth C. 1989."On the rise of epistemic meanings in English: an example of subjectification in semantic change". *Language* 65(1): 31-55.
Traugott, Elizabeth C. 1995."Subjectification in grammaticalisation". In: Dieter Stein and Susan Wright (eds.), *Subjectivity and Subjectivisation*, Cambridge: Cambridge University Press, 31-54.
Travis, Lisa. 1984. *Parameters and Effects of Word Order Variation*. (Unpublished Ph.D. Dissertation, Massachusetts Institute of Technology).
Vallduví, Enric. 1992. *The Informational Component*. New York: Garland.
Vennemann, Theo. 1974."Topics, subjects, and word order: from SXV to SVX via TVX". In: J. M. Anderson and C. Jones (eds.), *Historical Linguistics I: Syntax, Morphology, Internal and Comparative Reconstruction*, Proceedings of the First International Conference on Historical Linguistics, Amsterdam: North-Holland, 339-376.
Virtanen, Tuija. 1988. *Discourse Functions of Adverbial Placement in English: Clause-initial Adverbials of Time and Place in Narratives and Procedural Place Descriptions*, Turku/Abo: Abo Akademi University Press.
Virtanen, Tuija. 1992a."Given and new information in adverbials: clause initial adverbials of time and place". *Journal of Pragmatics* 17: 99-115.
Virtanen, Tuija. 1992b."Issues of text typology: narrative - a 'basic' type of text?". *Text* 12(2): 293-310.
Ward, Gregory L. 1988. *The Semantics and Pragmatics of Preposing*. New York: Garland.
Ward, Gregory L. 1990."The discourse functions of VP preposing". *Language* 66(4): 742-63.
Ward, Gregory L. and Birner, Betty J. 1992."VP inversion and aspect in written texts". In: Dieter Stein (ed.), *Cooperating with Written Texts: The Pragmatics and Comprehension of Written Texts*, Berlin: Mouton, 575-588.
Ward, Gregory and Birner, Betty J. 1994."A unified account of English fronting constructions". *Penn Working Papers in Linguistics*, University of Pennsylvania 1: 159-165.
Wardhaugh, Ronald. 1992. *An Introduction to Sociolinguistics, 2nd edition*. Oxford: Blackwell.
Werlich, Egon. 1976. *A Text Grammar of English*. Heidelberg: Quelle Meyer.

REFERENCES

Wikberg, Kay. 1992."Discourse category and text type classification: procedural discourse in the Brown and LOB corpora". In: Gerhard Leitner (ed.), *New Directions in English Language Corpora - Methodology, Results, Software Developments*, Berlin: Mouton, 247-262.

Yokoyama, Olga T. 1986. *Discourse and Word Order.* Amsterdam & Philadelphia: John Benjamins.

Name Index

A
Aissen 206
Algeo 209
Ariel 8

B
Bain 142
Banfield 99, 118, 210
Bell 126
Biber 125ff., 135ff., 139, 148, 152, 155, 158, 160, 162, 164, 211
Birner 9, 20, 23-26, 35, 40ff., 52, 55ff., 67, 76, 82, 86, 88, 98, 105, 129f., 204, 207ff.
Bock 16
Bolinger 20, 44f., 52f., 75, 83, 87, 207
Bresnan 24, 36ff., 42, 103, 207
Brinker 140, 142
Brinton 108, 209
Brown 8f.
Bühler 142

C
Carroll 191
Chafe 8f., 12, 47, 69, 109, 128ff., 164ff., 189, 210
Chomsky 10
Coopmans 24, 36, 51
Creider 8, 51
Culicover 10, 36, 40f., 51

D
de Beaugrande 145
de Haan 147
Declerck 39
Denison 14, 29, 205
Diewald 141, 211
Dik 10
Dimter 141
Downing 13, 17
Dressler 145
Drubig 40, 44ff., 51ff., 68, 74f., 110, 207, 209f.
Dryer 11
Dudley-Evans 145

E
Ehrlich 98ff.
Ellegard 147, 212
Emonds 34f., 97, 210
Enkvist 10, 40, 55, 66, 80, 91, 145f., 198, 212
Erdmann 10, 19, 22, 40, 46, 52, 207, 210

F
Faigley 142f., 211
Fillmore 116
Finegan 160, 162, 164
Firbas 17, 72f., 78, 80
Ford 18, 58f.
Fox 14, 117

G
Garcia 15, 84
Gazdar 34
Geluykens 8, 59ff., 208
Giora 179f., 192
Givón 8, 14ff., 18, 97, 117, 193
Green 19ff., 28, 34f., 40, 48, 65, 67ff., 77, 80, 97ff., 118f., 128ff., 204, 207, 210
Greenberg 13f., 16
Grice 63, 66
Große 140, 142
Gülich 126, 211
Gundel 9, 11, 50, 78, 84, 113

H

Haegeman 34
Halliday 11ff., 67tff., 115, 142f., 188, 204, 208
Hammond 13
Hankamer 206
Hartvigson 40, 48, 51f., 210
Hasan 11, 67ff., 115, 143, 208
Hawkins 13
Hooper 34, 97, 102, 210
Hopper 30, 32, 66, 205f.

I

Isenberg 126

J

Jackendoff 10
Jacobsson 205
Jakobsen 40, 48, 51f., 210
Johansson 212
Jones 156, 170ff.
Jucker 147, 211

K

Kanerva 36
Kaplan 50
Kathol 34
Kemmer 11, 42, 104, 106
Kinneavy 142f., 211f.
Kintsch 105
Kjellmer 40, 91ff.
König 19, 26, 40, 91, 95
Kuno 103ff.

L

Labov 110
Lambrecht 18
Langacker 38, 40, 45, 80, 102ff., 118, 167, 204f.
Lehmann 13ff., 33
Levine 34, 36
Li 17f.
Linde 110
Longacre 85, 88, 208, 212
Lowe 59, 96

Lüger 150, 152f., 155, 158, 166, 212f.
Lux 140

M

Malinowski 142
Mervis 145
Meyer 142f.
Miller 144
Mithun 14, 17
Morris 1

N

Noonan 13, 17
Nystrand 129, 145f., 211

O

Olson 127
Osgood 16

P

Partee 39
Payne 13ff.
Penhallurick 10, 40, 46ff., 51f., 82
Prideaux 14
Prince 8ff., 39, 48, 50, 56, 61, 75, 207
Pu 14

Q

Quirk 4, 25ff., 52, 84, 90, 95, 148, 205, 207f.

R

Raible 126, 211
Ramsey 18, 58
Rapoport 81, 85
Reape 34
Reinhart 99
Rochemont 10, 36, 40f., 51
Rosch 145
Rouse 3, 47
Rudanko 95

S

Safir 36, 40
Schachter 36

Name Index

Schiffrin 188ff.
Schmidt 21f., 29ff., 67, 74, 118, 205, 209
Searle 142
Siewierska 13f.
Stein 29, 31f., 66, 106, 117f., 130, 205, 208f.
Stockwell 19, 29ff., 65f., 194, 205f.
Sundby 85f., 209
Svartvik 4, 85, 148
Swales 145

T
Tannen 127f.
Thompson 15, 17f., 35, 50, 58, 97, 102, 210
Tomlin 13
Toulmin 155
Traugott 32, 66, 71, 205f.
Travis 34

V
Vallduví 11
Van Dijk 105, 212
van Oosten 13
Vennemann 19, 29
Virtanen 56f., 139, 142f., 145f., 155, 190
von Stutterheim 191

W
Waller 3
Ward 12, 53ff., 86, 207f.
Wardhaugh 128
Werlich 126, 142, 211f.
Wikberg 152, 155, 158, 160, 162, 211

Y
Yokoyama 13
Yule 8f.

Subject Index

accessibility 8
activation cost 8
agent; *also*: actor 12, 87
American English 126, 135ff.
anchor(ing) 17f., 58, 66, 106, 108, 112ff., 119ff., 130, 182, 184
argument structure 37
argumentation 142ff., 155ff., 163, 175, 183f., 189ff.
  argumentative discourse 155, 158, 160, 170, 183, 192
aspect 86
assertion 98, 100
audience involvement 128
author (*or* speaker) comment 156, 161ff., 170ff., 185, 190

B

backgrounding 30, 59, 102, 117, 179ff., 192
basic word order 4, 7, 16ff., 19
  basic constituent order 7, 14
be-inversion 24, 26f., 38f., 65, 79ff., 87
bi-focal 43, 79, 90
biography136, 138, 148ff., 160ff.
British English 126, 135ff.

C

c-construability 41f.
canonical situation of utterance 141
categorial structure 37ff.
children's tales 3
clefts 50
Cognitive Grammar 38, 40, 45, 80, 105
coherence 9
cohesion 69, 91, 111
colloquial (style) 69, 128, 131ff.

comment, newspaper 151, 170, 174f., 182ff.
  commentary 175
  leader 175
communicative dynamism 16, 72, 78
compound tenses (in inversion) 118
conceptualisation 69, 106ff., 119, 129, 191
  conception 106f., 109
connective (function of inversion) 48, 90, 92ff.
consciousness; proximal, displaced 165ff., 172
construal (of topic entities) 106ff., 129
  topic construal 113, 123
contrastiveness 61, 80
  contrast 42, 61, 82, 114, 162
  contrastive focus 41ff.
  contrastive semantics 39
conversation 58ff., 128f., 134, 188ff.
criminal stories 3

D

description 142ff., 152, 158, 160, 175, 190ff.
desituated (discourse) 129, 189
digressions 117, 179ff., 189
discourse marker 5, 57, 105, 188ff.
discourse model 49
discourse organisation 5, 58, 72, 127, 130, 150, 166, 170, 179, 182ff., 192
  text organisation 56
discourse structure 56, 109, 112f., 122f., 142ff, 146, 150, 189ff.
  text structure 111, 117
  textual surface structure 143
discourse type 60, 139ff., 189

text type 14, 139ff.
type of discourse 3, 126
discourse typology 139ff.
text typology 126
displaced immediacy 76, 109, 158, 165ff., 178f., 184, 192
displacement 5, 44, , 69, 109, 146, 164ff., 173, 187
   displaced (discourse) 88, 129, 137
   displaced speech 164ff.
displacement of self 168f.
displacement, spatiotemporal 168f.
do-periphrasis 16, 29, 31
dynamic semantic functions 72f.

E
Early Modern English 30ff.
editorial 136ff., 148ff., 155ff., 170, 175
embedded inversion 35, 64, 97ff., 118
emotivity; *also*: emotive meaning 5, 64, 116ff., 130, 132, 139, 151
   emotionality 32, 94, 130, 134
empathy 103ff, 108, 169
emphasis 32, 35, 67, 91, 94, 98, 137
   emphatic (meaning) 48, 66, 91, 96
   emphatic focus 55, 66, 91, 94, 101
endophoric (reference) 68ff., 190
   textual reference 68ff., 77
epistemic 32
equative sentences 85
essay 131, 133, 136, 138, 148ff., 160ff.
evaluation 114f., 155f., 170f, 179ff., 183f., 190
exclamatory inversion 21
existential scale 72f., 75ff., 89, 118, 120
exophoric (reference) 67ff.
   situational reference 67ff.
exposition 142ff., 176, 186, 189ff.
   expository discourse 160, 162ff., 170, 186, 192
expressive discourse 142
expressive syntax 118
external conjunctive (relations) 71, 112
extraposition 20, 173, 180

F
fictional (discourse) 136, 176
   fiction 130, 152
   fictional texts 2, 130
focus constructions 40f., 51
   focus inversion 36
   focus movement 75
   focus preposing 55
   focus-marking 41ff.
   presentational focus 37, 41ff.
focus 4, 7, 10ff., 40, 46, 89
   information(al) focus 10, 41, 55, 75, 87, 89
   sentence focus 10f., 27, 55, 76
focus management 64, 105ff., 129, 137, 152
focus of attention 5, 11, 45, 49f., 67, 84, 105ff., 115, 117, 129, 156, 164, 189
foregrounding 30, 117
formality 127f., 134
free indirect discourse 99, 108, 116, 133
function (of a discourse) 139f., 141ff., 190ff.
   intention 143
   purpose 143
functions of language 11ff., 142
   ideational 11f., 142f., 174, 189ff.
   interpersonal 11f., 142f., 157, 184, 190ff.
   textual 11f.

G
genre 3f., 126f., 135ff., 139ff., 144ff., 148ff., 174ff., 189
genre conventions 137ff., 144ff., 151, 189
Government and Binding theory 34
grammatical relations 13f.
   grammatical functions 36f.
   grammatical roles 7f., 12, 39
   grammatical word order languages 15ff., 50
   rigid word order languages 15, 19

SUBJECT INDEX

grammaticalisation 5, 29ff., 64, 66f., 86
ground(ing) 18, 58, 75, 79, 84, 106, 113ff., 122f.
guidebook 3, 110, 145, 161

H
head-driven phrase structure grammar 34
hearer-orientation; *also*: hearer-involvement 128, 188
receiver-orientation 145
Heavy-NP-Shift 36

I
ideational (meaning) 11, 19, 59, 63, 112, 188
illocution 140
illocutionary types 142
immediacy 165ff., 182, 186f.
immediate experience 164, 166, 169
implicature 66, 86
indirect object movement 50
information (status) 47ff., 56ff., 60, 78, 105
brand-new 48
discourse-familiar(ity) 9, 40, 48ff., 56f., 66, 73, 76, 78, 114
discourse-new 56
discourse-old 49f., 56, 78
evoked 41f., 46, 48f., 56, 61
given(ness) 9, 17, 30, 48ff., 73, 78
hearer familiar(ity) 9, 40, 49f.
hearer-old 50, 78
inferrable 43, 48f., 56, 78, 106
irrecoverable 60f.
new 40, 75
recoverable 30
rhematic 17f.
thematic 17
unused 48f.
information-packaging (function of inversion) 9, 40, 47ff., 66, 77, 130
informative discourse 138, 175, 189
information-based (discourse) 150, 152, 174

initial adverbial placement 20, 53ff., 66
innovation (of inversion types) 30ff., 39, 65, 89, 121
instruction 11, 49f., 67, 69, 83, 105, 113, 145, 170, 192
interactional; *also*: interactive 59, 61, 127ff., 134, 136
internal conjunctive (relations) 71, 74, 111, 134
interpersonal (meaning) 11, 19, 59, 63, 67, 71, 96, 112, 188ff.
interspeaker variation 126f., 135ff.
intonation 52, 130, 135
intraspeaker variation 126, 131
inversion after additive adverbs 26, 28, 33, 91ff.
inversion after affective constituents 33
inversion after deictic adverbs 44, 53, 67ff., 109, 119ff., 129, 134, 158, 190
inversion after directional adverbs 75, 88, 103, 113, 133f., 158, 161
inversion after manner adverbs 33
inversion after negative constituents 26, 28, 33, 91ff., 119, 132ff., 156f.
inversion after pronominal elements 26, 89ff., 115f., 134f., 157
inversion following lexical phrases 44, 74ff., 119ff., 129
inversion in correlative constructions 27f., 89f., 115, 133, 157
inverted conditional 21

J
juridicial writing 131, 164

L
left-dislocation 20, 50, 59ff.
letters 131, 133
Lexical Functional Grammar 37
lexical-verb-inversion 24, 26, 38, 79, 87
limiting (of inversion types) 32f., 66
linguistic co-occurence 125, 140
literary (style) 99, 131ff.
literature 128
locative inversion 24, 36ff., 45, 81

232 SUBJECT INDEX

locativity; *also*: locative (meaning) 25, 33, 39, 52, 65, 83, 132
logical subject 12, 204

M
main clause phenomenon 35, 97ff.
marked constructions 29
　marked focus 10, 40f., 76, 82
　marked theme 12
　marked word order 63, 132, 139
markedness 14ff., 21, 63, 116ff., 137
　markedness reversal 14
maxim of quantity 63
Middle English 31ff.
modality172f., 180
mode of discourse 51, 127ff., 134
　mode of communication 130
monograph 138, 160
monologue discourse 61, 141

N
narration 142ff., 152, 190ff.
narrative (texts) 30, 77, 132ff., 136, 143
natural word order 4, 7, 16ff.
negation 54, 95
news analysis 170f., 174, 176, 184ff.
news 153ff., 164, 175, 177ff.
　hard news 166ff., 174
　soft news 174
newsworthy-first-principle 17
nominal style 138
non-fictional discourse 130f., 147ff., 164ff.
　non-fictional texts 4
novel 3, 131

O
Old English 29ff., 74
open proposition 55, 207

P
passive 50, 147
patient 88
perception 70, 109, 119, 134
　perceptual field 44, 68f., 129

persuasive discourse 142, 155ff.
phrase structure grammar 34
planning time 128
point of view 3, 5, 97, 99ff., 106ff., 138
　perspective 3, 17, 75, 102ff., 106ff., 117ff., 157, 170
　viewpoint 35, 96, 102ff., 117ff., 168
pragmatic word order languages 15, 18
　flexible word order languages 15, 17
Prague School (of Linguistics) 16, 72
pre-signals 146, 175f.
preposing 8, 15, 21, 50, 53ff., 57, 65
prepositional subject 38
prescriptivism 137
presentative (function of inversion) 40ff., 68ff., 117, 190
presupposition10, 100
presuppositional set 50, 80, 82, 84, 114
printed (discourse) 142
　printed texts 4
profiled 45, 80, 103, 107
propositional meaning (*or* content) 1, 4, 31
　truth-value; *also*: truth-conditional meaning 63, 70ff., 118, 188
prosody 33
prototypes 142f., 145

Q
quality scale 72f., 78ff., 120
quotation inversion 22f.

R
reference point 38, 45, 47, 75ff., 103, 105ff., 113ff., 122f.
reflexives 42, 103f.
reportage 136f., 148ff., 152, 174
reported speech 99f., 131
representative discourse 142
review 110, 133, 136f., 148ff., 158ff.
right-dislocation 20
root transformation 34f., 97, 100

S
salience 9f., 16ff., 48, 106, 112, 120,

130
scientific writing 131, 135ff., 148ff.
semantic role structure 36f.
shared knowledge 42f., 55
situatedness 129, 136
speaker roles (*or* attitudes) 166ff., 174ff., 187
speaker's agreement 98f.
speaker-orientation 99f., 102
split intransitivity 103
spoken (mode) 127ff.
  oral communication 129
  oral (language) 68f., 134, 160ff.
  speech 127ff., 134
  spoken discourse (*or* language) 18, 60, 188f.
staged activity 75, 104
  deictic effect 113, 134
story-telling 134
  (short-)stories 47, 131f.
structure-preserving hypothesis 35f.
  structure-preserving constraint 35, 97
structure-preserving transformation 35, 118
style 127f., 130ff., 190
  register 126, 130
subject extraction 36, 38
subject raising 36, 37
subject-orientation 99f., 102
subject-prominent languages 17f.
subject-shift 30f.
subject-verb agreement 12, 36, 38
subjectification 71f., 94
subjectivity 5, 35, 66, 96ff., 102ff., 106ff., 118, 130, 137, 151, 167ff., 176f., 188ff.

T
tag formation 36
technical writing 164
textual (meaning) 11, 19, 31, 59, 63, 67, 71, 112, 188
textual metaphor 71, 74, 134, 183, 190
theme 7, 12, 17f., 204
there-insertion 20, 44, 50ff., 83, 147

expletive (*or* unstressed) *there* 52f.
existential *there* 20, 51f.
top-down processing 145
topic change 82, 105f., 110ff., 117, 122f., 129f., 145f., 150, 154ff., 179
  thematic shift 30
  topic shift 31, 57, 117
topic 4, 7ff., 18, 30, 61, 74, 106ff.
  discourse topic 9, 141f., 158f., 163, 180
  sentence topic 9
  topic entity 9, 55
topicalisation 8f., 36, 55, 60
  topic preposing 55
topicality 8f., 46, 111
  thematicity 8
  topic continuity 8, 16, 117
  topichood 9
turn-taking 59f., 189

U
universe of discourse 5, 69, 77, 88, 103, 107, 118, 123, 129, 164, 189
  discourse world 5, 61, 69, 74, 119

V
verbs in inversion 34, 88, 122f.
  dynamic verbs 83, 191
  intransitive verbs 31, 33
  static verbs 75, 79ff., 83, 89
  transitive verbs 54, 118
  verbs of appearance or existence 73, 79
viewing; static, dynamic 143f., 152, 190
visual-impact reading (of inversion) 44, 46, 110f., 145, 152f., 155, 161

W
wh-clefts 39
word order flexibility 15, 17
word order rigidity 15, 18f., 74
word order (*or* language) type 7, 13ff.
written (mode) 127ff.
  writing 127ff.

written texts 4, 108, 129
written discourse 5, 60f., 69, 74, 141, 147ff., 164ff.
written language 5, 133

Z
zero-topic constructions 18

In the series STUDIES IN DISCOURSE AND GRAMMAR (SiDaG) the following titles have been published and will be published:

1. GELUYKENS, Ronald: *From Discourse Process to Grammatical Construction: On Left-Dislocation in English.* Amsterdam/Philadelphia, 1992.
2. IWASAKI, Shoichi: *Subjectivity in Grammar and Discourse: Theoretical Considerations and a Case Study of Japanese Spoken Discourse.* Amsterdam/Philadelphia, 1993.
3. WEBER, Elizabeth G.: *Varieties of Questions in English Conversation.* Amsterdam/Philadelphia, 1993.
4. DOWNING, Pamela: *Numerical Classifier Systems: The Case of Japanese.* Amsterdam/Philadelphia, 1996.
5. TAO, Hongyin: *Units in Mandarin Conversation: Prosody, Discourse, and Grammar.* Amsterdam/Philadelphia, 1996.
6. DORGELOH, Heidrun: *Inversion in Modern English: Form and function.* Amsterdam/Philadelphia, 1997.
7. LAURY, Ritva: *Demonstratives in Interaction. The emergence of a definite article in Finnish.* Amsterdam/Philadelphia, n.y.p.